Monitoring Microservices and Containerized Applications

Deployment, Configuration, and Best Practices for Prometheus and Alert Manager

Navin Sabharwal
Piyush Pandey

Apress®

Monitoring Microservices and Containerized Applications

Navin Sabharwal
New Delhi, Delhi, India

Piyush Pandey
New Delhi, India

ISBN-13 (pbk): 978-1-4842-6215-3
https://doi.org/10.1007/978-1-4842-6216-0

ISBN-13 (electronic): 978-1-4842-6216-0

Managing Director, Apress Media LLC: Welmoed Spahr
Acquisitions Editor: Celestin Suresh John
Development Editor: Matthew Moodie
Coordinating Editor: Aditee Mirashi

Cover designed by eStudioCalamar

Cover image designed by Pixabay

Distributed to the book trade worldwide by Springer Science+Business Media New York, 233 Spring Street, 6th Floor, New York, NY 10013. Phone 1-800-SPRINGER, fax (201) 348-4505, email orders-ny@springer-sbm.com, or visit www.springeronline.com. Apress Media, LLC is a California LLC and the sole member (owner) is Springer Science+Business Media Finance Inc (SSBM Finance Inc). SSBM Finance Inc is a **Delaware** corporation.

For information on translations, please e-mail booktranslations@springernature.com; for reprint, paperback, or audio rights, please e-mail bookpermissions@springernature.com.

Apress titles may be purchased in bulk for academic, corporate, or promotional use. eBook versions and licenses are also available for most titles. For more information, reference our Print and eBook Bulk Sales web page at http://www.apress.com/bulk-sales.

Any source code or other supplementary material referenced by the author in this book is available to readers on GitHub via the book's product page, located at www.apress.com/978-1-4842-6215-3. For more detailed information, please visit http://www.apress.com/source-code.

Printed on acid-free paper

Table of Contents

About the Authors

Navin Sabharwal: Navin has more than twenty years of industry experience and is an innovator, thought leader, patent holder, and author in the areas of cloud computing, artificial intelligence and machine learning, public cloud, DevOps, AIOps, infrastructure services, monitoring and management platforms, big data analytics, and software product development. Navin is responsible for DevOps, artificial intelligence, cloud lifecycle management, service management, monitoring and management, IT Ops analytics, AIOps and machine learning, automation, operational efficiency of scaled delivery through Lean Ops, strategy, and delivery for HCL Technologies. He is reachable at navinsabharwal@gmail.com and https://www.linkedin.com/in/navinsabharwal.

Piyush Pandey: Piyush has more than ten years of industry experience. He is currently working at HCL Technologies as automation architect, delivering solutions catering to hybrid cloud using cloud native and third-party solutions. Automation solutions cover use cases like enterprise observability, infra as code, server automation, runbook automation, cloud management platform, cloud native automation, and dashboard/visibility. He is responsible for designing end-to-end solutions and architecture for enterprise automation adoption. You can reach him at piyushnsitcoep@gmail.com and https://www.linkedin.com/in/piyush-pandey-704495b.

About the Technical Reviewer

Amit Agrawal: Amit is principal data scientist and researcher delivering solutions in field of AI and machine learning. He is responsible for designing end-to-end solutions and architecture for enterprise products. He is reachable at agrawal.amit24@gmail.com and https://www.linkedin.com/in/amit-agrawal-30383425.

Acknowledgments

To my family, Shweta and Soumil, for being always there by my side and letting me sacrifice their time for my intellectual and spiritual pursuits. For taking care of everything while I am immersed in authoring. This and other accomplishments of my life wouldn't have been possible without your love and support. To my Mom and my sister for the love and support as always, without your blessings nothing is possible.

To my coauthor Piyush, thank you for the hard work and quick turnarounds to deliver this. It was an enriching experience. Also to Siddharth Choudhary & Saurabh Tripathi, thank you for your research input for this book which helped in shaping up practical examples for readers.

To my team here at HCL who has been a source of inspiration with their hard work, ever engaging technical conversations and their technical depth. Your everflowing ideas are a source of happiness and excitement every single day. Piyush Pandey, Sarvesh Pandey, Amit Agrawal, Vasand Kumar, Punith Krishnamurthy, Sandeep Sharma, Amit Dwivedi, Gauarv Bhardwaj, Nitin Narotra, and Vivek thank you for being their and making technology fun.

To Celestine and Aditee and the entire team at Apress for turning our ideas into reality. It has been an amazing experience authoring with you and over the years, the speed of decision making and the editorial support has been excellent.

To all that I have had the opportunity to work with my co-authors, colleagues, managers, mentors and guides, in this world of 7 Billion, it was conincidence that brought us together it was and is an enriching experience to be associated with you and learn from you. All ideas and paths are an assimilation of conversations that I have had and epxeriences I have shared. Thank you.

ACKNOWLEDGMENTS

Thank you goddess Saraswati, for guiding me to the path of knowledge and spirituality and keep me on this path.

असतो मा साद गमय, तमसो मा ज्योतिर् गमय, मृत्योर मा अमृतम् गमय

(Asato Ma Sad Gamaya, Tamaso Ma Jyotir Gamaya, Mrityor Ma Amritam Gamaya)

Lead us from ignorance to truth, lead us from darkness to light, Lead us from death to immortality.

CHAPTER 1

Container Overview

This first chapter will introduce readers to the world of containers, microservice applications, and their associated monitoring and management tools ecosystem. We will also look into how containers and the ecosystem around them are assembled. The chapter will cover the following topics:

- Introducing Containers
- Evolution of Container Technology
- Docker and Kubernetes Architecture
- Container Monitoring Ecosystem Overview

Introducing Containers

Over the past few years, worldwide digital transformation has accelerated by leaps and bounds, as companies of all sizes find new ways to leverage technology to boost their agility and provide better services to their customers. Fueling this fire is the need to survive in a changing environment. For many companies, an initial step toward digital transformation is modernizing their applications and taking advantage of automated environments in the cloud. Modernization empowers companies with the following:

© Navin Sabharwal, Piyush Pandey 2020
N. Sabharwal and P. Pandey, *Monitoring Microservices and Containerized Applications*,
https://doi.org/10.1007/978-1-4842-6216-0_1

- **Elasticity:** the ability to respond to spikes in customer demand

- **Availability:** the ability to serve customers' requests wherever and whenever

- **Agility:** the ability to quickly fix a problem or deploy new functionality that customers want

When cloud computing first started gaining traction among enterprises, one major motivation was cost reduction. Many organizations began to recognize that cloud computing's capability to transform IT offered a vision of infrastructure as a dynamic, self-service-based, and pay-as-you-go consumption of resources that would augment their aspirations to become twenty-first-century business enterprises. Containers are taking the innovations introduced by virtualization and cloud computing to the next level.

Containers provide a portable, consistent, and lightweight software environment for applications to easily run and scale anywhere. Throughout its lifecycle, an application will operate in many different environments, from development to testing, to integration, to pre-production and production. An application may be hosted on either physical infrastructure or virtual on-premises infrastructure, or may be ported to a public cloud infrastructure. Before containers, IT teams had to consider the compatibility restrictions of each new environment and write additional code to ensure the application would function in all the different environments. To solve this problem of portability and to ensure that an application can run irrespective of the changes in underlying infrastructure components, containers were developed to package the application with its dependencies, configuration files, and interfaces— allowing developers to use a single image that moves seamlessly between different hosts.

What Are Containers?

Containers are a way to wrap up an application into its own isolated package. Everything the application requires to run successfully as a process is now captured and executed within the container.

A container enables bundling of all application dependencies, like library dependencies, runtimes, and so forth. This allows for the concept of standardization and consistency across environments, as the container will always come pre-loaded with all the pre-requisites/dependencies required to run the application service. Now you can develop the application code on your personal work station and then safely deploy it to run on production infrastructure.

A container is an instance of a container image. A container image is a way to package an app or service (like a snapshot) and then deploy it in a reliable and reproducible way.

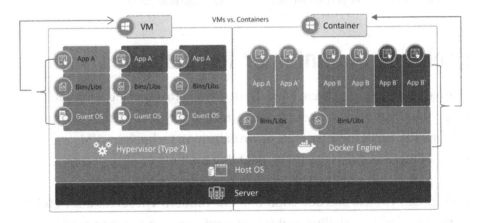

Figure 1-1. *Container vs VM comparison*

Building applications with containers helps bring in agility for developing, testing, and deploying an application across any cloud. With containers, you can take an app from development to production with little or no code change. However, when you deploy to VMs, you have to either do it manually or use a CI/CD tool with Infra as Code solutions (see Figure 1-1). You might need to perform tasks like modifying configuration items, copying application content between servers, and running interactive setup programs based on application setup, followed by testing. In case of manual setup, this can consume significant time. With an automated setup, the amount of time may be less than that required by the manual approach, but the reduction when a container is used is even more significant. Below Figure 1-1 shows how applications are segregated with a separate Operating System layer and only share the hardware using the hypervisor in virtualization. This also shows how containers are sharing the operating system and there is no separate OS for each application, only the components which are different for each application are deployed separately, the OS image is shared.

Evolution of Container Technology

The earliest computers were typically dedicated to a specific task that might take days or even weeks to run, which is why in the 1960s and through the 1970s there was rise of virtualization technology. VM partitioning is as old as the 1960s, enabling multiple users to access a computer concurrently. The following decades were marked by widespread VM use and development. The modern VM serves a variety of purposes, such as installing multiple operating systems on one machine to enable it to host multiple applications with specific, unique OS requirements that differ from each other.

In 1979, the chroot system call was introduced, which allowed one to change the root directory of a process and its children to a new location in the file system. Chroot was a significant step toward the rise of containers, as it allowed process isolation by restricting an application's file access to a specific directory. This helped improve system security.

Introduced in 2001, Linux VServer is an operating system virtualization technology that is implemented by patching the Linux kernel. In 2004, the first public beta of Solaris Containers was released; it combined system resource controls and boundary separation provided by zones. Process containers, or control groups (cgroups), were introduced by Google in 2006 and were designed for limiting, accounting for, and isolating the resource usage (CPU, memory, disk I/O, network) of a collection of processes.

LXC (LinuX Containers) was the first mature implementation of Linux Container Manager. It was implemented in 2008 using cgroups and Linux namespaces.

Finally, Docker emerged in 2013, which led to a tectonic shift in the way applications are designed, developed, and deployed. Docker built its foundation on two systems, LXC and libcontainers. Libcontainers came from LMCTFY, which was an open source container stack where applications created and managed their own subcontainers. Docker also used LXC in its initial stages and later replaced that container manager with its own library, libcontainer. In addition to building on previous software, Docker had an easy-to-use GUI and was capable of running multiple applications with different requirements on a single OS.

Container technology's momentum continued in 2017 with the introduction of Kubernetes, which is a highly effective container orchestration technology. Container technology ramped up over the next few years as multiple players, such as Openshift, Pivotal, Azure, Google, AWS, and even Docker, changed gears to support the open source Kubernetes container scheduler and orchestration tool, making it the most popular and widely used container orchestration technology. In 2017, Microsoft enabled organizations to run Linux containers on Windows servers, which was a major development for Microsoft-based businesses that wanted to containerize applications and stay compatible with their existing systems.

Docker and Kubernetes Architecture

Containers are a way of packaging software, mainly the application's code, libraries, and dependencies. Containers group and isolate a set of processes and resources, such as memory, CPU, disk, and so forth, from the host and any other containers. The isolation ensures that any processes inside the container cannot see any processes or resources outside the container. Containers typically leverage Linux kernel features like namespaces (ipc, uts, mount, pid, network, and user) and cgroups, which provide an abstraction layer on top of an existing kernel instance, thus creating isolated environments similar to virtual machines.

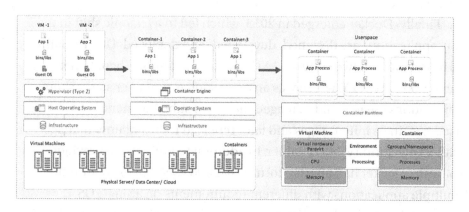

Figure 1-2. *Container architecture with respect to physical and virtual infrastructure*

Docker is a container-based technology where containers share the host OS kernel by using Linux kernel features like namespaces and control groups. Docker is available in two versions: Docker Community Edition (CE) and Docker Enterprise Edition (EE). Docker EE is designed for enterprise adoption and is recommended over Docker CE for running containerized business-critical applications in production.

Docker architecture is based on client–server architecture (Figure 1-3). The Docker client interacts with the Docker daemon, which in turn manages the lifecycle of the container from building and running to scaling.

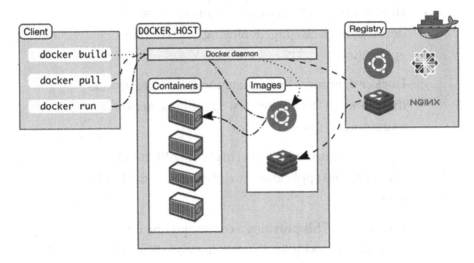

Figure 1-3. *Docker architecture*

- **Docker client:** Docker users can interact with Docker through a client.

- **Docker host:** The Docker host provides a base environment in which to run containerized applications. It provides all the necessary infrastructure base components right from the Docker daemon: images, containers, networks, and storage.

- **Docker images:** Docker images are equivalent to an OS template or an image, with the difference being that instead of packaging the OS it contains the application source code along with all the dependencies required to run the application. Using these images, we can achieve application portability across infrastructure without worrying about the underlying technologies used.

7

- **Registries:** Registries are used for managing Docker images. There are two major registry types: public and private.

- **Docker engine:** The Docker engine enables developing, packaging, deploying, and running applications.

- **Docker daemon:** Docker daemon is the core process that manages Docker images, containers, networks, and storage volumes.

- **Docker Engine REST API:** This is the API used by containerized applications to interact with the Docker daemon.

- **Docker CLI:** This provides a command line interface for interacting with the Docker daemon (Figure 1-4).

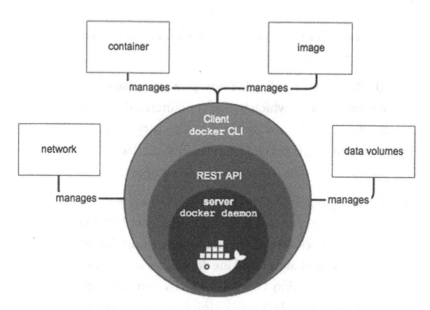

Figure 1-4. *Docker management interfaces (CLI & API)*

Kubernetes is an open-source container management (orchestration) tool that provides an abstraction layer over the container to manage the container fleets leveraging REST APIs. Kubernetes is portable in nature and is supported to run on various public or private cloud platforms, such as Physical Server, GCP, AWS, Azure, OpenStack, or Apache Mesos.

Similar to Docker, Kubernetes follows a client–server architecture. It has a master server, which could be one or more than one, that is used to manage target nodes where containerized applications are deployed. It also has the feature of service discovery.

The master server consists of various components, including a kube-apiserver, an etcd storage, a kube-controller-manager, a cloud-controller-manager, a kube-scheduler, and a DNS server for Kubernetes services. Node components include Kubelet and kube-proxy (Figure 1-5).

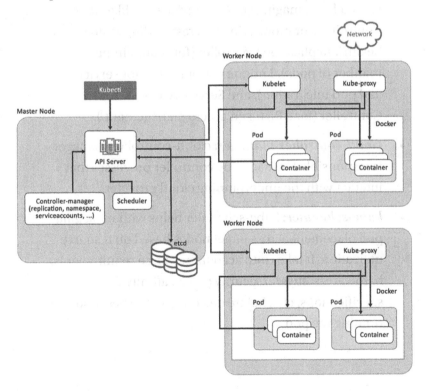

Figure 1-5. *Kubernetes architecture*

Master Node

The following are the main components on the master node:

- ***etcd cluster:*** etcd cluster is a distributed key–value storage used to store Kubernetes cluster data (such as number of pods, their state, namespace, etc.), API objects, and service discovery details.

- ***kube-apiserver:*** Kubernetes API server provides a programmatic interface for container management activities (like pods, services, replication sets/ controllers) using REST APIs.

- ***kube-controller-manager:*** kube-controller-manager is used for managing controller processes like Node Controller (for monitoring and responding to node health), Replication Controller (for maintaining number of pods), Endpoints Controller (for service and pod integration), and Service Account/Token Controller (for API/token access management).

- ***cloud-controller-manager:*** cloud-controller-manager is responsible for managing controller processes that interact with the underpinning cloud provider.

- ***kube-scheduler:*** kube-scheduler helps with managing pod placement across target nodes based on resource utilization. It takes into account resource requirements, hardware/software/security policy, affinity specifications, etc., before deciding on the best node for running the pod.

Node (Worker) Components

The following are the main components on a (worker) node:

- *Kubelet:* Kubelet is the agent component running on a worker node, and its main purpose is to ensure containers are running in the pod. Any containers that are outside the management of Kubernetes are not managed by Kubelet. It ensures that workers, pods, and their containers are in a healthy state, as well as reports these metrics back to the Kubernetes master node.

- *kube-proxy:* kube-proxy is a proxy service that runs on the worker node to manage inter-pod networking and communication. It's also a crucial component for service concept realization.

- **Kubectl:** kubectl is a command line tool used for Kubernetes cluster management and uses APIs exposed by kube-apiserver .

- **Pod:** A pod is a logical collection of one or more containers that formulates a single application and is represented as a running process on worker nodes. A pod packages application containers, storage, network and other configurations required for running containers. A pod can horizontally scale out and enable application deployment strategies like rolling updates and blue/green deployment, which aim to minimize application downtime and risk during upgrades.

- **Service:** A service provides an interface for the collection of one or more pods bound by policy. Since a pod's lifecycle is ephemeral in nature, services help to ensure application access without worrying even if a backend pod dies abruptly .

- **Namespace:** A namespace is a logical construct used for dividing cluster resources across multiple users. You can use resource quotas with a namespace to manage resource consumption by multiple application teams.

- **Deployment:** Deployment represents a collection of one or more running pods that formulate an application as per the pod specification. It works closely with Deployment Controller to ensure the pod is available as per the user specification mentioned in the pod specification.

Microservices Architecture

Microservices architecture is an approach to building an application using a set of small services. Each service runs in its own process and communicates with other processes. Each microservice represents a functionality that can now be developed, deployed, and managed independently. Each of these smaller services has its individual data model, logic, data storage technologies (SQL, NoSQL), and programming language.

Additionally, microservices can now scale out independently, meaning you can scale out a specific service instead of the entire application based on utilization patterns. This approach helps organizations save money on infrastructure components that may remain unutilized in the traditional monolithic application world (Figure 1-6).

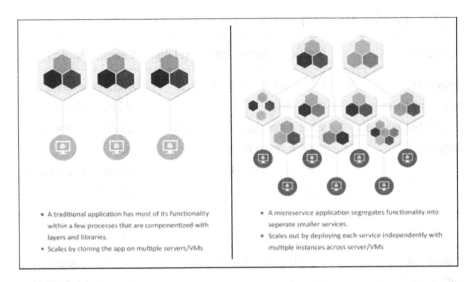

Figure 1-6. *Monolithic vs microservice application comparison*

Containers are pretty much the accepted norm for managing microservice architectures. That's true for hosted services that have adopted Kubernetes and offer services based on a container infrastructure. It's also true for organizations that increasingly use containers to manage their workloads and adapt to new market conditions. Advancements in container technology ecosystems are opening new avenues of monitoring. For example, service mesh technologies, when paired with Kubernetes, enable traffic management, service identity, policy enforcement, and telemetry for microservices.

Monitoring and health management of application services and infrastructure is an important aspect of operational stability, especially for the production environment.

Health monitoring allows near-real-time visibility into the state of your application services, pods, containers, and underlying infrastructure. Microservices-based applications often leverage health checks to keep track of application availability, performance, faults, etc. Table 1-1 shows the monitoring areas to be considered for microservices-based applications.

Table 1-1. *Monitoring Areas*

Architecture	Metric Selection Decision Logic	Sample Metrics
Microservice In general, there is one process to track per container.	Where are the new services deployed? What percentage of time is the service reachable? How many requests are enqueued?	Average percentage of time a request-servicing thread is busy. Number of enqueued requests. Percentage of time a service is reachable
Application Multiple microservices running simultaneously constitute an application	Does the database respond quickly? Are the message queues fast enough? How does heap memory usage change over time? Are application services responsive?	Query execution frequency, response time, and failure rate. Response time, failure rate
Container Separate from the underlying process being run within it, containers are also monitored	How responsive are the processes within container? Which images have been deployed? Are specific containers associated with over-utilization of host?	CPU throttle time. Container disk I/O. Memory usage. Network (volume, dropped packets)
Container Cluster Multiple containers deployed to run as group. Many of the metrics of individual containers can also be summarized.	Are your clusters healthy and properly sized? Can applications be effectively run on fewer nodes?	Percentage of clusters remaining operational compared to those originally deployed

(*continued*)

Table 1-1. (*continued*)

Architecture	Metric Selection Decision Logic	Sample Metrics
Host Also called a node, multiple hosts can support a cluster of containers	Do changes in utilization indicate a problem with a process or application?	Percentage of total memory capacity in use. Percentage of time CPUs are utilized
Infrastructure Cloud in which hosts are running	How much does it cost to run each service or deployment? What is the ratio of microservices and/or containers per instance?	Network traffic Utilization of databases, storage, and other shared services
End user The users using the application or other applications using APIs.	What is the average web/transaction response time experienced by users or by target application?	Response time. Number and percentage of failed user actions/transactions

Container Monitoring Ecosystem Overview

With the rise of container technology, there was a requirement to have a supporting ecosystem via which enterprises could run mission-critical workloads on the container. With the introduction of container technology and microservices architecture, monitoring solutions now need to manage data for both non-ephemeral and ephemeral services. Collecting data from applications composed of so many services has now become vastly complex. In a DevOps world, monitoring containerized applications and environments is not just needed for the operations team but also as a feedback mechanism for developers to understand their application performance bottlenecks/faults/bugs/etc. The following are the nuances to be considered when it comes to container monitoring:

- **Short lifespan of containers:** Containers are constantly provisioned and decommissioned based on demand. This can lead to cycles, where in the morning a container host cluster is filled up with microservices belonging to Workload A, while in the afternoon this same host is serving Application B. This means that a security breach, slow performance, or downtime on a certain host will have a very different business impact depending on when it happens.

- **One microservice can be leveraged by numerous applications:** As different applications often share the same microservices, monitoring tools must be able to dynamically map which instance of a microservice impacts which application.

- **Temporary nature of containers:** When the assembly of a new container is triggered based on a container image, networking connections, storage resources, and integration with other required services have to be instantly provided. This dynamic provisioning can impact the performance of related and unrelated infrastructure components.

- **More levels to watch:** In the case of Kubernetes, enterprise IT needs to monitor at the level of nodes (host servers), pods (host clusters), and individual containers. In addition, monitoring has to happen on the VM and storage levels, as well as on the microservices level.

- **Different container management frameworks:**
  Amazon EC2 Container Services run on Amazon's
  proprietary management platform, while Google
  naturally supports Kubernetes (so does VMware),
  and Docker supports Swarm. Container monitoring
  solutions need to be aware of the differences between
  these container management platforms.

- **Microservices change fast and often:** Anomaly
  detection for microservices-based applications is much
  more difficult than that for standard apps, as apps
  consisting of microservices are constantly changing.
  New microservices are added to the app and existing
  ones are updated in a very quick sequence, leading to
  different infrastructure usage patterns. The monitoring
  tool needs to be able to differentiate between "normal"
  usage patterns caused by intentional changes and
  actual anomalies that have to be addressed.

Per Host Metrics Explosion			
Component	# of Metrics for a Traditional Stack	for 10 Container Cluster with 1 Underlying Host	for 10 Container Cluster with 1 Underlying Host
Operating System	100	100	200
Orchestrator	n/a	50	50
Container	n/a	500 (50 per container)	5,000 (50 per container)
Application	50	500 (50 per container)	5,000 (50 per container)
Total # of Metrics	150	1,150	10,250

Figure 1-7. Metrics explosion view with container technology evolution

In order to have complete visibility of containerized applications, you need to have data from the various components that formulate the base infrastructure for running containers. This means you need to monitor the following:

- Application services

- Pods and containers

- Clusters running the containers

- Network for service/pod/cluster communication

- Host OS/machine running the cluster

Choosing the right monitoring toolset is certainly important and should be based upon the pros and cons of the solution. The following are the options available in the market for container monitoring:

- **Prometheus:** Prometheus is one of the oldest and most popular open source container monitoring solutions available. It's a graduated cloud native computing foundation (CNCF) project that offers powerful querying capabilities, visualization, and alerting.

- **Grafana:** Grafana is a popular reporting dashboarding tool for container environments. It has the capability to leverage data feeds from Prometheus and other sources for visualizing information from the Kubernetes environment.

- **cAdvisor:** cAdvisor is another container resource monitoring tool that works at the worker node level instead of the pod level. It has the capability to discover all the containers running on worker nodes and to provide metrics about CPU, memory, filesystem, etc. This solution does not provide long-term storage of metric data or analytics services on top, which would be useful for driving insights for the operations team.

- **Heapster:** Heapster aggregates monitoring data across multiple nodes using Kubelet and cAdvisor at the backend. Unlike cAdvisor, Heapster works at the pod level instead of the worker node level.

- **Sysdig:** Sysdig Monitor helps in monitoring container applications by providing end-to-end visibility—from application service to pod to container to node level— of the availability, performance, and faults across multiple container technologies and clouds.

- **Dynatrace:** Dynatrace has a new suite of tools available for container monitoring and alerting. Leveraging an agent-based approach, it can discover and fetch data about containerized application services, pods, containers, worker nodes, etc.

- **AppDynamics:** Application and business performance software that collects data from agents installed on the host using Docker APIs.

- **Fluentd:** Open source data collector for unified logging layers.

- **Collectd:** A small daemon that periodically collects system information and provides mechanisms to store and monitor container metrics.

- **Cloud native:** Leading cloud providers like AWS (Cloudwatch), Azure (Azure Monitor), and Google Cloud (Stackdriver) have their own native mechanisms to monitor container ecosystems on AWS EKS, Azure AKS, and Google GKE.

Summary

In this chapter, we have seen the container ecosystem evolution, Docker and Kubernetes architecture, and the benefits and challenges of container technology. We have also looked at monitoring and management tools and metrics for effective container monitoring. In the next chapter, we will start with practical exercises to set up Docker and Kubernetes, and we will end with deploying our first containerized application to kickstart the container monitoring journey.

CHAPTER 2

Getting Started with Containers

This chapter will provide hands-on steps for installing Docker and Kubernetes. We also look into how to deploy a containerized application on Kubernetes. This will set us up for the following chapters, where we will monitor this setup using Prometheus. This chapter will cover the following topics:

- Setting Up Docker CE and Running First Container
- Setting Up Kubernetes
- Deploying the Sample Application

Lab Environment Setup

For our lab environment, we will be using two Redhat 7 virtual machines (VMs). We recommend that readers use at minimum two CPUs, 8 GB RAM, and 80 GB hard disk (under/location) for the exercises here in Chapter 2. VMs can be hosted on VMware Workstation, VMware, Hyper V, or a public cloud like AWS, Azure, or GCP. Kindly ensure both VMs are able to communicate with each other on a private IP address and have outbound internet connectivity to download packages for installation.

Figure 2-1 represents the lab environment we will be setting up as part of this chapter.

N. Sabharwal and P. Pandey, *Monitoring Microservices and Containerized Applications*, https://doi.org/10.1007/978-1-4842-6216-0_2

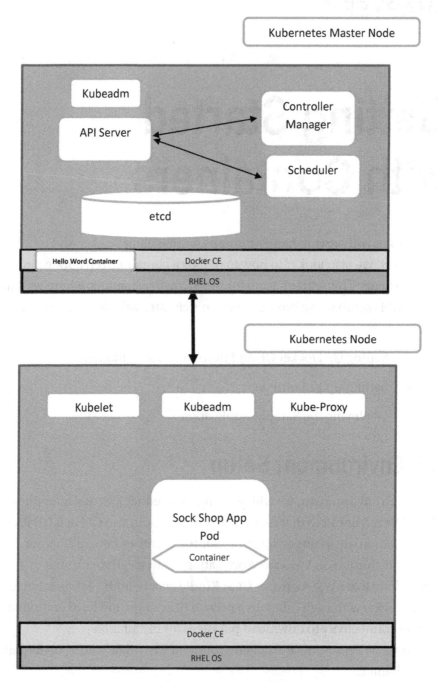

Figure 2-1. *Lab environnement setup for Chapter 2*

As part of this chapter, we will be performing the following steps:

- We will begin with installation of Docker CE engine on two nodes.

- After Docker CE engine setup, we will run a "Hello World" sample on the master Kubernetes node to validate our setup.

- We will install the core Kubernetes components on the master node using the Kubeadm utility.

- We will install Kubernetes components on the worker/target node.

- We will join the worker/target node with the master node.

- Finally, we will deploy the containerized application Sock-shop on the worker/target node.

Setting Up Docker CE

To start with container monitoring using Prometheus and Alert Manager, the first step will be to set up the container ecosystem. We will set up Docker CE 18.09.0 on both of our Redhat VMs. This will serve as the container engine for our applications.

Note   Please make sure all the commands mentioned in Steps 1 through 8 are executed successfully on both Redhat VMs. Steps 9 and 10 will be only executed on the master node.

---

1. SSH into Redhat VMs. We will begin with cleaning
    up any older version of Docker (if any) present
    on the system. It is recommended to clean any
    pre-existing installation in case readers are using
    existing VMs for this exercise. If readers are using
    fresh VMs then kindly proceed to Step 2.

    ```
    $ sudo yum remove docker docker-common docker-
    selinux docker-engine-selinux
    ```

2. Execute the following command to install pre-
    requisite packages for Docker CE. The yum-config-
    manager utility is used to manage the main yum
    configuration options like enabling/disabling/
    adding repositories. device-mapper-persistent-
    data and lvm2 are needed for the device mapper
    storage driver. The device mapper storage driver
    for containers enables capabilities like thin
    provisioning and snapshotting, which are useful for
    image and container management.

    ```
    $ sudo yum install -y yum-utils device-mapper-
    persistent-data lvm2
    ```

3. Configure the docker-ce repo by executing the
    following command:

    ```
    $ sudo yum-config-manager --add-repo https://
    download.docker.com/linux/centos/docker-ce.repo
    ```

    Docker CE repo configuration will occur after the
    execution of the preceding command. It will save
    the repo under _/etc/yum.repos.d/docker-ce.
    repo as mentioned in Figure 2-2.

```
[root@devops0088 ~]# yum-config-manager --add-repo https://download.docker.com/linux/centos/docker-ce.repo
Loaded plugins: langpacks, product-id, subscription-manager
adding repo from: https://download.docker.com/linux/centos/docker-ce.repo
grabbing file https://download.docker.com/linux/centos/docker-ce.repo to /etc/yum.repos.d/docker-ce.repo
repo saved to /etc/yum.repos.d/docker-ce.repo
```

Figure 2-2. *Docker CE repo configuration*

4. Execute the following command to update the yum
    cache. This will ensure yum configuration is updated
    as per the command executed in the previous step.

    ```
    $ sudo yum makecache fast
    ```

5. Run the following command for SELinux policies for
    container runtimes. This package is needed for setting
    up container SELinux policy on Redhat systems. This
    is required to setup the security policies for Docker
    containers to access and share the resources.

    ```
    $ sudo yum install -y http://mirror.centos.
    org/centos/7/extras/x86_64/Packages/container-
    selinux-2.107-3.el7.noarch.rpm
    ```

    The SELinux policy gets updated after the execution
    of the preceding command.

6. Run the following command to install Docker
    community edition:

    ```
    $ sudo yum install docker-ce-18.09.0-3.el7 -y
    ```

    Installation of Docker CE is completed after the
    execution of the preceding command.

7. Run the following command to enable the Docker service:

    ```
    $ sudo systemctl enable docker.service
    ```

    Enable the service of Docker after executing the
    preceding command.

8. Execute the following commands to start and then validate the status of Docker service (see Figure 2-3):

```
$ sudo systemctl start docker.service
$ sudo systemctl status docker.service
```

```
[root@devops0088 ~]$ sudo systemctl status docker.service
● docker.service - Docker Application Container Engine
   Loaded: loaded (/usr/lib/systemd/system/docker.service; enabled; vendor preset: disabled)
   Active: active (running) since Wed 2019-10-30 15:37:28 IST; 16s ago
     Docs: https://docs.docker.com
 Main PID: 20937 (dockerd)
    Tasks: 10
   Memory: 42.1M
   CGroup: /system.slice/docker.service
           └─20937 /usr/bin/dockerd -H fd:// --containerd=/run/containerd/containerd.sock
```

Figure 2-3. *Start and verify Docker CE service. Look for the active (running) status of the docker service*

9. Pull the Docker image from Docker Hub by executing the following command. Docker Hub is a service provided by Docker for searching and sharing container images. Docker Hub provides repositories with access to push and pull container images. Additionally, Docker Hub provides official images managed by Docker and publisher images managed by external vendors.

```
$ docker pull hello-world
```

10. Now, let's validate our installation of the Docker Engine by running the first Docker container on our master node. Execute the following command after logging in to the master node. You can verify the installation as shown in Figure 2-4.

```
$ docker run hello-world
```

```
[root@devops0088 ~]# docker run hello-world

Hello from Docker!
This message shows that your installation appears to be working correctly.

To generate this message, Docker took the following steps:
 1. The Docker client contacted the Docker daemon.
 2. The Docker daemon pulled the "hello-world" image from the Docker Hub.
    (amd64)
 3. The Docker daemon created a new container from that image which runs the
    executable that produces the output you are currently reading.
 4. The Docker daemon streamed that output to the Docker client, which sent it
    to your terminal.

To try something more ambitious, you can run an Ubuntu container with:
 $ docker run -it ubuntu bash

Share images, automate workflows, and more with a free Docker ID:
 https://hub.docker.com/

For more examples and ideas, visit:
 https://docs.docker.com/get-started/
```

Figure 2-4. *Running first Docker container*

If you see the response as "Hello from the Docker!" the Docker
container is running successfully.

Setting Up Kubernetes

The following steps elaborate the commands needed to set up Kubernetes
master and worker nodes. In the previous section, we set up Docker
Engine on both nodes.

Installing Kubernetes on RHEL 7

Let's start:

1. Disable SELinux and set up firewall rules on the master
    node. Setting SELinux in permissive mode effectively
    disables it and thereby enables containers to access
    the host filesystem. The br_netfilter and net.
    bridge.bridge-nf-call-iptables modules are used
    for setting up Kubernetes networking options.

Navigate to the Kubernetes master node and execute
the following commands to set the hostname and
disable SELinux:

```
$ hostnamectl set-hostname 'k8s-master'
$ exec bash
$ setenforce 0
$ sed -i --follow-symlinks 's/SELINUX=enforcing/
SELINUX=disabled/g' /etc/sysconfig/selinux
```

```
~]# hostnamectl set-hostname 'k8s-master'
~]# exec bash
~]# setenforce 0
~]# sed -i --follow-symlinks 's/SELINUX=enforcing/SELINUX=disabled/g'
/etc/sysconfig/selinux
```

Figure 2-5. *SELinux policy update*

Set the following firewall rules on your master node
by executing the following commands:

```
firewall-cmd --permanent --add-port=6443/tcp
firewall-cmd --permanent --add-port=2379-2380/tcp
firewall-cmd --permanent --add-port=10250/tcp
firewall-cmd --permanent --add-port=10251/tcp
firewall-cmd --permanent --add-port=10252/tcp
firewall-cmd --permanent --add-port=10255/tcp
firewall-cmd --reload
modprobe br_netfilter
echo '1' > /proc/sys/net/bridge/bridge-nf-call-iptables
```

Table 2-1 lists the relevance of the inbound TCP
ports enabled on the master node. See Figure 2-6.

Table 2-1. *Ports required for Kubernetes*

Port Range	Purpose
6443*	These ports are used for Kubernetes API access.
2379-2380	These ports are used for etcd server client API.
10250	This port is used for Kubelet API.
10251	This port is used for kube-scheduler.
10252	This port is used for kube-controller-manager.

```
[root@k8s-master ~]# firewall-cmd --permanent --add-port=6443/tcp
success
[root@k8s-master ~]# firewall-cmd --permanent --add-port=2379-2380/tcp
success
[root@k8s-master ~]# firewall-cmd --permanent --add-port=10250/tcp
success
[root@k8s-master ~]# firewall-cmd --permanent --add-port=10251/tcp
success
[root@k8s-master ~]# firewall-cmd --permanent --add-port=10252/tcp
success
[root@k8s-master ~]# firewall-cmd --permanent --add-port=10255/tcp
success
[root@k8s-master ~]# firewall-cmd --reload
success
[root@k8s-master ~]# modprobe br_netfilter
[root@k8s-master ~]# echo '1' > /proc/sys/net/bridge/bridge-nf-call-iptables
```

Figure 2-6. *Firewall policy update*

Note   In the absence of a DNS server in your lab environment, you need to update the /etc/hosts file on the master and worker nodes manually with entries as depicted below.

- <Master node IP > k8s-master
- <Worker node IP > worker-node1

For example, in our environment, the hosts file had the following entries on both servers (see Figure 2-7).

```
10.1.150.126    k8s-master
10.1.150.150    worker-node1
```

Figure 2-7. */etc/hosts file entry sample*

2. Configure the Kubernetes repository on the master node. Execute the following command to configure the repositories needed for Kubernetes installation:

```
cat <<EOF > /etc/yum.repos.d/kubernetes.repo
[kubernetes]
name=Kubernetes
baseurl=https://packages.cloud.google.com/yum/repos/
kubernetes-el7-x86_64
enabled=1
gpgcheck=1
repo_gpgcheck=1
gpgkey=https://packages.cloud.google.com/yum/doc/yum-
key.gpg https://packages.cloud.google.com/yum/doc/rpm-
package-key.gpg
EOF
```

3. Install Kubeadm on the master node (Figure 2-8). This will be used to deploy Kubernetes components in an automated fashion on the master and worker/target nodes. Execute the following command to install kubeadm:

```
$ yum install kubeadm -y
Start and enable kubectl service by executing below
command

$systemctl restart kubelet && systemctl enable kubelet
$systemctl status  kubelet
```

```
systemctl restart kubelet && systemctl enable kubelet
systemctl status  kubelet
kubelet.service - kubelet: The Kubernetes Node Agent
 Loaded: loaded (/usr/lib/systemd/system/kubelet.service; enabled; vendor preset: disabled)
Drop-In: /usr/lib/systemd/system/kubelet.service.d
         └─10-kubeadm.conf
 Active: active (running) since Wed 2020-05-13 19:01:02 IST; 2min 31s ago
   Docs: https://kubernetes.io/docs/
```

Figure 2-8. *Kubeadm installation*

4. Execute the following command to initialize
   Kubernetes kubeadm on the master node:

```
$sudo swapoff -a
$sudo sed -i '/ swap / s/^\(.*\)$/#\1/g' /etc/fstab
$kubeadm init
```

Execute the following commands to use the cluster as a
root user:

```
$mkdir -p $HOME/.kube
$cp -i /etc/kubernetes/admin.conf $HOME/.kube/config
$chown $(id -u):$(id -g) $HOME/.kube/config
```

5. Deploy the pod network to the cluster on the master
   node.

   Run the following command to get the status of the cluster and
   pods (Figure 2-9):

```
$kubectl get nodes
$kubectl get pods --all-namespaces
```

```
[root@k8s-master ~]# kubectl get nodes
NAME         STATUS     ROLES    AGE     VERSION
k8s-master   NotReady   master   13m     v1.16.2
[root@k8s-master ~]# kubectl get pods --all-namespaces
NAMESPACE     NAME                                      READY   STATUS    RESTARTS   AGE
kube-system   coredns-5644d7b6d9-mwhbf                  0/1     Pending   0          13m
kube-system   coredns-5644d7b6d9-vkqgq                  0/1     Pending   0          13m
kube-system   etcd-k8s-master                           1/1     Running   0          12m
kube-system   kube-apiserver-k8s-master                 1/1     Running   0          12m
kube-system   kube-controller-manager-k8s-master        1/1     Running   0          12m
kube-system   kube-proxy-57kfh                          1/1     Running   0          13m
kube-system   kube-scheduler-k8s-master                 1/1     Running   0          12m
```

Figure 2-9. *List Kubernetes nodes and namespaces*

Execute the following commands to deploy the network (Figure 2-10):

```
$export kubever=$(kubectl version | base64 | tr -d '\n')
$kubectl apply -f "https://cloud.weave.works/k8s/net?k8s-
version=$kubever"
```

```
[root@k8s-master ~]# kubectl apply -f "https://cloud.weave.works/k8s/net?k8s-version=$kubever"
serviceaccount/weave-net created
clusterrole.rbac.authorization.k8s.io/weave-net created
clusterrolebinding.rbac.authorization.k8s.io/weave-net created
role.rbac.authorization.k8s.io/weave-net created
rolebinding.rbac.authorization.k8s.io/weave-net created
daemonset.apps/weave-net created
```

Figure 2-10. *Kubernetes network deployment*

Execute the following command to get the status of the cluster and pods; this time, the statuses should come as "Ready" and "Running" states, respectively (Figure 2-11).

```
$kubectl get nodes
$kubectl get pods --all-namespaces
```

```
[root@k8s-master ~]# kubectl get nodes
NAME         STATUS   ROLES    AGE     VERSION
k8s-master   Ready    master   21m     v1.16.2
[root@k8s-master ~]# kubectl get pods --all-namespaces
NAMESPACE     NAME                                  READY   STATUS    RESTARTS   AGE
kube-system   coredns-5644d7b6d9-mwhbf              1/1     Running   0          21m
kube-system   coredns-5644d7b6d9-vkqgq              1/1     Running   0          21m
kube-system   etcd-k8s-master                       1/1     Running   0          20m
kube-system   kube-apiserver-k8s-master             1/1     Running   0          20m
kube-system   kube-controller-manager-k8s-master    1/1     Running   0          20m
kube-system   kube-proxy-57kfh                      1/1     Running   0          21m
kube-system   kube-scheduler-k8s-master             1/1     Running   0          20m
kube-system   weave-net-dxfqc                       2/2     Running   0          2m47s
```

Figure 2-11. *List Kubernetes nodes and namespaces*

Add Worker Node to the Kubernetes Master Node

Now, we'll add a worker node:

1. Update the /etc/hosts file on the worker node
    (10.1.150.150):

    - <Master node IP > k8s-master1

    - <Worker node IP > worker-node1

    For example, in our environment the hosts file had the following
    entries on the worker node (Figure 2-12):

    ```
    10.1.150.126    k8s-master
    10.1.150.150    worker-node1
    ```

Figure 2-12. */etc/hosts file entry sample*

2. Disable SELinux and configure the firewall rules on the worker node:

```
$setenforce 0
$sed -i --follow-symlinks 's/SELINUX=enforcing/
SELINUX=disabled/g' /etc/sysconfig/selinux
$firewall-cmd --permanent --add-port=10250/tcp
$firewall-cmd --permanent --add-port=10255/tcp
$firewall-cmd --permanent --add-port=30000-32767/tcp
$firewall-cmd --permanent --add-port=6783/tcp
$firewall-cmd   --reload
$echo '1' > /proc/sys/net/bridge/bridge-nf-call-iptables
```

Table 2-2 lists the relevance of each inbound TCP port on the worker/target node (see Figure 2-13).

Table 2-2. *Port ranges required for Kubernetes*

Port Range	Purpose
10250	This port is used by the Kubelet API.
30000-32767	This port is used by NodePort Services.

```
[root@devops0088 ~]# setenforce 0
[root@devops0088 ~]# sed -i --follow-symlinks 's/SELINUX=enforcing/SELINUX=disabled/g' /etc/sysconfig/selinux
[root@devops0088 ~]# firewall-cmd --permanent --add-port=10250/tcp
success
[root@devops0088 ~]# firewall-cmd --permanent --add-port=10255/tcp
success
[root@devops0088 ~]# firewall-cmd --permanent --add-port=30000-32767/tcp
success
[root@devops0088 ~]# firewall-cmd --permanent --add-port=6783/tcp
success
[root@devops0088 ~]# firewall-cmd   --reload
success
[root@devops0088 ~]# echo '1' > /proc/sys/net/bridge/bridge-nf-call-iptables
```

Figure 2-13. *SELinux and firewall policy update*

3. Configure Kubernetes repositories on the worker
    node (10.1.150.150)(Figure 2-14):

    ```
    cat <<EOF > /etc/yum.repos.d/kubernetes.repo
    [kubernetes]
    name=Kubernetes
    baseurl=https://packages.cloud.google.com/yum/repos/
    kubernetes-el7-x86_64
    enabled=1
    gpgcheck=1
    repo_gpgcheck=1
    gpgkey=https://packages.cloud.google.com/yum/doc/
    yum-key.gpg https://packages.cloud.google.com/
    yum/doc/rpm-package-key.gpg
    EOF
    ```

```
[root@devops0088 ~]# cat <<EOF > /etc/yum.repos.d/kubernetes.repo
> [kubernetes]
> name=Kubernetes
> baseurl=https://packages.cloud.google.com/yum/repos/kubernetes-el7-x86_64
> enabled=1
> gpgcheck=1
> repo_gpgcheck=1
> gpgkey=https://packages.cloud.google.com/yum/doc/yum-key.gpg https://packages.cloud.google.com/yum/doc/rpm-package-key.gpg
> EOF
```

Figure 2-14. *Kubernetes repository configuration*

4. Install kubeadm on worker node(10.1.150.150).

    Execute the following command to install kubeadm:

    ```
    $install kubeadm -y
    ```

    Then start and enable the kubectl service:

    ```
    $systemctl  restart kubelet && systemctl enable kubelet
    ```

5. Join the worker node (10.1.1.50.150) to the master
    node (10.1.150.126) using the token ID. Navigate
    to Kubernetes master (10.1.150.126) and fetch the
    token by executing the following command:

```
$kubeadm token list
```

Execute the following command in the worker node
(10.1.1.50.150):

```
$sudo swapoff -a
$sudo sed -i '/ swap / s/^\(.*\)$/#\1/g' /etc/fstab
$kubeadm join --token ahh26d.8sl6ey1l9h4eawl7
10.1.150.126:6443 --discovery-token-unsafe-skip-
ca-verification
```

Run the kubectl get nodes command on the master
node (101.1.150.126) to see the worker node machine join
(Figure 2-15):

```
$kubectl get nodes
```

```
[root@k8s-master ~]# kubectl get nodes
NAME            STATUS      ROLES     AGE       VERSION
devops0088      Ready       <none>    3m53s     v1.16.2
k8s-master      Ready       master    91m       v1.16.2
```

Figure 2-15. *List Kubernetes nodes*

Kubernetes master and worker nodes are configured
successfully.

Deploying an Application

Now that we have our container ecosystem ready, it's time to deploy our
first application. We will deploy a microservice-based application called
Sock Shop (Figure 2-16).

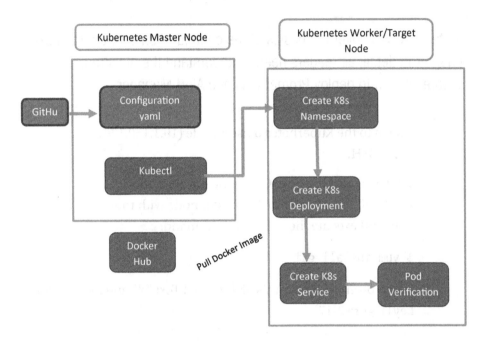

Figure 2-16. *Sock Shop application deployment flow*

The following is the flow for the Sock Shop application deployment we will follow in this chapter:

1. We will first clone the configuration scripts for Sock Shop from GitHub.

2. We will then use Kubectl to create a namespace on the worker/target node and then deploy the configuration as a pod.

3. We will then create a service for our application for end-user access.

4. Finally, we will test the status of our application using command line and web browser access.

Note   We will cover the basics of the configuration script in the next
chapter in detail, as readers need to understand the file structure
before using it to deploy Prometheus and Alert Manager.

Log in to the Kubernetes master node (10.1.150.126)
using SSH.

5. First, we need to set up Git on the master node
   (10.1.150.126). Log in to the master node with root
   user and execute the following command:

   ```
   $ yum install git
   ```

   When prompt asks "Is this ok [y/d/N]", Text "Y" and press Enter
   key (Figure 2-17).

```
Transaction Summary
================================================================================
Install  1 Package (+3 Dependent packages)

Total download size: 4.5 M
Installed size: 22 M
Is this ok [y/d/N]: y
```

Figure 2-17. *Install Git*

Check that Git installed successfully by executing the following
command:

```
$ git version
```

You will get a result like that in Figure 2-18, which means Git was
installed successfully.

```
[root@devops0088 ~]# git version
git version 1.8.3.1
```

Figure 2-18. *Verify Git version*

6. Clone the Sock Shop application from GitHub from
   the following URL into the /home/prometheus folder.
   You will see a microservices-demo folder after
   command execution.

```
$ git clone https://github.com/dryice-devops/
microservices-demo.git
$ll
```

Navigate into the microservices-demo folder. You will be able to
view the following files and folder:

```
$ cd microservices-demo/
```

7. Navigate to the Deploy folder within the
   microservices-demo folder. Then, navigate to the
   kubernetes folder.

```
$ cd deploy/kubernetes/
```

In the kubernetes folder you will be able to view the files and
folder shown in Figure 2-19.

```
[root@devops0087 kubernetes]# ll
total 16
-rw-r--r-- 1 root root 13112 Dec 18 19:45 complete-demo.yaml
```

Figure 2-19. *Navigate to Deploy folder*

8. Create the namespace sock-shop by executing
   the following inline command from the /home/
   prometheus/microservices-demo/deploy/
   kubernetes folder (Figure 2-20):

```
$ kubectl create namespace sock-shop
```

```
[root@k8s-master kubernetes]# kubectl create namespace sock-shop
namespace/sock-shop created    _
```

Figure 2-20. *Namespace creation for container application Sock Shop*

9. Deploy Sock Shop by executing the following
   inline command from the /home/prometheus/
   microservices-demo/deploy/kubernetes folder
   (Figure 2-21):

   ```
   $ kubectl apply -f complete-demo.yaml
   ```

```
[root@k8s-master kubernetes]# kubectl apply -f complete-demo.yaml
deployment.apps/carts-db created
service/carts-db created
deployment.apps/carts created
service/carts created
deployment.apps/catalogue-db created
service/catalogue-db created
deployment.apps/catalogue created
service/catalogue created
deployment.apps/front-end created
service/front-end created
deployment.apps/orders-db created
service/orders-db created
deployment.apps/orders created
service/orders created
deployment.apps/payment created
service/payment created
deployment.apps/queue-master created
service/queue-master created
deployment.apps/rabbitmq created
service/rabbitmq created
deployment.apps/shipping created
service/shipping created
deployment.apps/user-db created
service/user-db created
deployment.apps/user created
service/user created
```

Figure 2-21. *Deploy container application Sock Shop*

10. To get the status of all the components of the Sock Shop application, please execute the following command:

```
$ kubectl get all -n sock-shop
```

The result would be as shown in Figure 2-22 (all the components' statuses should be "Running").

```
[root@k8s-master kubernetes]# kubectl get all -n sock-shop
NAME                                    READY   STATUS    RESTARTS   AGE
pod/carts-7989595fd6-8d8m2              1/1     Running   0          14m
pod/carts-db-6b5bd9cfd9-hrvvp           1/1     Running   0          14m
pod/catalogue-894664bb5-wz8lz           1/1     Running   0          14m
pod/catalogue-db-7cb7cdf884-qxj8d       1/1     Running   0          14m
pod/front-end-5cf4fc84cd-44g2r          1/1     Running   0          14m
pod/orders-78b875776c-k75pk             1/1     Running   0          14m
pod/orders-db-66847d5fc-bdfwl           1/1     Running   0          14m
pod/payment-5f7dcddf5-tqnzd             1/1     Running   0          14m
pod/queue-master-b8b6d9f97-ftz5t        1/1     Running   0          14m
pod/rabbitmq-568f768447-1tt56           1/1     Running   0          14m
pod/shipping-6965fd459-h4dh7            1/1     Running   0          14m
pod/user-6d7cffc456-gtrdp               1/1     Running   0          14m
pod/user-db-85c858465d-bf54s            1/1     Running   0          14m

NAME                    TYPE        CLUSTER-IP       EXTERNAL-IP   PORT(S)        AGE
service/carts           ClusterIP   10.109.121.210   <none>        80/TCP         14m
service/carts-db        ClusterIP   10.98.68.250     <none>        27017/TCP      14m
service/catalogue       ClusterIP   10.96.50.238     <none>        80/TCP         14m
service/catalogue-db    ClusterIP   10.105.221.162   <none>        3306/TCP       14m
service/front-end       NodePort    10.110.154.63    <none>        80:31010/TCP   14m
service/orders          ClusterIP   10.104.255.248   <none>        80/TCP         14m
service/orders-db       ClusterIP   10.110.94.108    <none>        27017/TCP      14m
service/payment         ClusterIP   10.103.40.167    <none>        80/TCP         14m
service/queue-master    ClusterIP   10.99.71.24      <none>        80/TCP         14m
service/rabbitmq        ClusterIP   10.104.53.156    <none>        5672/TCP       14m
service/shipping        ClusterIP   10.104.201.147   <none>        80/TCP         14m
service/user            ClusterIP   10.103.202.136   <none>        80/TCP         14m
service/user-db         ClusterIP   10.108.246.238   <none>        27017/TCP      14m
```

Figure 2-22. *Verify container application Sock Shop*

11. Open your browser and open the following URL: `http://Kubernetes-Cluster-IP:` 31010; e.g., in our case, it is `http://10.1.150.126:31010` (Figure 2-23).

Figure 2-23. *Sock Shop application page*

Summary

In this chapter, we have provided hands-on steps for setting up Docker and Kubernetes. We also deployed our first containerized application. In the next chapter, we will show how to install Prometheus and Alert Manager.

CHAPTER 3

Getting Started with Prometheus and Alert Manager

In this chapter, we will go through the Prometheus monitoring tool, including its architecture and deployment. We will also be installing Prometheus and Alert Manager on Kubernetes and integrating the two. The chapter will cover the following topics:

- Overview of Prometheus
- Architecture of Prometheus and Alert Manager
- Prometheus and Alert Manager Setup and Configuration on Kubernetes Cluster
- Integration of Prometheus and Alert manager

Overview of Prometheus

Container-based technologies also affect elements of infrastructure management services, like backup, patching, security, high availability, disaster recovery, and so forth. Monitoring is one such element that has evolved in leaps and bounds with the rise of container technology.

© Navin Sabharwal, Piyush Pandey 2020
N. Sabharwal and P. Pandey, *Monitoring Microservices and Containerized Applications*,
https://doi.org/10.1007/978-1-4842-6216-0_3

Prometheus is one of the container monitoring tools that comes up as
a go-to open source monitoring and alerting solution. Prometheus was
initially conceived at SoundCloud, and slowly it became a favorite tool for
container monitoring. It's predominantly written in GO language and is
one of the first Cloud Native Computing Foundation (CNCF)–graduated
projects.

Prometheus supports multi-dimensional data models based on
key–value pairs, which helps in collecting container monitoring as
time-series data. It also provides a powerful query language called
Prometheus Query Language (PromQL). PromQL allows the selection and
aggregation of time-series data in real time, which can either be viewed as
a graph, viewed as tabular data, or used by external systems via API call.
Prometheus also supports various integrations with third-party systems
for reporting, alerting, and dashboarding, along with exporters for fetching
data from various sources.

Prometheus and Alert Manager Architecture

The Prometheus and Alert Manager architecture diagram in Figure 3-1
illustrates the architecture of Prometheus and its components.

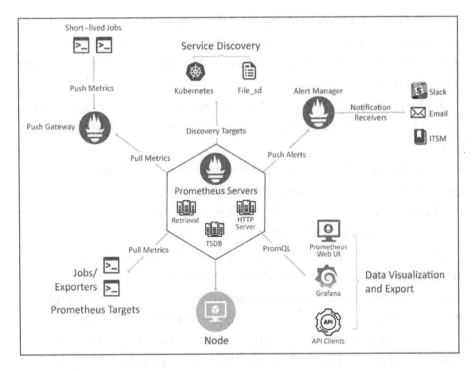

Figure 3-1. *Prometheus and Alert Manager architecture*

Now, let's look more closely at the following components:

Prometheus Server: This component is the central component that collects the metrics from multiple container cluster nodes. The metrics data is stored locally. Prometheus monitoring leverages the concept of scraping, where target systems' metric endpoints are contacted to fetch data at regular intervals.

This means that your application needs to expose an endpoint where metrics are available, and Prometheus should have a mechanism to scrape it. If the application service is not designed to provide Prometheus with metrics because the code either can't be modified or is not written to send metrics we can leverage the Prometheus exporter to fetch metrics.

Push Gateway: Push Gateway is used for scraping metrics from applications and passing on the data to Prometheus. Push Gateway captures the data and then transforms it into the Prometheus data format before pushing.

Exporter: Exporter is equivalent to a plugin or monitoring agent that runs on the target host to fetch data and then export it to the metric in Prometheus.

Alert Manager: Alert Manager is used to send the various alerts based upon the metrics data collected in Prometheus.

Web UI: The web UI layer of Prometheus provides the end user with an interface to visualize data collected by Prometheus.

Kubernetes APIs provide metrics regarding these infrastructure components from an availability, fault, performance, and security standpoint. Prometheus helps overcome many of the unique challenges that monitoring Kubernetes clusters can present. While the Kubernetes native API and the kube-state-metrics can fetch container, node, and application data by exposing the Kubernetes internal data (number of desired/running replicas in a deployment, schedulable nodes, etc.), Prometheus provides an aggregation layer above to enable operations teams to manage the container ecosystem seamlessly. A typical user would have to do computations of their own if they directly fetch metrics from Kubernetes for monitoring data in the absence of a tool like Prometheus.

Prometheus and Alert Manager Setup and Configuration

In the previous chapter, while deploying the Sock Shop application, we used a YAML (a recursive acronym for "YAML Ain't Markup Language") configuration file to provide the details required for deploying the application on a target/worker node. We will now look at how to install and configure Prometheus and Alert Manager using YAML-based definitions.

These days, Kubernetes objects, such as pods, services, and deployments, are created by using YAML files, and thus have a number of advantages over a kubectl command, which is an alternative way to create Kubernetes objects.

Advantages of using a YAML file to create Kubernetes Objects:

- YAML files are saved into source code management, like Github, to track the changes.

- It can be parameterized to make changes to Kubernetes objects at runtime.

Before installing Prometheus and Alert Manager, we want to give readers an overview of the basics of the YAML file structure. YAML is a human-readable data-serialization language. It is commonly used for configuration files and in applications where data is being stored or transmitted. YAML was created specifically for common use cases, such as the following:

- Configuration files

- Log files

- Cross-language data sharing

- Complex data structures

At a high level, the following are the building blocks of a YAML file, shown in Figure 3-2.

Key–Value Pair	Array/Lists	Dictionary/Map

Fruit: Apple
Vegetable: Radish
Liquid: Water
Meat: Goat
	Fruits:
	  - Orange
	  - Banana
	  - Mango
	Vegetables:
	  - Potato
	  - Tomato
	  - Carrot
		Banana:
		  Calories: 200
		  Fat: 0.5g
		  Carbs: 30g
		Grapes:
		  Calories: 100
		  Fat: 0.4g
		  Carbs: 20g

Figure 3-2. *YAML file building blocks*

- **Key–Value Pair:** The basic type of entry in a YAML file is a key–value pair. After the key and colon there is a space and then the value.

- **Arrays/Lists:** Lists would have a number of items listed under the name of the list. The elements of the list would start with a hyphen (-).

- **Dictionary/Map:** A more complex type of YAML file would be a dictionary and map.

In the upcoming sections, we will cover the creation of the deployment resource by using YAML and will provide readers with an overview of key fields used in that process.

Now, let's start with setting up Prometheus and Alert Manager on a Kubernetes cluster. We will use the same container environment setup seen in the previous chapter for this exercise.

Setting Up Prometheus on a Kubernetes Cluster

Figure 3-3 provides an overview of the task flows we will follow to deploy Prometheus.

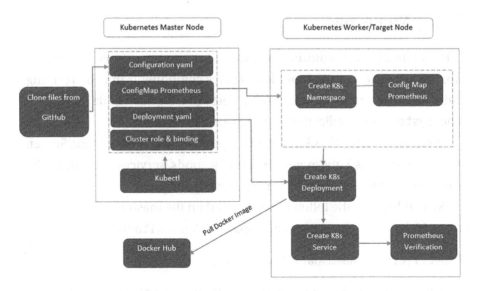

Figure 3-3. *Prometheus deployment flow*

The following is the flow for the Prometheus deployment that we will follow in this chapter:

- We will first clone the configuration files from GitHub.

- We will then use Kubectl to create a namespace on the worker/target node.

- We will create a cluster role and role binding.

- We will create a config map and then deploy the configuration as a pod.

- We will then create a service for Prometheus for end-user access.

- Finally, we will test the status of the Prometheus deployment using the command line and web browser access.

Create Namespace

As Prometheus is a monitoring tool, we will create a namespace to make
a logical segregation from other Kubernetes components that are running
under different namespaces on Kubernetes Cluster, such as default,
kube-system, Any Application Namespace etc.

Prometheus and Alert Manager components, e.g., Prometheus Server,
will be deployed as Kubernetes objects (e.g., pods, services, etc.) and will
also be created under the monitoring namespace.

Step 1: Execute the following command on the master node
(10.1.150.126) to create a new namespace called monitoring:

```
$kubectl create namespace monitoring
```

After executing the command, you will see the monitoring namespace
created, as shown in Figure 3-4.

```
[root@k8s-master /]# kubectl create namespace monitoring
namespace/monitoring created
```

Figure 3-4. *Namespace creation for Prometheus monitoring*

Step 2: Now we will create a cluster role and binding. Kubernetes
resources access is regulated via role-based access control (RBAC). RBAC
uses the rbac.authorization.k8s.io API to manage authorization. In the
RBAC API, a cluster role contains rules that represent a set of permissions
on the Kubernetes cluster. A cluster role will be used to provide access to
the following:

- Non-resource endpoints (like /healthz)

- Cluster-scoped resources (like nodes)

- Namespaced resources (like pods) across all
  namespaces (needed to run kubectl get pods --all-
  namespaces, for example)

Cluster role binding grants the permissions defined in a cluster role to a user or set of users. It holds a list of subjects (users, groups, or service accounts) and a reference to the role being granted. Permissions can be granted within a namespace cluster-wide using a cluster role binding. In this step, we will create the cluster role and role binding using the single YAML file clusterRole.yaml.

Log in to the Kubernetes master node and navigate to the /home directory. Execute the following commands in the Clone clusterRole. yaml file.

```
$ cd /home
```

```
$ git clone https://github.com/dryice-devops/prometheus.git
```

Now, let's have a look at the content of this YAML file and understand the sections and their relevance. The file has two sections: ClusterRole and ClusterRoleBinding.

ClusterRole Section Details

- **apiVersion:** The beginning section of the file defines apiVersion of Kubernetes so it can interact with the Kubernetes API server. It is typically used for creating the object. apiVersion varies depending upon the Kubernetes version you have in your environment.

- **Kind:** The Kind field defines the type of Kubernetes object; e.g., ClusterRole, deployment, service, pods, etc. In our case, we are using ClusterRole.

- **Metadata:** This section has name subcomponents defined in the file. The Name field specifies the name of the object. We are using Prometheus as the name in our example.

Figure 3-5 shows snapshots of these sections.

```
apiVersion: rbac.authorization.k8s.io/v1beta1
kind: ClusterRole
metadata:
    name: prometheus
```

Figure 3-5. *ClusterRole YAML file walkthrough*

- **Rules:** A rule is a set of operations (verbs) that can
  be carried out on a group of resources that belong
  to different API groups (also called *legacy*). In our
  example, we are creating a rule that allows a user to
  execute several operations on nodes, proxy, service,
  endpoints, and pods that belong to the core (expressed
  by "" in the YAML file), apps, and extensions. API
  Groups.Rule has several subcomponent elements in it.

  Resources: This field defines various Kubernetes
  resources.

  Verbs: This field defines the action to be performed
  on the resources.

  nonResourceURLs: NonResourceURLs is a set
  of partial URLs that a user should have access to.
  Non-resource URLs are not namespaced; this field
  is only applicable for ClusterRoles referenced from
  a ClusterRoleBinding. Rules can either apply to API
  resources (such as pods or secrets) or non-resource
  URL paths (such as /api), but not both. Figure 3-6
  shows snapshot of above mentioned sections.

```
  rules:
- apiGroups: [""]
    resources:
    - nodes
    - nodes/proxy
    - services
    - endpoints
    - pods
    verbs: ["get", "list", "watch"]
- apiGroups:
    - extensions
    resources:
    - ingresses
    verbs: ["get", "list", "watch"]
- nonResourceURLs: ["/metrics"]
    verbs: ["get"]
```

Figure 3-6. *ClusterRole YAML file walkthrough*

ClusterRoleBinding Section

- **apiVersion:** The beginning section of the file defines
  the apiVersion of Kubernetes so it can interact with the
  Kubernetes API server. It is typically used for creating
  the object. apiVersion varies depending upon the
  Kubernetes version you have in your environment.

- **Kind:** The Kind field defines the types of Kubernetes
  objects; e.g., ClusterRole, deployment, service, pods,
  etc. In our case, we are using ClusterRoleBinding.

- **Metadata:** This section has name subcomponents
  defined in the file. The Name field specifies the name of
  the object. We are using Prometheus as the name in our
  example. See Figure 3-7.

```
apiVersion: rbac.authorization.k8s.io/v1beta1
kind: ClusterRoleBinding
metadata:
  name: prometheus
```

Figure 3-7. *ClusterRole YAML file walkthrough*

- **RoleRef:** In this field, we are binding the Prometheus ClusterRole to the default service account provided by Kubernetes inside the `monitoring` namespace. This section has further subcomponents in it.

  apiGroup: This field defines the rbac.authorization. k8s.io API to interact with the API group.

  kind: This field defines the object type.

  Name: Name of the ClusterRole; e.g., Prometheus

- **Subjects:** This section defines the set of users and processes that needs to access the Kubernetes API. This section has further subcomponents in it.

  Kind: This field defines the object type service account.

  Name: As every Kubernetes installation has a service account called `default` that is associated with every running pod, we used the same `default`.

  Namespace: This field defines the namespace name for cluster role binding; e.g., `monitoring` (which we created in previous step). Figure 3-8 shows snapshot of above mentioned sections.

```
roleRef:
  apiGroup: rbac.authorization.k8s.io
  kind: ClusterRole
  name: prometheus
subjects:
- kind: ServiceAccount
  name: default
  namespace: monitoring
```

Figure 3-8. *ClusterRole YAML file walkthrough*

Step 3: Now, let's create the role using the following command on the master node (10.1.150.126) in the /home directory:

`$kubectl create -f clusterRole.yaml`

After executing the preceding command, the cluster role and cluster role binding will be created as per Figure 3-9.

```
[root@k8s-master prometheus]# kubectl create -f clusterRole.yaml
clusterrole.rbac.authorization.k8s.io/prometheus created
clusterrolebinding.rbac.authorization.k8s.io/prometheus created
```

Figure 3-9. *Cluster role creation for Prometheus*

Create a Config Map

A config map will be used to decouple any configuration artifacts from image content and alerting rules, which will be mounted to the Prometheus container in the /etc/prometheus as prometheus.yaml and prometheus.rules files.

Step 1: In the previous step, while creating the cluster role and binding, we cloned a file on the Kubernetes master node called config-map.yaml in /home/Prometheus. We will use this file to create a config map. Now, let's review the content of this YAML file. The config map incorporates the prometheus.rules and prometheus.yml files under the data section. See the snapshot of configmap.yaml in Figure 3-10.

- **apiVersion:** The beginning section of the file defines the apiVersion of Kubernetes with which to interact with the Kubernetes API server. It is typically used for creating the object. apiVersion varies depending upon the Kubernetes version you have in your environment.

- **Kind:** This field defines the types of the Kubernetes objects; e.g., ClusterRole, deployment, service, pods, etc. In our case, the object is a config map.

- **Metadata:** This section has name subcomponents defined in the file that have data about the config map.

Name: This field has the name of the config map. In our example, we are using `prometheus-server-conf`.

Label: This field defines the label for the config map; e.g., `prometheus-server-conf`.

Namespace: This field defines the namespace where the config map will be created; e.g., `monitoring`.

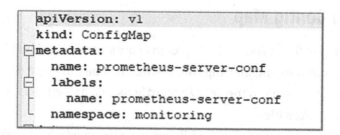

```
apiVersion: v1
kind: ConfigMap
metadata:
  name: prometheus-server-conf
  labels:
    name: prometheus-server-conf
  namespace: monitoring
```

Figure 3-10. *Config map YAML file walkthrough*

- **Data:** This field defines the `prometheus.rules` and `prometheus.yaml` content and passes their information at runtime to the config map.

  prometheus.rules: This section contains the alerting rules used to generate alerts on the basis of various conditions; e.g., out of memory, out of disk space, etc. In this case, we used high pod memory usage.

  prometheus.yml: This file is used for configuring Prometheus. It defines scraping jobs and their instances, as well as which rule files to load. The `prometheus.yaml` file contains all the configuration information that would help to dynamically discover pods and services running in the Kubernetes cluster. The following are scrape jobs in our Prometheus scrape configuration:

  - **kubernetes-apiservers:** It gets all the metrics from the API servers.

  - **kubernetes-nodes:** All Kubernetes node metrics will be collected with this job.

  - **kubernetes-pods:** All the pod metrics will be discovered if the pod metadata is annotated with `prometheus.io/scrape` and `prometheus.io/port` annotations.

  - **kubernetes-cadvisor:** Collects all cAdvisor metrics.

  - **kubernetes-service-endpoints:** All the service endpoints will be scraped if the service metadata is annotated with `prometheus.io/scrape` and `prometheus.io/port` annotations. Service endpoints when annotated with the prometheus annotations are used by prometheus to select and scrape data from.

- **prometheus.rules:** This contains all the alert rules for sending alerts to Alert Manager.

- **Global:** The global configuration specifies parameters that are valid in all other configuration contexts. This has various subcomponents, as follows:

  scrape_interval: How frequently to scrape targets by default; we took 20s in our example.

  evaluation_interval: How long until a scrape request times out; we took 20s in our example.

- **rule_files:** This specifies a list of globs. Glob provides method for traversing file systems and find pathname or files matching a specific pattern. Using this Rules and alerts are read from all matching files that we defined under prometheus.rules and the path defined as /etc/prometheus/prometheus. rules. See Figure 3-11.

```
data:
  prometheus.rules: |-
    groups:
    - name: devopscube demo alert
      rules:
      - alert: High Pod Meory
        expr: sum(container_memory_usage_bytes) > 1
        for: 1m
        labels:
          severity: slack
        annotations:
          summary: High Memory Usage
  prometheus.yml: |-
    global:
      scrape_interval: 20s
      evaluation_interval: 20s
    rule_files:
      - /etc/prometheus/prometheus.rules
    alerting:
      alertmanagers:
      - scheme: http
        static_configs:
        - targets:
          - "alertmanager.monitoring.svc:9093 |"
```

Figure 3-11. *Config map YAML file walkthrough*

Alerting: This section specifies settings related to Alert Manager.

- **alertmanagers:** This section defines how to integrate with Alert Manager for sending alerts from Prometheus.

- **Scheme:** This configures the protocol scheme used for making the requests to send the requests; e.g., http, https; we used http in our case.

- **static_configs:** Using Static_Configs, Alertmanagers configuration can be defined as a static value. Another option available is to use dynamic discovery mechanism for configuring Alertmanagers.

- **targets:** This defines the static target value (IP address and port) xxx.xxx.xxx.xxx:port on which Alert Manager is running.

  scrape_configs: This section specifies a set of targets and parameters for how to scrape them. Prometheus needs some targets to scrape application metrics from.

- **job_name:** The job name assigned to scraped metrics; in our case we use prometheus as a job name, the same used by Prometheus to monitor itself.

- **static_configs:** In this Static_config we can define the list of Targets that will be used for scrapping metrics using above mentioned Job.

- **Targets:** Targets may be statically configured via the static_configs parameter or dynamically discovered using one of the supported service-discovery mechanisms; e.g., Consul, Kubernetes, etc. In our case, we use a static target (IP & port); e.g., xxx.xxx.xxx.xxx:port.

Step 2: Execute the following command to create the config map in Kubernetes on the master node (10.1.150.126) in the /home/Prometheus directory:

```
kubectl create -f config-map.yaml
```

After executing the preceding command, a config map with the name prometheus-server-conf will be created, as shown in Figure 3-12.

```
[root@k8s-master prometheus]# kubectl create -f config-map.yaml
configmap/prometheus-server-conf created
```

Figure 3-12. *Config map creation for Prometheus*

Create a Prometheus Deployment

Step 1: In a previous step, while creating the cluster role and binding, we cloned a file on the Kubernetes master node called prometheus-deployment.yaml in /home/Prometheus. We will use the official Prometheus Docker image v2.12.0 from the Docker hub. In this configuration, the Prometheus config map is mounted as a file inside /etc/Prometheus. The following are the details of the Prometheus-deployment.yaml file (Figure 3-13):

- **apiVersion:** The beginning section of the file defines the apiVersion of Kubernetes with which to interact with the Kubernetes API server. It is typically used for creating the object. The apiVersion varies depending upon the Kubernetes version you have in your environment.

- **kind:** This field defines the types of the Kubernetes objects; e.g., ClusterRole, deployment, service, pods, etc. In our case, we are using a deployment object.

- **Metadata:** This section has name subcomponents defined in the file.

  - **Name:** This field specifies the name of the service object; e.g., `prometheus-deployment`.

  - **Namespace:** This field specifies the namespace of the service object; e.g., `monitoring`.

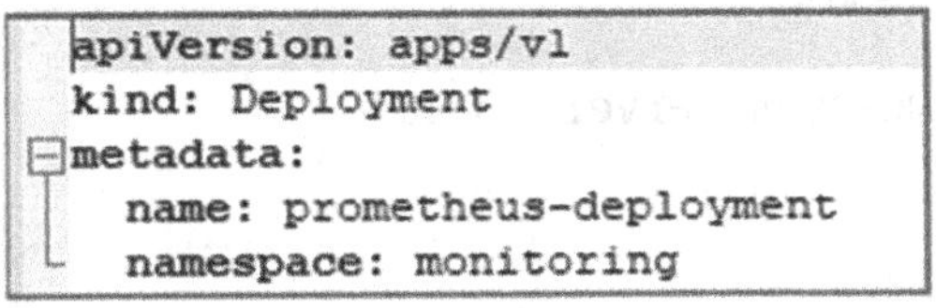

```
apiVersion: apps/v1
kind: Deployment
metadata:
    name: prometheus-deployment
    namespace: monitoring
```

Figure 3-13. *Prometheus-deployment YAML file walkthrough*

- **Spec:** This field provides the specification of service.

  Replicas: This field provides data about the number of pods to be made available at a particular instance.

  Selector: This section provides details about the service selector. Service Selector enables grouping of set of Pods (in this case Prometheus pod) which will be exposed as a Service for external network access.

- **matchLabels:** The name will be used to match and identify the service (Figure 3-14).

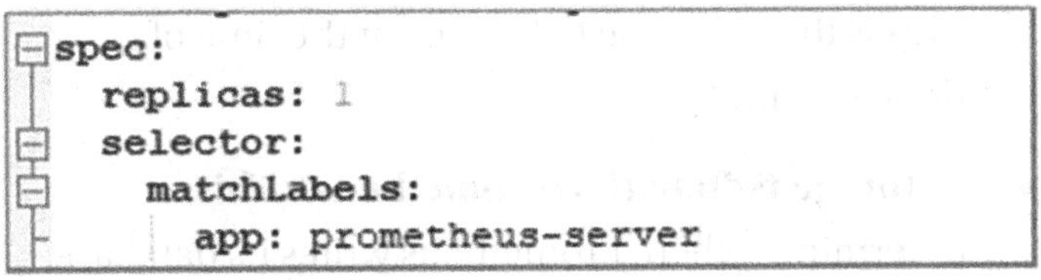

```
spec:
  replicas: 1
  selector:
    matchLabels:
      app: prometheus-server
```

Figure 3-14. *prometheus-deployment YAML file walkthrough*

- **Template:** type of port used by the service (Figure 3-15)

  Metadata: Name will be used to match and identify the service

  - **Labels:** key–value pair that is attached to object intended to be used to specify identifying attributes. See here:

    app — key

    prometheus-server — value

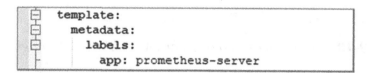

Figure 3-15. *prometheus-deployment YAML file walkthrough*

- **Spec:** See Figure 3-16.

  - **Containers:** detail of container object

  Name: name of the container

  Image: image with version

  Args: argument used at the time of container creation

  - **--config.file=/etc/prometheus/prometheus.yml:** This is the file name to be used at the time of deployment.

  - **--storage.tsdb.path=/prometheus/:** This determines where Prometheus writes its database.

Ports:

- **containerport:** application listening port

```
spec:
  containers:
    - name: prometheus
      image: prom/prometheus:latest
      args:
        - "--config.file=/etc/prometheus/prometheus.yml"
        - "--storage.tsdb.path=/prometheus/"
      ports:
        - containerPort: 9090
```

Figure 3-16. *prometheus-deployment YAML file walkthrough*

- **volumeMounts:** A storage volume allows an existing
  StorageOS volume to be mounted into your pod
  (Figure 3-17). Two volumeMounts are created:
  prometheus-config-volume and prometheus-storage-
  volume. The former will be using our config map to
  manage prometheus.yml. With prometheus-storage-
  volume, we create an empty directory in which to store
  the Prometheus data.

Name: name of the volume

mountPath: defines the mounted path

```
volumeMounts:
  - name: prometheus-config-volume
    mountPath: /etc/prometheus/
  - name: prometheus-storage-volume
    mountPath: /prometheus/
```

Figure 3-17. *prometheus-deployment YAML file walkthrough*

- **volume:** A volume is a directory with data that is accessible to all containers running in a pod and gets mounted into each container's file system. Its lifetime is identical to the lifetime of the pod. Decoupling the volume lifetime from the container lifetime allows the volume to persist across container crashes and restarts. Volumes can be backed by the host's file system, by persistent block storage volumes such as AWS EBS, or by a distributed file system.

  name: name of the volume

  configMap: config map used by the volume

- **defaultMode:** This defines the default file permissions for Volume.

- **name:** defined name of the config map that needs to be used

  name:

- **emptyDir:** The emptyDir volume is first created when a pod is assigned to a node, and it exists as long as that pod is running on the node we used to store the Prometheus data (Figure 3-18).

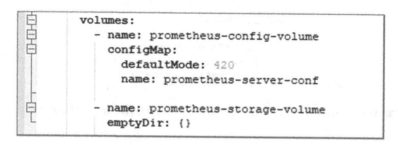

```
volumes:
  - name: prometheus-config-volume
    configMap:
      defaultMode: 420
      name: prometheus-server-conf

  - name: prometheus-storage-volume
    emptyDir: {}
```

Figure 3-18. *prometheus-deployment YAML file walkthrough*

Step 2: To create a deployment on the monitoring namespace using the prometheus-deployment.yaml file, execute the following command on the master node (10.1.150.126) in the /home/Prometheus folder:

```
$kubectl apply -f prometheus-deployment.yaml -n monitoring
```

Once the preceding command has run successfully, prometheus-deployment will be created under the monitoring namespace in the Kubernetes cluster, as shown in Figure 3-19.

```
[root@k8s-master prometheus]# kubectl apply -f prometheus-deployment.yaml -n monitoring
deployment.apps/prometheus-deployment created
```

Figure 3-19. *Prometheus deployment*

Step 3: You can check the created deployment using the following command on the master node (10.1.150.126) in the /home/Prometheus folder. It will return the name of the deployment—in our case, prometheus-deployment) and its states, as shown in Figure 3-20.

```
$kubectl get deployments --namespace=monitoring
```

```
[root@k8s-master prometheus]# kubectl get deployments --namespace=monitoring
NAME                    READY   UP-TO-DATE   AVAILABLE   AGE
prometheus-deployment   1/1     1            1           3m9s
```

Figure 3-20. *Prometheus deployment status verification*

Exposing Prometheus as a Service

To access the Prometheus dashboard over IP, we need to expose it as a Kubernetes service.

Step 1: In a previous section, while creating the cluster role and binding, we cloned a file on the Kubernetes master node called prometheus-service.yaml in /home/prometheus. It exposes Prometheus on all Kubernetes node IP addresses on port 30000. The following are the details of the `prometheus-service.yaml` file:

- **apiVersion:** The beginning section of the file defines the apiVersion of Kubernetes with which to interact with the Kubernetes API server. It is typically used for creating the object. apiVersion varies depending upon the Kubernetes version you have in your environment.

- **kind:** This field defines the types of the Kubernetes object; e.g., ClusterRole, deployment, service, pods, etc. In our case, we are using a service object.

- **Metadata:** This section has name subcomponents defined in the file.

  Name: Specifies the name of the service object; e.g., `Prometheus-service`.

  Namespace: The namespace of the service object; e.g., `monitoring`.

  Annotations: These are used for non-identifying information that is used by the other tools like AlertManager for scraping Promeheus endpoint (except K8).

  - **prometheus.io/scrape:** To scrape metrics for the specific service or pods, use the prometheus scrape annotation (Figure 3-21).

  - **prometheus.io/port:** This annotation indicates to Prometheus to scrape the specific port.

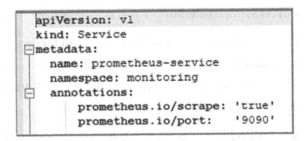

```
apiVersion: v1
kind: Service
metadata:
   name: prometheus-service
   namespace: monitoring
   annotations:
        prometheus.io/scrape:  'true'
        prometheus.io/port:    '9090'
```

Figure 3-21. *prometheus-service YAML file walkthrough*

- **spec:** Specification of the service

  selector: Service selector

- **App:** Pod name used by the service to communicate with this pod.

- **Type:** In this section, we define how the specific Kubernetes service will be exposed (the default value is ClusterIP). In our example, we are using NodePort, which exposes the service on each node's IP at a static port (the NodePort). A ClusterIP service, to which the NodePort service routes, is automatically created. You'll be able to contact the NodePort service from outside the cluster by requesting <NodeIP>:<NodePort> (Figure 3-22).

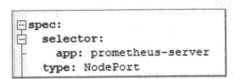

```
spec:
   selector:
       app: prometheus-server
   type: NodePort
```

Figure 3-22. *prometheus-service YAML file walkthrough*

Ports: Service selector

- **Port:** The port on which the service will be exposed internally within the cluster. Once the service is up on the defined port it starts sending requests to the port on the pods selected by the service.

- **targetPort:** This is a port via which the service will send the request to the specific pod; the pod must be run on the same port.

- **nodePort:** This port is used to expose the service externally to the cluster. NodePort is the default setting if the port field is not specified (Figure 3-23).

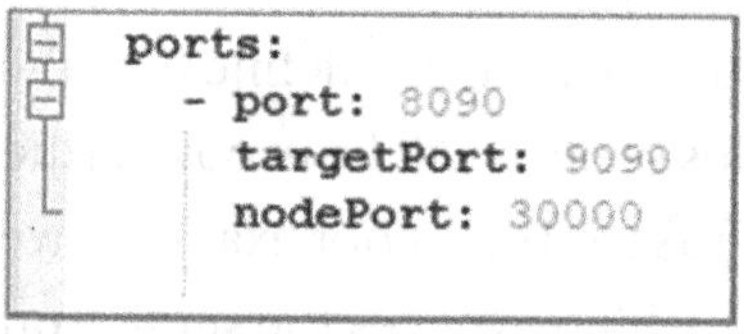

```
ports:
  - port: 8090
    targetPort: 9090
    nodePort: 30000
```

Figure 3-23. prometheus-service YAML file walkthrough

Step 2: Create the service using the following command on the master node (10.1.150.126). See Figure 3-24.

```
$kubectl create -f prometheus-service.yaml
--namespace=monitoring
```

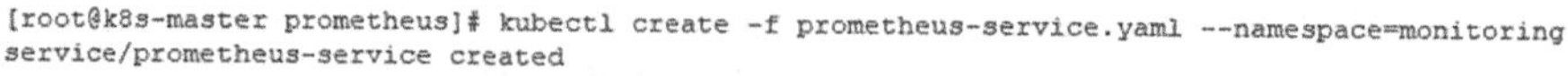

```
[root@k8s-master prometheus]# kubectl create -f prometheus-service.yaml --namespace=monitoring
service/prometheus-service created
```

Figure 3-24. Prometheus service creation

Step 3: Once the service is created, the Prometheus dashboard can be accessed by using any Kubernetes master node IP address (10.1.150.126) on port 30000 (Figure 3-25).

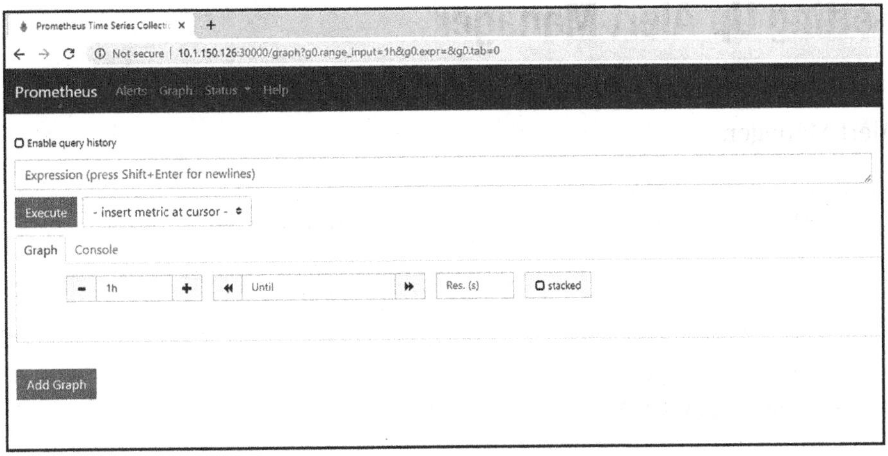

Figure 3-25. *Prometheus console access*

Step 4: Now, if you browse to Status ➤ Targets, you can see the Kubernetes endpoints are connected to Prometheus automatically using service discovery (Figure 3-26).

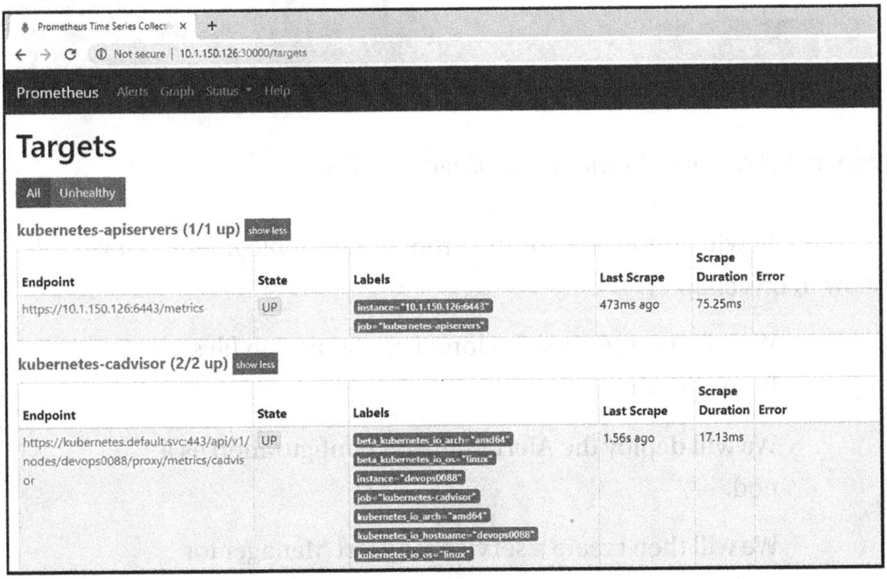

Figure 3-26. *Verify Prometheus console access*

Setting Up Alert Manager

Figure 3-27 provides an overview of the task flows we will follow to deploy Alert Manager.

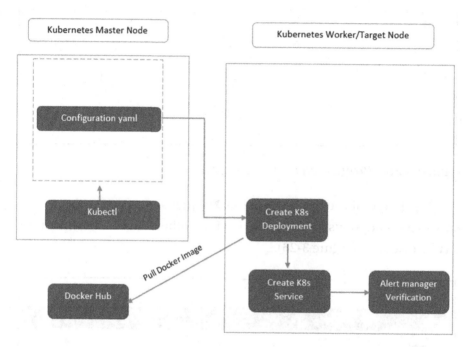

Figure 3-27. *Alert Manager deployment flow*

The following is the flow for the Prometheus deployment that we will follow in this chapter:

> We will use the already cloned configuration files from Github.

> We will deploy the Alert Manager configuration as a pod.

> We will then create a service for Alert Manager for end-user access.

Finally, we will test the status of the Alert Manager deployment using the command line and web browser access.

Create a Deployment

Step 1: In a previous section, while creating the cluster role and binding, we cloned a file on the Kubernetes master node called `alertmanager-deployment.yaml` in `/home/prometheus`. The following are the details of this YAML file:

- **apiVersion:** The beginning section of the file defines the apiVersion of Kubernetes with which to interact with the Kubernetes API server. It is typically used for creating the object. apiVersion varies depending upon the Kubernetes version you have in your environment.

- **kind:** This field defines the type of the Kubernetes object; e.g., ClusterRole, deployment, service, pod, etc. In our case, we are using a deployment object.

- **Metadata:** This section has name subcomponents defined in the file (Figure 3-28).

  Name: Specifies the name of the deployment object; e.g., `alertmanager`.

  Namespace: Specifies the namespace of the deployment object; e.g., `monitoring`.

```
apiVersion: apps/v1
kind: Deployment
metadata:
    name: alertmanager
    namespace: monitoring
```

Figure 3-28. *alertmanager-deployment YAML file walkthrough*

- **Spec:** Specification of service

  Replicas: Number of pods to be available on
  Kubernetes cluster; e.g., 1 or 2

  Selector: Service selector

- **matchLabels:** Name will be used to match and identify
  the service by key and value pair; e.g., we used app as
  the key and alertmanager as the value (Figure 3-29).

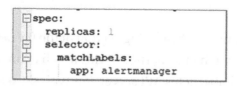

Figure 3-29. *alertmanager-deployment YAML file walkthrough*

  Template: Type of port used by the service

- **Metadata:** Name will be used to match and identify the
  service (Figure 3-30).

  - **Labels:** Key–value pair that is attached to the object
    intended to be used to specify identifying attributes.
    app is a key and alertmanager is the value.

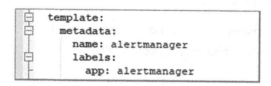

Figure 3-30. *alertmanager-deployment YAML file walkthrough*

- **Spec:** See Figure 3-31.

  - **Containers:** Detail of container object

    Name: Name of the container

    Image: Docker image with version

    Ports:

    - **containerPort:** Application listening port

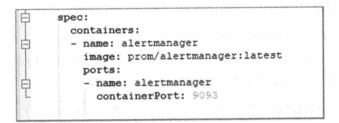

```
spec:
  containers:
  - name: alertmanager
    image: prom/alertmanager:latest
    ports:
    - name: alertmanager
      containerPort: 9093
```

Figure 3-31. *alertmanager-deployment YAML file walkthrough*

Step 2: Create the deployment using the following command on the master node (10.1.150.126) in the /home/Prometheus folder (Figure 3-32):

```
$kubectl create -f alertmanager-deployment.yaml
```

```
[root@k8s-master prometheus]# kubectl create -f alertmanager-deployment.yaml
deployment.apps/alertmanager created
```

Figure 3-32. *Alert Manager deployment*

Create a Service

Step 1: We need to expose the Alert Manager using NodePort just to access the web UI. Prometheus will talk to Alert Manager using the internal service endpoint. In a previous section, while creating the cluster role

and binding, we cloned a file on the Kubernetes master node called
`alertmanager-service.yaml`. The following outlines the details of the
YAML file:

- **apiVersion:** The beginning section of the file defines
  the apiVersion of Kubernetes with which to interact
  with the Kubernetes API server. It is typically used for
  creating the object. apiVersion varies depending upon
  the Kubernetes version you have in your environment
  (Figure 3-33).

- **Kind:** This field defines the type of the Kubernetes
  object; e.g., ClusterRole, deployment, service, pod, etc.
  In our case, we are using a service object.

- **Metadata:** This section has name subcomponents
  defined in the file.

  Name: Specifies the name of the service object; e.g..
  `alertmanager`

  Namespace: The namespace of the service object;
  e.g., `monitoring`

```
apiVersion: v1
kind: Service
metadata:
    name: alertmanager
    namespace: monitoring
```

Figure 3-33. *alertmanager-service YAML file walkthrough*

- **Spec:**

  Selector: Service selector

  - **app:** Pod name used by the service to communicate
    with this pod

Type: This field provides information about the type of the publishing services. Kubernetes service types allow you to specify what kind of service you want. In our example, we are using app: alertmanager, where app is a key and alertmanager is the value of the pod we defined in alertmanager-deployment. yaml. The same will be used by alertmanager-service to communicate with this pod name (Figure 3-34).

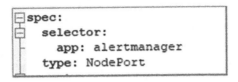

Figure 3-34. *alertmanager-service YAML file walkthrough*

ports: We explained about the port, targetPort, and nodePort fields in the "Exposing Prometheus as a Service" section (Figure 3-35).

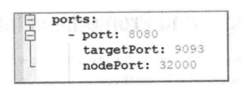

Figure 3-35. *alertmanager-service YAML file walkthrough*

Step 2: Create the service using the following command (Figure 3-36):

```
$kubectl create -f alertmanager-service.yaml
```

```
[root@k8s-master prometheus]# kubectl create -f alertmanager-service.yaml
service/alertmanager created
```

Figure 3-36. *Alert Manager service creation*

After creating the service, the Alert Manager dashboard is accessible on node port 32000 with the IP address of the Kubernetes master node (10.1.150.126) (Figure 3-37).

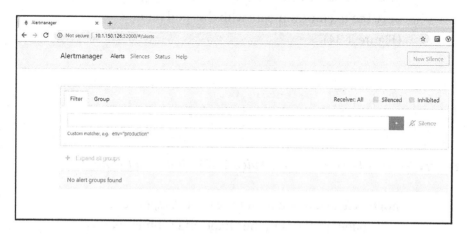

Figure 3-37. *Alert Manager dashboard access*

Alert Manager and Prometheus Integration

Figure 3-38 provides an overview of the task flows we will follow to integrate Alert Manager with Prometheus.

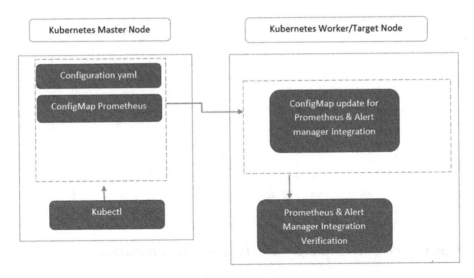

Figure 3-38. *Alert Manager and Prometheus integration flow*

The following is the flow for the Alert Manager and Prometheus integration that we will follow in this chapter:

We will use the already cloned configuration files from Github.

We will then use Kubectl to update the config map.

Finally, we will test the status of the integration using Prometheus web browser access.

Step 1: Log in to the Kubernetes master node (10.1.150.126), go to the /home/prometheus folder, and update the config-map.yaml file. Replace alertmanager.monitoring.svc:9093 with the Alert Manager URL, e.g., http://10.1.150.126:32000, under the targets section of prometheus. yml highlighted in the config-map.yaml file in Figure 3-39.

```
prometheus.yml: |-
  global:
    scrape_interval: 20s
    evaluation_interval: 20s
  rule_files:
    - /etc/prometheus/prometheus.rules
  alerting:
    alertmanagers:
    - scheme: http
      static_configs:
      - targets:
        - "10.1.150.150:32000"
```

Figure 3-39. *Alert Manager and Prometheus integration*

Step 2: Run the following command in the master node (10.1.150.126) under /home/prometheus to get the config map:

$kubectl get configmaps -n=monitoring

This command returns the config map list (Figure 3-40).

```
[root@k8s-master prometheus]# kubectl get configmaps -n=monitoring
NAME                     DATA   AGE
alertmanager-config      1      20h
prometheus-server-conf   2      21h
```

Figure 3-40. *Config map list*

Step 3: Run the following command in the master node (10.1.150.126) under /home/prometheus to get the prometheus-server-conf config map we updated in Step 1 (Figure 3-41).

$ kubectl delete configmaps prometheus-server-conf -n=monitoring

```
[root@k8s-master prometheus]# kubectl delete configmaps prometheus-server-conf -n=monitoring
configmap "prometheus-server-conf" deleted
```

Figure 3-41. *Config map delete*

Step 4: Once you have deleted `prometheus-server-conf`, create the same with the updated `config-map.yaml` file in the master node (10.1.150.126) by executing the following command from the `/home/Prometheus` directory (Figure 3-42):

```
$ kubectl create -f config-map.yaml
```

```
[root@k8s-master prometheus]# kubectl create -f config-map.yaml
configmap/prometheus-server-conf created
```

Figure 3-42. *Config map create*

Step 5: Execute the following command to identify the Prometheus pod and then delete to get the updated config map changes:

```
$kubectl get pods -n=monitoring
```

The preceding command will return all the pods running under the monitoring namespace (Figure 3-43).

```
alertmanager-564d4884bd-mjjft                 1/1   Running   0   18h
prometheus-deployment-5c4f4f5779-p6pcm        1/1   Running   0   62s
```

Figure 3-43. *List Prometheus pods*

Select `Prometheus-deployment-5c4f4f5779-p6pcm` and delete the same with the following command (Figure 3-44):

```
$kubectl delete pods prometheus-deployment-5c4f4f5779-zgkkf
-n=monitoring
```

```
[root@k8s-master prometheus]# kubectl delete pods  prometheus-deployment-5c4f4f5779-zgkkf -n=monitoring
pod "prometheus-deployment-5c4f4f5779-zgkkf" deleted
```

Figure 3-44. *Delete pods*

Check the running pods again by using the following command:

```
$kubectl get pods -n=monitoring
```

It will return the newly created Prometheus pods by Kubernetes deployment (Figure 3-45).

```
[root@k8s-master prometheus]# kubectl get pods -n=monitoring
NAME                                     READY   STATUS    RESTARTS   AGE
alertmanager-564d4884bd-mjjft            1/1     Running   0          20h
prometheus-deployment-5c4f4f5779-zhmdt   1/1     Running   0          90m
```

Figure 3-45. *List pods*

Step 6: Check the Prometheus URL to verify Alert Manager is configured correctly:

- Open Prometheus URL http://10.1.150.126:30000.

- Go to Status ➤ Runtime & Build Information.

- Check the Alert Manager section. The Alert Manager end point should be mentioned http://10.1.150.126:32000/api/v1/alerts (Figure 3-46).

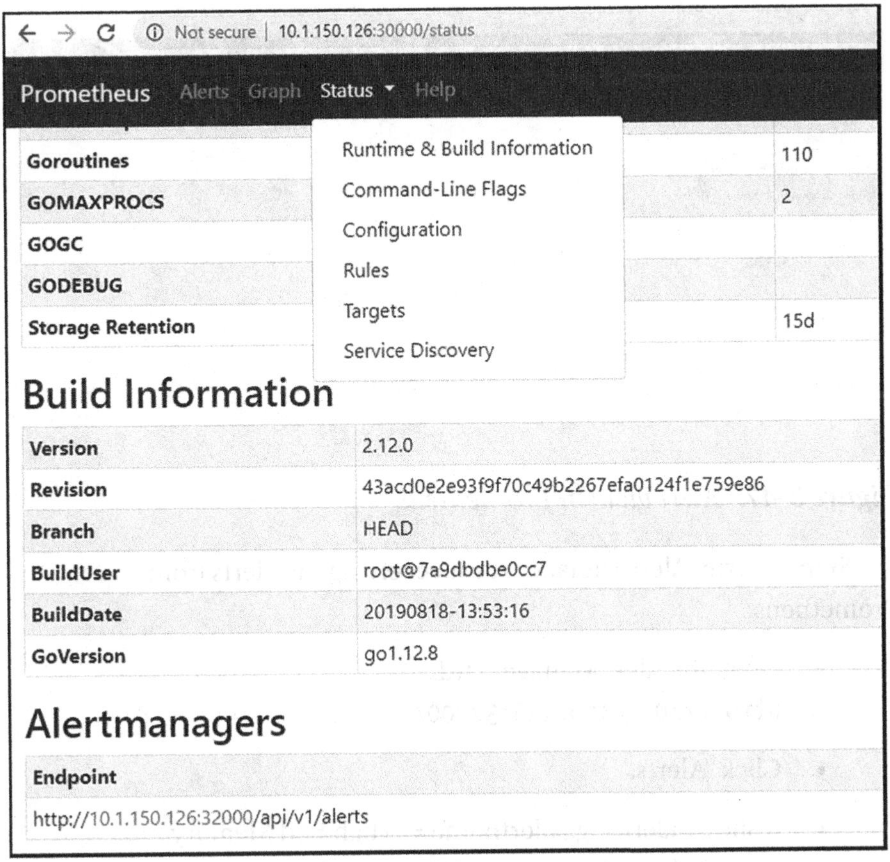

Figure 3-46.   *Verify Alert Manager endpoint in Prometheus*

- Prometheus starts sending the alert after five seconds (configured in config map) to Alert Manager, and the State would be "FIRING" in the Prometheus URL under the Alert section (Figure 3-47).

Figure 3-47. *Alert view in Prometheus*

Step 7: Verify Alert Manager starts receiving the alerts from
Prometheus:

- Open the Alert Manager URL
  `http://10.1.150.126:32000/`

- Click "Alerts."

- It shows alert, e.g., alertname = "High Pod Memory,"
  sending from Prometheus (Figure 3-48).

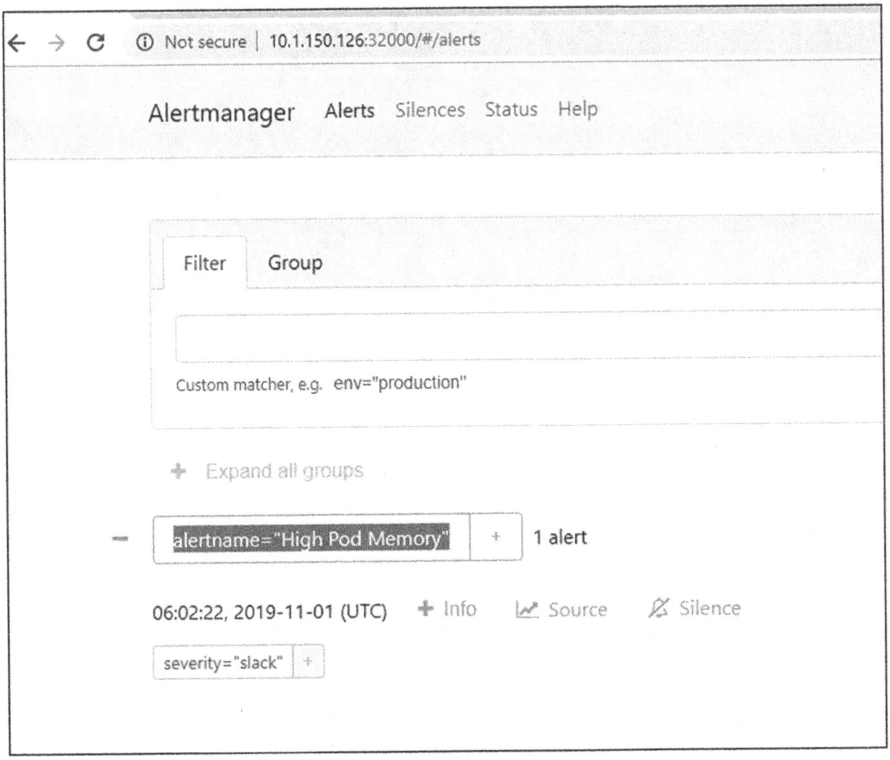

Figure 3-48. Alert view in Alert Manager

Summary

In this chapter, we have learned the basics of Prometheus, its architecture, and various components. We set up Prometheus and Alert Manager and integrated the two to work together. In the next chapter, we will start with a deep-dive understanding of Prometheus and Alert Manager solutions for container monitoring, starting with infrastructure parameter monitoring.

CHAPTER 4

Container Infrastructure Monitoring

This chapter will provide hands-on steps to the readers on container infrastructure monitoring using Prometheus. We will also learn how to deploy a containerized application using a Helm chart. A Helm chart is a package manager for Kubernetes that helps developers and operators to more easily package, configure, and deploy applications and services onto Kubernetes clusters. This chapter will cover the following topics:

- Container Infrastructure Monitoring Using Parameters
- Labels
- Helm and Tiller Installation
- Using Exporters for Container Monitoring

© Navin Sabharwal, Piyush Pandey 2020
N. Sabharwal and P. Pandey, *Monitoring Microservices and Containerized Applications*,
https://doi.org/10.1007/978-1-4842-6216-0_4

Container Infrastructure Monitoring Using Parameters

Before we jump into using Prometheus to monitor a Kubernetes-managed container ecosystem, let's look at the key aspects that need to be monitored from an infrastructure perspective. Monitoring and alerting at the container orchestration level works on two levels. On one side, we need to monitor whether the services handled by Kubernetes do meet the requirements we defined. On the other side, we need to make sure all the components of Kubernetes are up and running. From an infrastructure perspective, the following are the key layers that need to be monitored:

- Containers

- Clusters running the containers, such as Kubernetes

- Communication and telemetry between containers (this can be done via contracts or by collecting logs from tools like ISTIO)

- Host OS/machine running the cluster

- Server running the hosts

To monitor Kubernetes, we need to ensure the status of certain services and components that are core to Kubernetes' functionality. Let's look at some of the key monitoring areas.

Service Discovery

In microservices apps, services are added and removed all the time. Containers move between hosts; autoscaling groups add and remove instances dynamically. Additionally, there's failover and auto-replication adding to the complexity of container monitoring. Manually validating the availability of services every time their network location changes is not feasible. Hence, there is a need for a monitoring solution for this.

Node Availability

Providing alerts regarding node availability is not very different from monitoring VMs or machines. Essentially, it involves checking if the host is up or down/unreachable, as well as the resources' availability (CPU, memory, disk, etc.).

Node Health

A node failure is not so much a critical event in Kubernetes, as its scheduler service will spin off containers in other available nodes. However, it's crucial to monitor scenarios where we could be running out of nodes, or where the resource requirements for the deployed applications exhaust existing nodes' resources. Another scenario could be to monitor quota limits configured at the resources level. To monitor node status, alerts on the metrics kube_node_status_ready and kube_node_spec_unschedulable can be scheduled. If you want to have an alert for capacity, you will have to sum each scheduled pod request for CPU and memory and then check that it doesn't go over the threshold for each of the nodes; this can be done using kube_node_status_capacity_cpu_cores and kube_node_status_capacity_memory_bytes.

Kubernetes Control Plane

The Kubernetes control plane constitutes the control plane of the cluster. Its service components (or "master" components) provide features like container orchestration, computing resource management, and the central API for users and services. An unhealthy control plane will sooner or later affect the availability of applications or the ability of users to manage their workloads. The control plane components include the following:

- Kubernetes API server

- Controller manager

- Scheduler

- etcd key–value store

Basic monitoring of these components would involve an HTTP check that queries the health-check endpoint (/healthz) exposed by instances of these services or by scraping the API endpoint in Kubernetes.

In addition to health checks, control plane components expose internal metrics via a Prometheus HTTP endpoint (/metrics) that can be added into a time-series database. While most of the metric data is useful for retrospective or live issue debugging/troubleshooting, some metrics, like latency, request, or error counts, can be used for proactive alerting.

Kubernetes Infrastructure Services

Beside the master components, there are a number of other services running in the cluster that play critical infrastructure service roles, like DNS and service discovery (kube-dns, coredns) or traffic management (kube-proxy). Just like control plane components, these components provide HTTP endpoints for health checks as well as internal metrics via a Prometheus endpoint.

Kubernetes Metrics

kube-state-metrics is a service that leverages Kubernetes APIs and provides metrics about the status/state of objects like pods, nodes, and deployments. The following are some of the key insights provided by kube-state that help operations to easily manage the container ecosystem state:

- Noting how many pods are running/stopped/terminated

- Noting how many times the specific pod has been restarted

- Analyzing the response time of a Kubernetes service

- Analyzing the slowest endpoints of a Kubernetes HTTP service

  - Noting the most frequently used HTTP endpoints

  - Noting the slowest HTTP endpoints

  - Looking at the average connection time

  - Noting any error codes

Labels

Labels enable us to capture additional attribute details of the data monitored. In the object, this is further stored as a key–value pair, where the key is the name of the attribute being captured and the value is the actual attribute data.

Labels work very well in Prometheus using PromQL. Let us consider a metric for getting the total number of HTTP requests received by the Kubernetes API server by differentiating based on the label, such as in the following:

```
instance ="10.1.150.150:30000", job = "federate" and
quantile="0.999"
```

PromQL:

```
http_requests{instance="10.1.150.150:30000",job="federate",
quantile="0.999"}
```

Now, let us see how we can execute the preceding example to generate the respective metrics on the Prometheus server.

Log in to the Prometheus UI and navigate to the Graph section, where you should type the following query:

```
http_requests{instance="10.1.150.150:30000",job="federate",
quantile="0.999"}
```

Click the Execute button, which will show the result in the form of a graph, as shown in Figure 4-1.

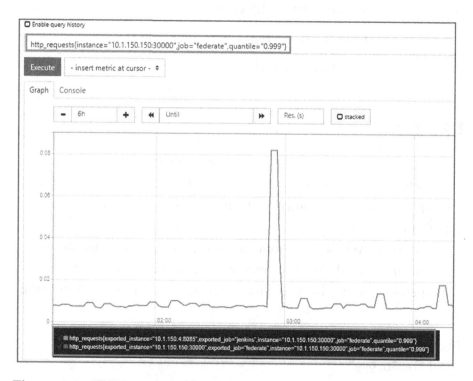

Figure 4-1. *HTTP request filterd by label*

Let us consider another example to find out the sum of the total number of requests handled by the Kubernetes API server per second by differentiating based on label, like component="apiserver",group="policy".

Here is the PromQL:

```
apiserver_request_duration_seconds_sum{component="apiserver",
group="policy"}
```

Again, type the following PromQL query:

```
http_requests{instance="10.1.150.150:30000",job="federate",
quantile="0.999"}
```

This will generate the respective metrics in Prometheus. Click the Execute button, which will show the result in the form of a graph, as shown in Figure 4-2.

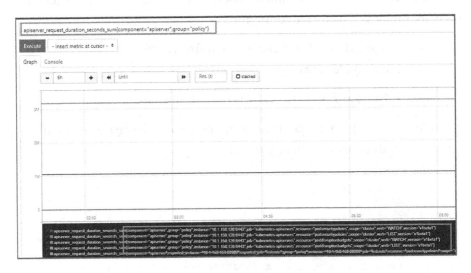

Figure 4-2. *Apiserver request duration in seconds, sum, filtered by label*

In the upcoming section, you will learn about the Prometheus exporters; e.g., cAdvisor, Blackbox. These exporters pull the metrics from various systems—e.g., Kubernetes, nodes, etc.—and push the data into Prometheus for further analysis. To install exporters on the Kubernetes cluster we need a Helm chart–based installation.

Helm and Tiller Setup

Helm consists of two components: Helm and Tiller. Helm itself is the client-side component that you run in your command line, while Tiller resides on target node cluster.

Before continuing, you will need to download and install Helm. For this exercise we are using the following Linux version of Helm: `helm-v2.16.0-rc.2-linux-amd64.tar.gz`. Helm should be installed on master node 10.1.150.126.

Step 1: Download Helm on the master node in the `/home/prometheus` folder and unpack the tar. After unpacking this, the `linux-amd64` folder should be created. Below commands download the tar file using wget and then are unpacked using tar command:

- `$ wget https://get.helm.sh/helm-v2.16.0-rc.2-linux-amd64.tar.gz`

- `$ tar zxvf helm-v2.16.0-rc.2-linux-amd64.tar.gz`

After executing the preceding commands, you will see the Helm and Tiller executables, as seen in Figure 4-3.

```
/home/prometheus/linux-amd64
[root@k8s-master linux-amd64]# ll
total 79692
-rwxr-xr-x. 1 root root 40460288 Oct 31 21:19 helm
-rw-r--r--. 1 root root    11343 Oct 31 21:20 LICENSE
-rw-r--r--. 1 root root     3444 Oct 31 21:20 README.n
-rwxr-xr-x. 1 root root 41127936 Oct 31 21:19 tiller
```

Figure 4-3. *Downloading Helm*

Step 2: After unzipping, copy the Helm binary from the `/home/prometheus/linux-amd64` directory to the `/usr/local/bin` directory using cp command for installing Helm on your local Linux VM:

`$ cp helm /usr/local/bin`

After copying the Helm executable, execute the following command from the /home/prometheus directory to verify that Helm was installed successfully.

The output should show the Helm version, as shown in Figure 4-4.

```
$helm version
```

```
[root@k8s-master prometheus]# helm version
Client: &version.Version{SemVer:"v2.16.0-rc.2", GitCommit:"e13bc94621d4ef666270cfbe734aaabf342a49bb", GitTreeState:"clean"}
Error: could not find tiller
```

Figure 4-4. Verifying Helm version

Note   Please ignore the error related to Tiller, as Tiller will be installed later on the Kubernetes master node.

Installing Tiller

Tiller is used to deploy the Helm chart on the Kubernetes cluster. Tiller requires a Kubernetes service account and permissions to access Kubernetes resources using role-based access and control (RBAC). The Kubernetes service account is used by Tiller for Kubernetes API server authentication. RBAC is used to give access to Kubernetes resources—e.g., pods, services, etc.—at the cluster level or within Kubernetes namespaces.

Kubernetes provides the following types of RBAC permission:

> **Role and ClusterRole:** A set of permissions over a user or group of users. A role is always confined to a single namespace, while a ClusterRole is cluster-scoped.

> **RoleBinding and ClusterRoleBinding:** Grants the permissions defined in a Role/ClusterRole respectively to a user or group of users. RoleBindings are bound to a certain namespace, and ClusterRoleBindings are cluster-global.

In the following steps we will create a Kubernetes service account and ClusterRoleBinding for Tiller to deploy the Helm charts on the Kubernetes cluster.

Step 1: Navigate to the /home/prometheus directory. You will find the tiller-helm.yaml file on the Kubernetes master node (10.1.150.126). This will be used for creating the service account in kube-system and for the ClusterRoleBinding, which will provide Tiller access to the cluster.

The kube-system is a namespace used by Kubernetes to manage objects or resources created by the Kubernetes components, so typically it contains pods like kube-dns, kube-proxy, kubernetes-dashboard, and so on.

Next is the explanation of the various sections of the tiller-helm. yaml file. It has two sections: ClusterRole and ClusterRoleBinding.

ClusterRole Section Details

- **apiVersion:** The beginning section of the file defines the apiVersion of Kubernetes with which to interact with the Kubernetes API server. It is typically used for creating the object. apiVersion varies depending upon the Kubernetes version you have in your environment.

- **Kind:** This field defines the type of the Kubernetes object; e.g., ClusterRole, deployment, service, pod, service account, etc. In our case, we defined kind as ServiceAccount.

- **Metadata:** This section has name subcomponents defined in the file. The name field specifies the name of the object. We are using tiller as the name in our example. For the namespace, we are using kube-system.

These sections are explained in Figure 4-5.

```
apiVersion: v1
kind: ServiceAccount
metadata:
    name: tiller
    namespace: kube-system
```

Figure 4-5. *tiller-helm.yaml file walkthrough*

ClusterRoleBinding Section

- **apiVersion**: The beginning section of the file defines the apiVersion of Kubernetes with which to interact with the Kubernetes API server. It is typically used for creating the object. apiVersion varies depending upon the Kubernetes version you have in your environment.

- **Kind:** This field defines the type of the Kubernetes object; e.g., ClusterRole, deployment, service, pods, etc. In our case, we are using `ClusterRoleBinding`, as per the explanation covered in the section "Installing Tiller."

- **Metadata:** This section has `name` subcomponents defined in the file. The `name` field specifies the name of the object. We are using `tiller` as the name in our example. See Figure 4-6.

```
apiVersion: rbac.authorization.k8s.io/v1beta1
kind: ClusterRoleBinding
metadata:
    name: tiller
```

Figure 4-6. *tiller-helm.yaml file walkthrough*

- **RoleRef:** In this field, we are binding the Prometheus cluster role to the default service account provided by Kubernetes inside the `monitoring` namespace. This section has further subcomponents in it.

  apiGroup: In Kubernetes, the API group is specified with the apiVersion to make a REST API call for a serialized object. Kubernetes RBAC uses the `rbac.authorization.k8s.io` API group to communicate with the Kubernetes API server. For detailed information about the apiGroup and Kubernetes REST API please refer to the following links: [1]

  kind: This field defines the object type.

  name: This is the name of the cluster role; e.g., `cluster-admin`.

See Figure 4-7.

```
roleRef:
    apiGroup: rbac.authorization.k8s.io
    kind: ClusterRole
    name: cluster-admin
```

***Figure 4-7.** tiller-helm.yaml file walkthrough*

Subjects: This section defines the set of users, such as service accounts and processes, that need to access the Kubernetes API. Here, we have to give the reference of the `tiller` service account, as shown in Figure 4-8 under the following subsections.

---

[1]https://kubernetes.io/docs/reference/using-api/api-overview/
https://kubernetes.io/docs/reference/

- **Kind:** This field defines the object type. Here it is
  ServiceAccount because ServiceAccount was created
  for Tiller to make a connection with the Kubernetes API
  server.

- **Name:** We are using name as tiller.

- **Namespace:** This field defines the namespace for the
  cluster role binding; e.g., kube-system.

Please see Figure 4-8.

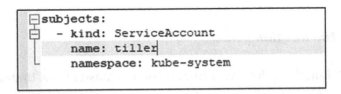

Figure 4-8. *tiller-helm.yaml file walkthrough*

Step 2: Use the following command to create the cluster role shown in
Figure 4-9:

```
$ kubectl create -f tiller-helm.yaml
```

```
[root@k8s-master ~]# kubectl create -f tiller-helm.yaml
serviceaccount/tiller created
clusterrolebinding.rbac.authorization.k8s.io/tiller created
```

Figure 4-9. *Configuring role for installing Tiller*

Step 3: Once the service account is created, deploy Tiller to your
cluster and assign it the service account you just created.

```
$ helm init --service-account tiller --history-max 200
```

The --service-account flag signifies that Tiller should run under
the tiller service account previously created. The --history-max flag
specifies the maximum number of objects Helm persists in its history.

If this flag isn't specified, history objects are not purged. Over a period of time, this can build up to a huge number of objects in your cluster and thereby make administration tasks difficult. Please refer to Figure 4-10.

```
[root@k8s-master ~]# helm init --service-account tiller --history-max 200
Creating /root/.helm
Creating /root/.helm/repository
Creating /root/.helm/repository/cache
Creating /root/.helm/repository/local
Creating /root/.helm/plugins
Creating /root/.helm/starters
Creating /root/.helm/cache/archive
Creating /root/.helm/repository/repositories.yaml
Adding stable repo with URL: https://kubernetes-charts.storage.googleapis.com
Adding local repo with URL: http://127.0.0.1:8879/charts
$HELM_HOME has been configured at /root/.helm.

Tiller (the Helm server-side component) has been installed into your Kubernetes Cluster.

Please note: by default, Tiller is deployed with an insecure 'allow unauthenticated users' policy.
To prevent this, run `helm init` with the --tiller-tls-verify flag.
For more information on securing your installation see: https://docs.helm.sh/using_helm/#securing-your-helm-installation
```

Figure 4-10. *Installing Tiller*

Step 4: Run the following command on the master node under /home/ Prometheus. You should now see both the client and the server version information, as shown in Figure 4-11.

```
$helm version
```

```
[root@k8s-master ~]# helm version
Client: &version.Version{SemVer:"v2.16.0-rc.2", GitCommit:"e13bc94621d4ef666270cfbe734aaabf342a49bb", GitTreeState:"clean"}
Server: &version.Version{SemVer:"v2.16.0-rc.2", GitCommit:"e13bc94621d4ef666270cfbe734aaabf342a49bb", GitTreeState:"clean"}
```

Figure 4-11. *Verifying Helm version*

Exporters

An exporter helps in fetching the state/logs/metrics from the application/ Kubernetes service and providing data to Prometheus. This concept is similar to that of adapters or plugins in other monitoring tools available in the market. Prometheus provides a list of official and externally contributed exporters. Let's explore some of these exporters, which are useful for container infrastructure monitoring:

```
https://prometheus.io/docs/instrumenting/exporters/
```

Node Exporter

Node Exporter is a Prometheus exporter for fetching metrics for hardware and OS metrics exposed by Unix/Linux kernels. It is written in Go language with pluggable metric collectors. Collectors differ as per operating system type. Table 4-1 provides a few examples.

Table 4-1. *Types of Collectors*

Name	Description	OS
Arp	Exposes ARP statistics from `/proc/net/arp`	Linux
Boottime	Exposes system boot time derived from `kern.boottime sysctl`	Darwin, Dragonfly, FreeBSD, NetBSD, OpenBSD, Solaris
Cpu	Exposes CPU statistics	Darwin, Dragonfly, FreeBSD, Linux, Solaris
Cpufreq	Exposes CPU frequency statistics	Linux, Solaris
Diskstats	Exposes disk I/O statistics	Darwin, Linux, OpenBSD
Filesystem	Exposes filesystem statistics, such as disk space used	Darwin, Dragonfly, FreeBSD, Linux, OpenBSD
Hwmon	Exposes hardware monitoring and sensor data from `/sys/class/hwmon/`	Linux
Meminfo	Exposes memory statistics	Darwin, Dragonfly, FreeBSD, Linux, OpenBSD
Netclass	Exposes network interface info from `/sys/class/net/`	Linux

(continued)

Table 4-1. (*continued*)

Name	Description	OS
netdev	Exposes network interface statistics such as bytes transferred	Darwin, Dragonfly, FreeBSD, Linux, OpenBSD
netstat	Exposes network statistics from `/proc/net/netstat`. This is the same information as `netstat -s`.	Linux
Nfs	Exposes NFS client statistics from `/proc/net/rpc/nfs`. This is the same information as `nfsstat -c`.	Linux
Nfsd	Exposes NFS kernel server statistics from `/proc/net/rpc/nfsd`. This is the same information as `nfsstat -s`.	Linux
uname	Exposes system information as provided by the uname system call	Darwin, FreeBSD, Linux, OpenBSD

Now, let's start with configuring Node Exporter on the environment we set up in the previous chapter. We will install Node Exporter on the Kubernetes master node (10.1.150.126) using Helm.

Step 1: Log in to the Kubernetes master node (10.1.150.126), navigate to the /home/prometheus folder, and execute the following command. It will download the exporter from the GitHub URL given below, as shown in Figure 4-12.

```
$ helm install --name node-exporter stable/prometheus-node-
exporter
```

```
https://github.com/helm/charts/tree/master/stable/prometheus-
node-exporter
```

```
[root@k8s-master prometheus]# helm install --name node-exporter stable/prometheus-node-exporter
NAME:    node-exporter
LAST DEPLOYED: Tue Nov 12 15:10:28 2019
NAMESPACE: default
STATUS: DEPLOYED

RESOURCES:
==> v1/ClusterRole
NAME                                            AGE
psp-node-exporter-prometheus-node-exporter      <invalid>

==> v1/ClusterRoleBinding
NAME                                            AGE
psp-node-exporter-prometheus-node-exporter      <invalid>

==> v1/DaemonSet
NAME                                       AGE
node-exporter-prometheus-node-exporter     <invalid>

==> v1/Pod(related)
NAME                                            AGE
node-exporter-prometheus-node-exporter-p2b5j    <invalid>
node-exporter-prometheus-node-exporter-t5pr6    <invalid>

==> v1/Service
NAME                                       AGE
node-exporter-prometheus-node-exporter     <invalid>
```

Figure 4-12. *Configuring Node Exporter*

Step 2: Now, let's verify the Node Exporter service is running by executing the following command from the /home/prometheus folder. The node-exporter-prometheus-node-exporter service should be visible in a running state, as highlighted in Figure 4-13. Also note the cluster IP address for the service, as it will be used in the next step.

```
$kubectl get svc
```

```
[root@k8s-master prometheus]# kubectl get svc
NAME                                       TYPE        CLUSTER-IP       EXTERNAL-IP   PORT(S)                        AGE
frontend                                   NodePort    10.105.20.144    <none>        80:30186/TCP                   7d19h
kubernetes                                 ClusterIP   10.96.0.1        <none>        443/TCP                        12d
myblog-wordpress                           NodePort    10.105.37.135    <none>        8081:31000/TCP,443:31020/TCP   4d23h
node-exporter-prometheus-node-exporter     ClusterIP   10.102.155.199   <none>        9100/TCP                       22s
redis-master                               ClusterIP   10.102.38.252    <none>        6379/TCP                       7d19h
redis-slave                                ClusterIP   10.108.54.154    <none>        6379/TCP                       7d19h
```

Figure 4-13. *Verifying Node Exporter status*

Step 3: The next step is to configure Node Exporter. Navigate to the /home/prometheus folder on the master Kubernetes node and open the config-map.yml file. Under the scarpe_config section find the job_name: node-exporter section and details for the job name and static configs, as shown in Figure 4-14.

```
- job_name: node-exporter
  static_configs:
  - targets: ['10.102.155.199:9100']
```

Figure 4-14. Node Exporter section

- **job_name:** This field represents the job name for Node Exporter. In this example, we are using node-exporter as job_name.

- **static_configs:** This section has a subsection named targets in it. Targets refers to the job target, which is 10.102.155.199 (cluster IP) and 9100, which is the service port on which the Node Exporter service is running. You can use the following command to verify your cluster IP and port information, as shown in Figure 4-15.

```
$ kubectl get svc
```

```
[root@k8s-master prometheus]# kubectl get svc
NAME                                           TYPE        CLUSTER-IP       EXTERNAL-IP   PORT(S)                        AGE
frontend                                       NodePort    10.105.20.144    <none>        80:30186/TCP                   7d19h
kubernetes                                     ClusterIP   10.96.0.1        <none>        443/TCP                        12d
myblog-wordpress                               NodePort    10.105.37.135    <none>        8081:31000/TCP,443:31020/TCP   4d23h
node-exporter-prometheus-node-exporter         ClusterIP   10.102.155.199   <none>        9100/TCP                       22s
redis-master                                   ClusterIP   10.102.38.252    <none>        6379/TCP                       7d19h
redis-slave                                    ClusterIP   10.108.54.154    <none>        6379/TCP                       7d19h
```

Figure 4-15. Verifying Node Exporter status

Step 3: Execute the following commands to reflect the Prometheus config map changes made in previous steps:

```
kubectl delete configmaps prometheus-server-conf -n=monitoring
kubectl create -f config-map.yaml
kubectl delete deployment prometheus-deployment -n monitoring
kubectl apply -f prometheus-deployment.yaml -n monitoring
```

Step 4: Verify Node Exporter's status from within the Prometheus UI by logging in and navigating to Status and then to Targets (`http://masternodeip:30000`)

Search for `node-exporter` on the page and verify that its state is UP, as shown in Figure 4-16.

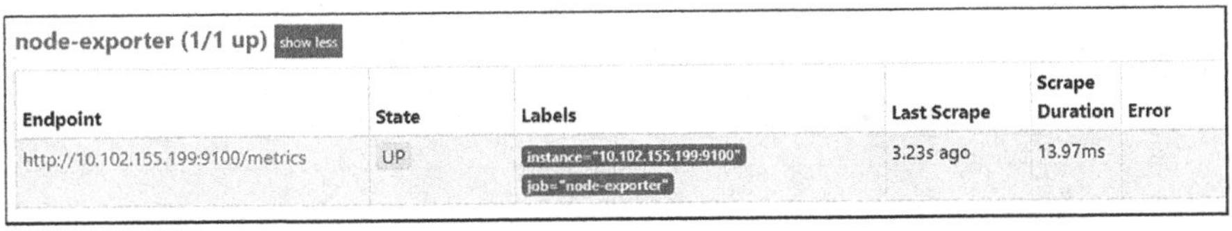

| node-exporter (1/1 up) show less | | | | | | |
Endpoint	State	Labels		Last Scrape	Scrape Duration	Error
http://10.102.155.199:9100/metrics	UP	instance="10.102.155.199:9100" job="node-exporter"		3.23s ago	13.97ms	

Figure 4-16. *Verifying Node Exporter status on Prometheus console*

Step 5: Now, let's execute a query to start collecting and displaying the node metrics. Click on the Graph tab. In the Expression section, in the text box, write `node_load15` and click on the Execute button, as shown in Figure 4-17.

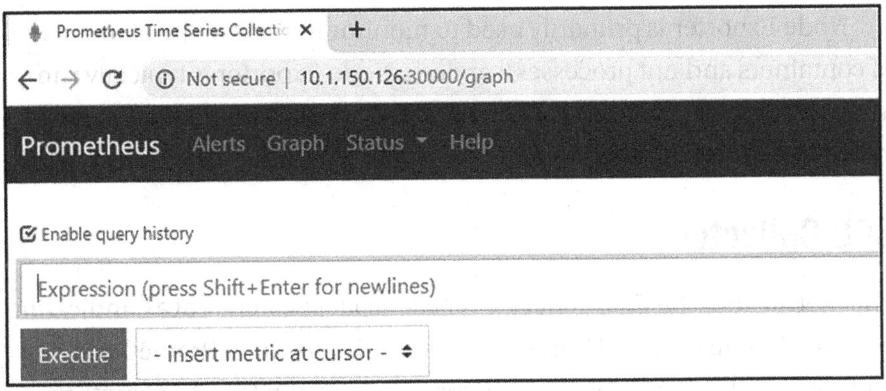

Figure 4-17. *Node Exporter–based query sample*

You will see a graph showing metrics similar to the one shown in Figure 4-18.

103

Figure 4-18. *Node Exporter–based graph*

Node Exporter is primarily used to monitor infrastructure elements of containers and not processes/services. Node Exporter is typically run as a privilege user instead of a root user. We will explore some of the key collectors as part of this chapter.

CPU Collector

The metric from the CPU collector is node_cpu_seconds_total, indicating how much time each CPU spent in each mode. Log in to Prometheus and click on the Graph tab. In the Expression section (text box) write the following query and click on the Execute button:

```
node_cpu_seconds_total{cpu="0", mode="idle"}
```

The following are the various aspects of CPU data collected by the CPU collector:

- **Latency:** Average or maximum delay in CPU scheduler

- **Traffic:** CPU utilization

- **Errors:** Processor-specific error events, faulted CPUs

- **Saturation:** Run-queue length

After execution, you will get the result shown in Figure 4-19.

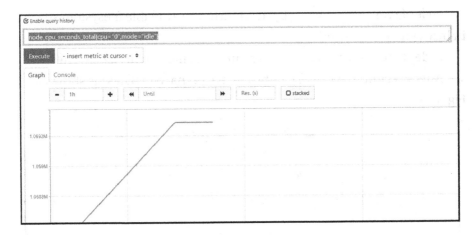

Figure 4-19. *CPU collector–based graph*

Node Exporter provided the following CPU-based metrics that tell us how many seconds each CPU spent doing each type of work:

```
node_cpu_seconds_total{cpu="0",mode="guest"} 0
node_cpu_seconds_total{cpu="0",mode="idle"} 2.03442237e+06
node_cpu_seconds_total{cpu="0",mode="iowait"} 3522.37
node_cpu_seconds_total{cpu="0",mode="irq"} 0.48
node_cpu_seconds_total{cpu="0",mode="nice"} 515.56
node_cpu_seconds_total{cpu="0",mode="softirq"} 953.06
```

```
node_cpu_seconds_total{cpu="0",mode="steal"} 0
node_cpu_seconds_total{cpu="0",mode="system"} 6605.46
```

Filesystem Collector

This collector exposes filesystem statistics, such as disk space used. Log in to Prometheus and click on the Graph tab. In the Expression section (text box), write the following query and click on the Execute button:

```
(node_filesystem_avail_bytes / node_filesystem_size_bytes)
```

node_filesystem_avail_bytes returns the available filesystem space in bytes for on-root users.

node_filesystem_size_bytes returns the filesystem size in bytes.

After execution, you will get the used disk space in bytes, as shown in Figure 4-20.

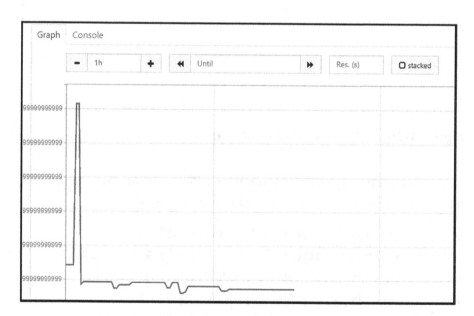

Figure 4-20. *Filesystem collector–based graph*

Diskstats Collector

This collector exposes disk I/O statistics. Log in to Prometheus and click on the Graph tab. In the Expression section (text box), write the following query and click on the Execute button:

```
node_disk_io_now
```

After execution, you will get the result as per Figure 4-21.

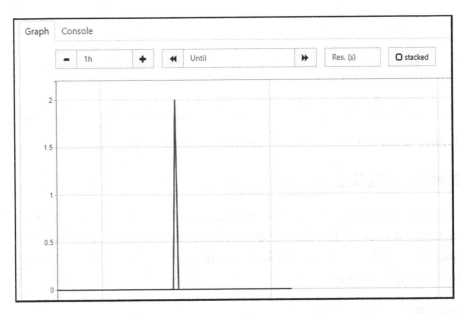

Figure 4-21. *Diskstats collector–based graph*

Netdev Collector

This collector exposes network interface statistics such as bytes transferred. Log in to Prometheus and click on the Graph tab. In the Expression section (text box), write the following query and click on the Execute button. This query will calculate network bandwidth usage of cluster.

```
rate(node_network_receive_bytes_total[1m])
```

After execution, you will get the result shown in Figure 4-22.

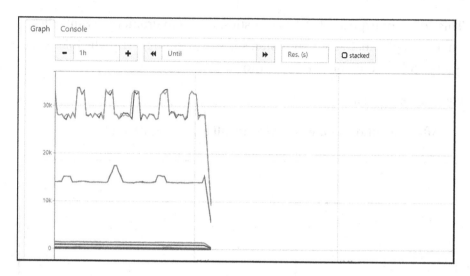

Figure 4-22. *Netdev collector–based graph*

Meminfo Collector

This collector exposes memory statistics. Log in to Prometheus and click on the Graph tab. In the Expression section (text box), write the following query and click on the Execute button. This query will calculate and show free available memory.

```
node_memory_MemFree_bytes
```

The following are the various aspects of memory data collected by the Meminfo collector:

- **Latency:** (none—difficult to find a good method of measuring and not actionable)

- **Traffic:** Amount of memory being used

- **Errors:** Out-of-memory errors

- **Saturation:** Out of Memory (OOM) killer events, swap usage

After execution, you will get the result shown in Figure 4-23.

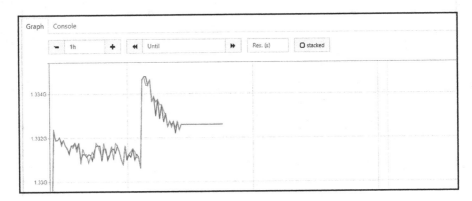

Figure 4-23. *Meminfo collector–based graph*

The following are some useful memory-based metrics provided by Node Exporter:

- node_memory_Active_anon_bytes (gauge) return memory information field Active_anon_bytes

- node_memory_Active_bytes (gauge) return memory information field Active_bytes

- node_memory_Active_file_bytes (gauge) return memory information field Active_file_bytes

Uname Collector

This collector exposes system information as provided by the uname system call. Log in to Prometheus and click on the Graph tab. In the Expression section (text box), write the following query and click on the Execute button. This query will show the count of machines run, along with the kernel version.

```
count by(release)(node_uname_info) from prometheus GUI.
```

After execution, you will get the result shown in Figure 4-24.

Figure 4-24. *Uname collector–based graph*

cAdvisor Exporter

cAdvisor is an open source container resource usage and performance monitoring exporter. Let's now configure the cAdvisor exporter in our container setup.

Step 1: We will configure cAdvisor on the Kubernetes master node (10.1.150.126). Navigate to the /home/prometheus folder and open the config-map.yaml file. Find the section with job_name: 'kubernetes-cadvisor' and review the following sections:

- **job_name:** This field defines the job name assigned to scraped metrics; in our case, we use kubernetes-cadvisor as the job name to fetch to gets metrics using the Kubernetes APIs.

- **kubernetes_sd_configs:** This field represents a list of Kubernetes service discovery configurations. Kubernetes SD configurations help in fetching targets from Kubernetes' REST API. We are using nodes in our case because every node has Docker containers that are running under Kubernetes pods, and cAdvisor provides Docker container–related metrics. The node role discovers one target per cluster node.

- **tls_config:** This field provide details for configuring TLS connections. Under this field there is a subfield for ca_file. This field provides details of the CA certificate used for API authentication.

- **metrics_path:** Defined cAdvisor metrics endpoint that is used by Prometheus to collect the container data, as shown in Figure 4-25.

```
- job_name: 'kuberntes-cadvisor'
    kubernetes_sd_configs:
    - role: node
    scheme: https
    tls_config:
      ca_file: /var/run/secrets/kubernetes.io/serviceaccount/ca.crt
    metrics_path: /metrics/cadvisor
```

Figure 4-25. *Config-map.yaml file review for cAdvisor exporter*

Step 2: Execute the following commands to apply the changes made to the Prometheus configuration:

```
$kubectl delete configmaps prometheus-server-conf -n=monitoring
$kubectl create -f config-map.yaml
$kubectl delete deployment prometheus-deployment -n monitoring
$kubectl apply -f prometheus-deployment.yaml -n monitoring
```

Step 3: To verify that all the components related to Prometheus are running fine, execute the following command, as shown in Figure 4-26:

```
$ kubectl get all -n=monitoring
```

```
[root@k8s-master prometheus]# kubectl get all -n=monitoring
NAME                                       READY    STATUS     RESTARTS   AGE
pod/alertmanager-564d4884bd-mjjft          1/1      Running    0          13d
pod/prometheus-deployment-5c4f4f5779-7rpbt 1/1      Running    0          69m

NAME                          TYPE       CLUSTER-IP       EXTERNAL-IP   PORT(S)           AGE
service/alertmanager          NodePort   10.111.165.123   <none>        8080:32000/TCP    13d
service/prometheus-service    NodePort   10.97.107.57     <none>        8080:30000/TCP    13d

NAME                                     READY   UP-TO-DATE   AVAILABLE   AGE
deployment.apps/alertmanager             1/1     1            1           13d
deployment.apps/prometheus-deployment    1/1     1            1           69m

NAME                                           DESIRED   CURRENT   READY   AGE
replicaset.apps/alertmanager-564d4884bd        1         1         1       13d
replicaset.apps/prometheus-deployment-5c4f4f5779  1      1         1       69m
```

Figure 4-26. *cAdvisor exporter configuration*

Step 4: Log in to Prometheus GUI at `http://kubernetes_master_nodeip: 30000`.

Click Status, and then choose "Targets." You will find the cAdvisor details as in Figure 4-27. Here, the number of endpoints depends on the number of nodes in the Kubernetes cluster, as shown in Figure 4-27.

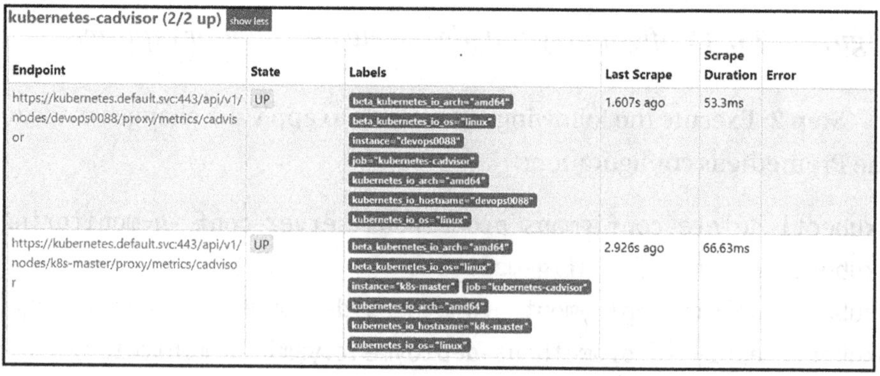

Figure 4-27. *cAdvisor exporter verification*

In our example, we are using a two-node cluster.

Step 5: Click the Graph tab in the Prometheus GUI and execute the following query to view the cumulative count of reads merged:

```
container_fs_reads_merged_total
```

After executing the query, you will see the result, as per Figure 4-28.

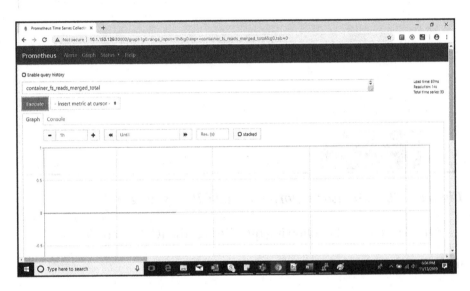

Figure 4-28. *cAdvisor exporter–based filesystem read graph*

Step 6: Execute the following query to get the CPU usage by Kubernetes namespaces:

```
sum(rate(container_cpu_usage_seconds_total{container_
name!="POD",namespace!=""}[5m])) by (namespace)
```

After executing the query, you will see the result as per Figure 4-29.

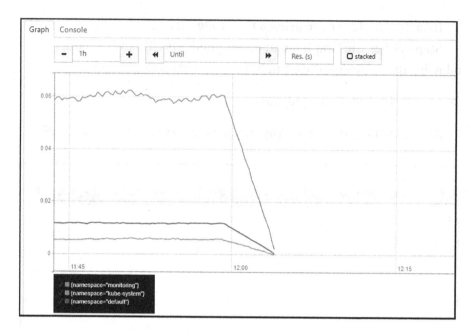

Figure 4-29. cAdvisor exporter–based CPU usage graph

Step 7: Execute the following query to get the ICMP statistics:

```
node_netstat_Icmp_InMsgs
```

After executing the query, you will see the result as shown in Figure 4-30.

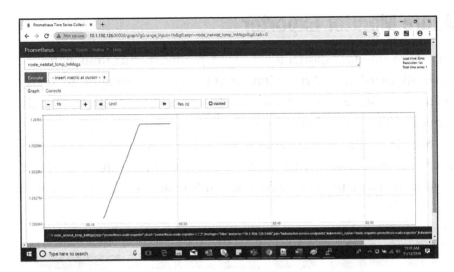

Figure 4-30. *cAdvisor exporter–based ICMP stats graph*

Step 8: Execute the following command to get a list of currently opened connections:

```
node_netstat_Tcp_ActiveOpens
```

After executing the query, you will see the result shown in Figure 4-31.

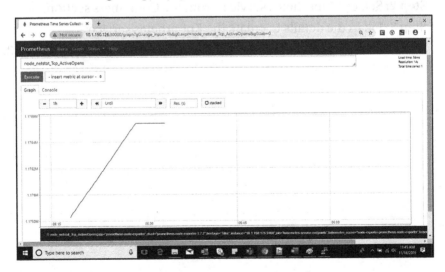

Figure 4-31. *cAdvisor exporter–based open connection graph*

Azure Monitor Exporter

The Azure Monitor exporter is used for exporting metrics from Azure applications using the Azure Monitor API. Now, let's configure an Azure container cluster and see how we can monitor it using Prometheus and leveraging the Azure Monitor exporter.

Step 1: This lab step assumes readers have an Azure account set up and have working knowledge of Azure. Log in to your Azure account and navigate to the Azure dashboard. Click on "Create a resource," as shown in Figure 4-32.

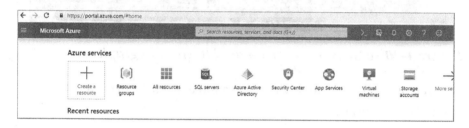

Figure 4-32. *Azure Console*

Step 2: Select "Kubernetes service" from the Containers section.

Step 3: Fill in the details to create the Kubernetes service:

Provide resource group name PrometheusPOC, as shown in Figure 4-33.

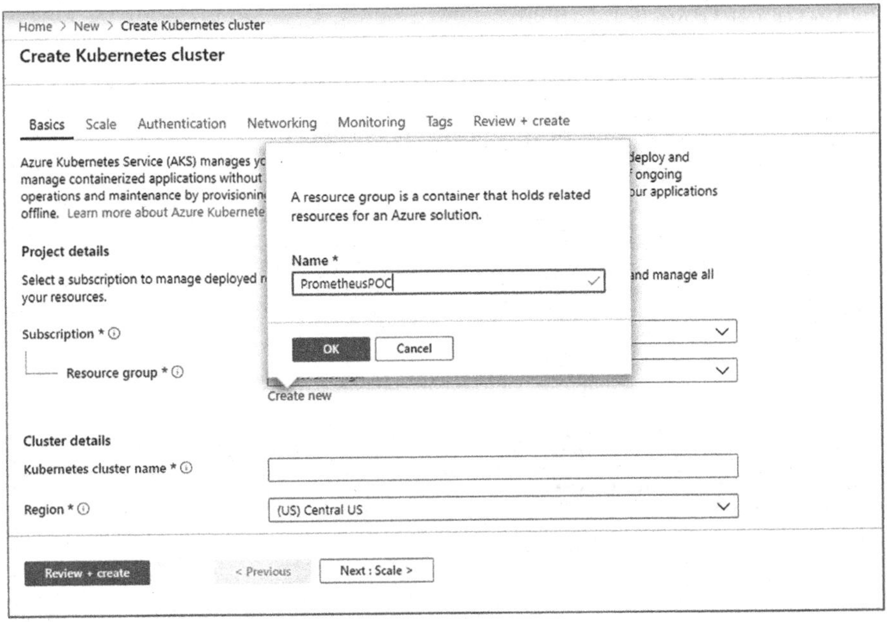

Figure 4-33. *Launching Azure AKS instance via Azure Console*

Note this value as it will be used in the exporter configuration.

Insert other required inputs like cluster name, location, pool size, etc. We are taking Node Count as "1" in this example, as shown in Figure 4-34.

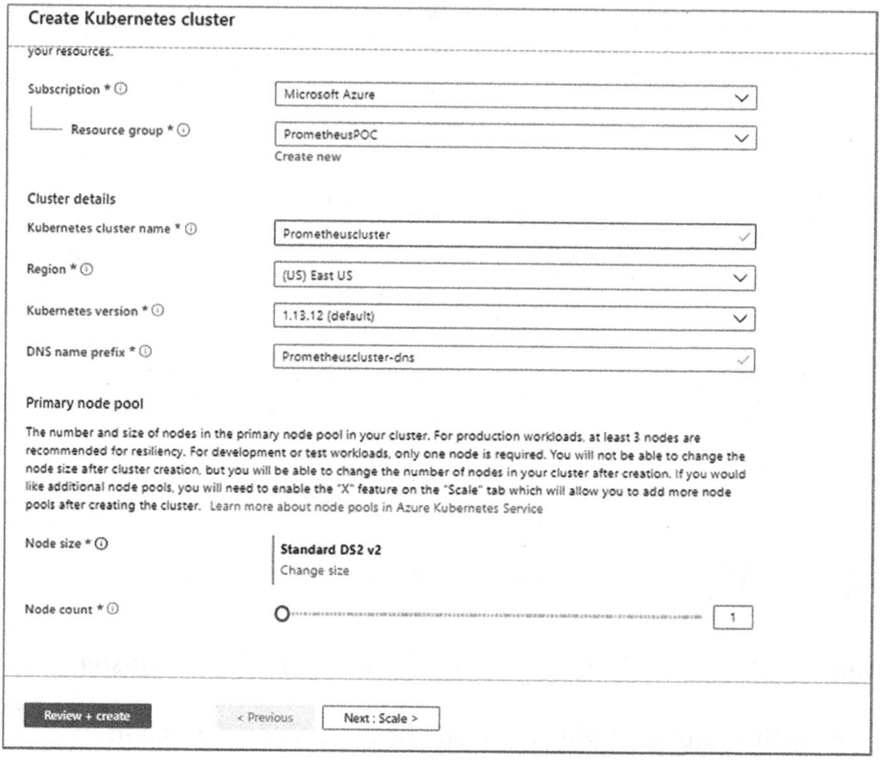

Create Kubernetes cluster

your resources.

Subscription * ⓘ

Microsoft Azure ⌄

└──── Resource group * ⓘ

PrometheusPOC ⌄
Create new

Cluster details

Kubernetes cluster name * ⓘ

Prometheuscluster ✓

Region * ⓘ

(US) East US ⌄

Kubernetes version * ⓘ

1.13.12 (default) ⌄

DNS name prefix * ⓘ

Prometheuscluster-dns ✓

Primary node pool

The number and size of nodes in the primary node pool in your cluster. For production workloads, at least 3 nodes are recommended for resiliency. For development or test workloads, only one node is required. You will not be able to change the node size after cluster creation, but you will be able to change the number of nodes in your cluster after creation. If you would like additional node pools, you will need to enable the "X" feature on the "Scale" tab which will allow you to add more node pools after creating the cluster. Learn more about node pools in Azure Kubernetes Service

Node size * ⓘ

Standard DS2 v2
Change size

Node count * ⓘ

◯·· 1

[Review + create]   < Previous   Next : Scale >

Figure 4-34. Launching Azure AKS instance via Azure Console

Now, click on the Scale tab and provide scaling settings by enabled VM scale sets, as shown in Figure 4-35.

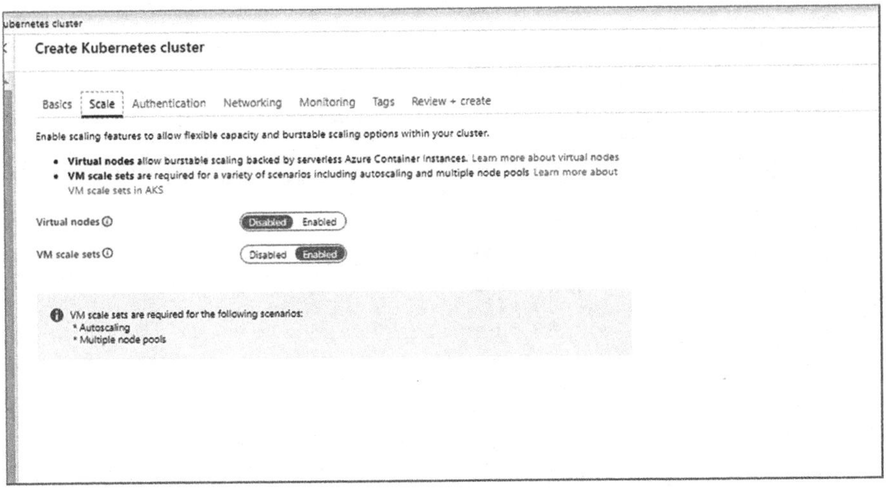

Figure 4-35. Launching Azure AKS instance via Azure Console

Click on the Authentication tab and provide either an existing service principal or create a new one. The service principal should have at least a read role on associated log analytics.

Then click on the Networking tab. Create a new virtual network and subnets, etc., or use the basic configuration, which will create a basic network with the default configuration, as shown in Figure 4-36.

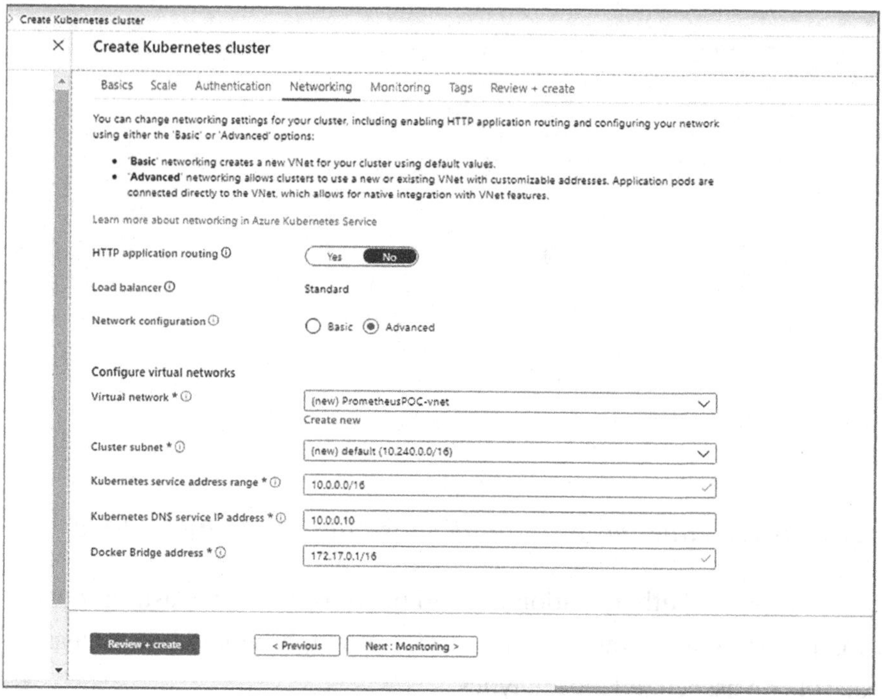

Figure 4-36. *Launching Azure AKS instance via Azure Console*

Click on the Monitoring tab and select "Yes" to enable container monitoring. Choose a workspace for the Log Analytics workspace. This workspace is used by Azure to monitor log data. In our example, we select the "DRYICEDEMOIAC" option for Log Analytics workspace, as shown in Figure 4-37.

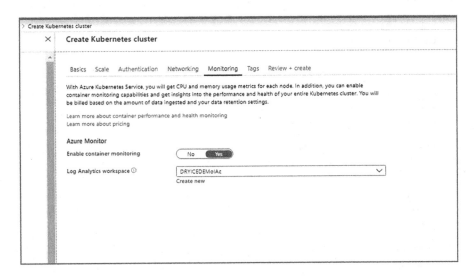

Figure 4-37. *Launching Azure AKS instance via Azure Console*

The Review+Create tab gives details about the information and options provided by the user to create the cluster. Now click the Create button to start the process of cluster creation, as shown in Figure 4-38.

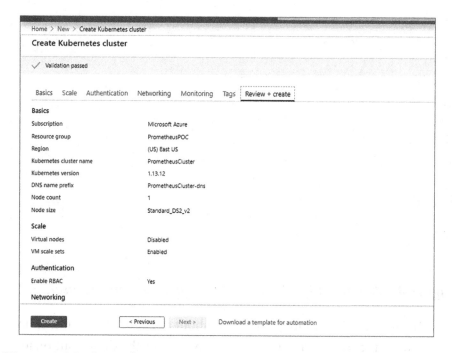

Figure 4-38. Launching Azure AKS instance via Azure Console

Step 4: After cluster creation, we will see the screen shown in Figure 4-39, which verifies the successful creation of the Azure AKS through Azure Console. We can see that a cluster by the name of `PrometheusCluster` is displayed on the Azure Console screen.

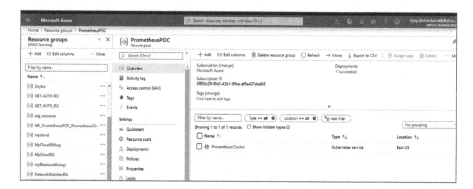

Figure 4-39. Verifying Azure AKS instance via Azure Console

After clicking on `PrometheusCluster`, the information related to the cluster is shown, as in Figure 4-40. Information would contain information like resource group name, location, tags, etc.

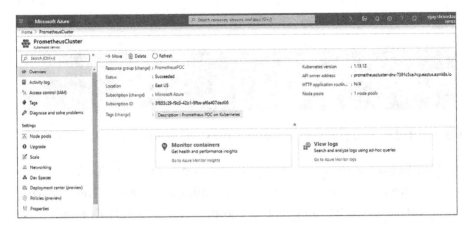

Figure 4-40. *Verifying Azure AKS instance via Azure Console*

Step 5: Now we will use the PowerShell AZ module to check nodes associated with the Kubernetes cluster. For this step, we will assume readers have PowerShell set up for Azure access. First, log in to the Azure PowerShell module using your credentials. Then, execute the following command to get the details of the nodes. For arguments, use the values used for provisioning the cluster in the previous step. You will need a Windows system with the PowerShell module installed on it to proceed, as shown in Figure 4-41.

```
az aks get-credentials --resource-group PrometheusPOC –name
PrometheusCluster
```

Figure 4-41. *Configuring Azure Powershell module for Azure AKS*

Step 6: Now we will push an application on Azure AKS. For this exercise, we will leverage a sample Azure voting application. The following is the URL for GitHub from which the container image will be pulled:

https://github.com/Azure-Samples/azure-voting-app-redis

Step 7: Create the namespace ms-votefront using the following command:

Kubectl create ns ms-votefront

Step 8: Check the associated nodes by executing the following command, as shown in Figure 4-42:

kubectl get ns

```
PS C:\MyWork\DockUbernetes\Git\azure-voting-app-redis> kubectl get ns
NAME            STATUS    AGE
default         Active    5h33m
kube-public     Active    5h33m
kube-system     Active    5h33m
ms-votefront    Active    22s
sock-shop       Active    3h21m
```

Figure 4-42. *Namespace verification for container application deployment on Azure AKS*

Step 9: Now let's apply the image to the Kubernetes cluster using the following command, as shown in Figure 4-43:

```
kubectl apply -f azure-vote-all-in-one-redis.yaml
```

```
PS C:\MyWork\DockUbernetes\Git\azure-voting-app-redis> kubectl apply -f azure-vote-all-in-one-redis.yaml
deployment.apps/azure-vote-back created
service/azure-vote-back created
deployment.apps/azure-vote-front created
service/azure-vote-front created
```

***Figure 4-43.** Deployment of container application on Azure AKS*

Step 10: Check the status and browser load balancer IP by executing the following command, as shown in Figure 4-44:

```
kubectl get all -n ms-votefront
```

```
PS C:\MyWork\DockUbernetes\Git\azure-voting-app-redis> kubectl get all -n  ms-votefront
NAME                                  READY   STATUS    RESTARTS   AGE
pod/azure-vote-back-847fc9bcb9-g7zc9  1/1     Running   0          2m57s
pod/azure-vote-front-5d945b4797-25v8l 1/1     Running   0          2m56s
kubectl :
At line:1 char:1
+ kubectl get all -n ms-votefront
+ ~~~~~~~~~~~~~~~~~~~~~~~~~~~~~~~~~
    + CategoryInfo          : NotSpecified: (:String) [], RemoteException
    + FullyQualifiedErrorId : NativeCommandError

NAME                       TYPE          CLUSTER-IP    EXTERNAL-IP   PORT(S)        AGE
service/azure-vote-back    ClusterIP     10.0.119.73   <none>        6379/TCP       2m57s
service/azure-vote-front   LoadBalancer  10.0.243.189  40.88.19.79   80:30980/TCP   2m56s
NAME                            READY   UP-TO-DATE   AVAILABLE   AGE
deployment.apps/azure-vote-back   1/1    1            1           2m58s
deployment.apps/azure-vote-front  1/1    1            1           2m57s
NAME                                      DESIRED   CURRENT   READY   AGE
replicaset.apps/azure-vote-back-847fc9bcb9   1       1         1       2m59s
replicaset.apps/azure-vote-front-5d945b4797  1       1         1       2m58s

PS C:\MyWork\DockUbernetes\Git\azure-voting-app-redis> |
```

***Figure 4-44.** Verification of container application on Azure AKS*

Step 11: Open the browser and type the IP address of the load balancer to verify the application is working, as shown in Figure 4-45.

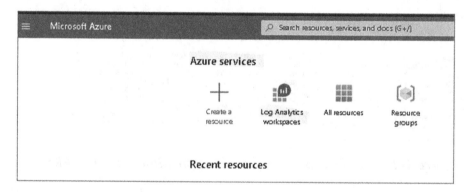

Figure 4-45. *Verification of container application on Azure AKS*

Step 12: To view the log, navigate to the Azure home page and click "Log Analytics workspaces," as shown in Figure 4-46.

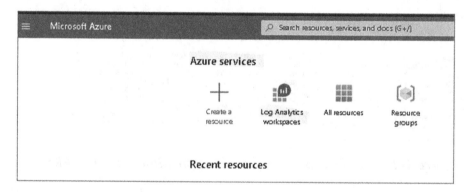

Figure 4-46. *Log Analytics workspaces*

Step 13: Once the Log Analytics workspaces page has opened, click the DRYICEDEMoIAC workspace as shown in Figure 4-47.

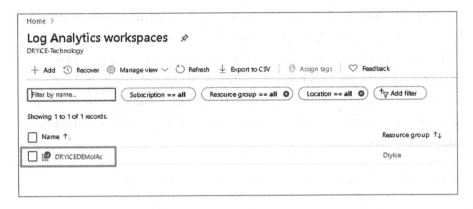

Figure 4-47. *Log Analytics workspaces page*

Now, click the "Logs" option, as shown in Figure 4-48, to see the Azure AKS logs.

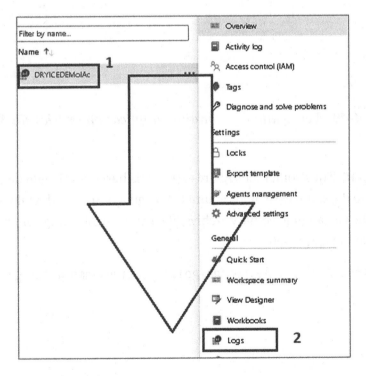

Figure 4-48. *Logs*

Step 14: Once the Logs page opens you can run the various queries to see the AKS cluster log. In our example, we type query `ContainerLog` in the query text box to see all the container logs running in our AKS cluster, then click the Run button, as shown in Figure 4-49. This query will return the deployed application container logs, such as details of the deployed Docker image, HTTP request `request(GET,POST)` handled by the application container, etc.

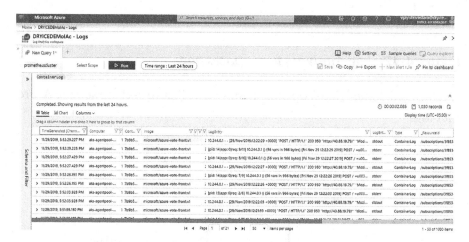

Figure 4-49. *Verification of container application metrics via Azure Console*

Step 15: The Prometheus Azure exporter is based on Go language. To configure the same we would require Go language. So, let's download and install the Go language binary archive file using the following command, as shown in Figure 4-50.

```
wget https://dl.google.com/go/go1.13.3.linux-amd64.tar.gz
```

```
[root@k8s-master home]# wget https://dl.google.com/go/go1.13.3.linux-amd64.tar.gz
--2019-12-02 18:26:54--  https://dl.google.com/go/go1.13.3.linux-amd64.tar.gz
Resolving dl.google.com (dl.google.com)... 173.194.219.190, 173.194.219.91, 173.194.219.93, ...
Connecting to dl.google.com (dl.google.com)|173.194.219.190|:443... connected.
HTTP request sent, awaiting response... 200 OK
Length: 120055279 (114M) [application/octet-stream]
Saving to: 'go1.13.3.linux-amd64.tar.gz'

100%[===================================================================================================>] 120,055,279 9.06MB/s   in 15s

2019-12-02 18:27:12 (7.42 MB/s) - 'go1.13.3.linux-amd64.tar.gz' saved [120055279/120055279]

[root@k8s-master home]# ll
total 117256
drwx------. 15 admin admin      4096 Jul  3 00:02 admin
----r-xr-x.  1 root  root        633 Nov 24 22:14 deployment.yml
-rw-r--r--.  1 root  root  120055279 Oct 18 04:07 go1.13.3.linux-amd64.tar.gz
drwx------.  3 root  root         78 Jul  2 23:59 monitor
drwxr-xr-x.  7 root  root       4096 Nov 20 16:23 prometheus
```

Figure 4-50. *Download package for Go installation*

For this command, download Go Linux version 1.13.3 from the following link: `https://dl.google.com`.

Step 16: Extract the downloaded archive and install it in the `/usr/local` Linux directory. You can also install this under the home directory (for shared hosting) or other location.

`tar -xzf go1.13.3.linux-amd64.tar.gz`

After extracting `go1.13.3.linux-amd64.tar.gz` move all the directories and files related to the Go language to `/usr/local` by using the `mv` command:

`mv go /usr/local`

Step 17: Now we need to set up the Go language environment variables for your project. Commonly, you need to set three environment variables: `GOROOT`, `GOPATH`, and `PATH`. `GOROOT` is the location where the Go package is installed on your system.

`export GOROOT=/usr/local/go`

Now set the `PATH` variable to access Go binary systemwide using the following command:

`export PATH=$GOPATH/bin:$GOROOT/bin:$PATH`

All the preceding environment setup will be set for your current session only. To make it permanent, add the preceding commands in the ~/.bash_profile file.

With this step, you have successfully installed and configured Go language on your system. Verify the setup by using the following command to check the Go version:

```
go version
```

Step 18: Clone the Azure exporter by executing the following inline command in the Kubernetes master server (10.1.150.126) from the home/prometheus directory:

```
git clone https://github.com/RobustPerception/azure_metrics_
exporter.git
```

Step 19: Navigate to the azure_metrics_exporter directory and create the azure.yaml file and copy the following content. You can download the sample Azure.yml file from the following link as well: https://github.com/RobustPerception/azure_metrics_exporter/blob/master/azure-example.yml. Add the details of your Azure subscription and credentials in the following section in the file (highlighted):

```
---
active_directory_authority_url: "https://login.
microsoftonline.com/"
resource_manager_url: "https://management.azure.com/"
credentials:
  subscription_id: <secret>
  client_id: <secret>
  client_secret: <secret>
  tenant_id: <secret>
```

Provide the resource group ID and valid metrics name in the targets section of the file.

The final content of file will look as follows:

```
---
active_directory_authority_url: "https://login.
microsoftonline.com/"
resource_manager_url: "https://management.azure.com/"
credentials:
  subscription_id: "xxxxxx"
  client_id: "xxxxxx"
  client_secret: "xxxxxx"
  tenant_id: "xxxxxx"

targets:
  - resource: "/resourcegroups/PrometheusRG/providers/Microsoft.
    ContainerService/managedClusters/prometheusclusterpoc"
    metrics:
        - name: "memoryRssBytes"
        - name: "cpuUsageNanoCores"
        - name: "cpuAllocatableNanoCores"
        - name: "memoryAllocatableBytes"
        - name: "cpuUsageNanoCores"
        - name: "memoryCapacityBytes"

resource_groups:
  - resource_group: "PrometheusRG"
    resource_types:
        - "Microsoft.Compute/virtualMachines"
    resource_name_include_re:
        - "aks-agentpool-75077965-vmss000000"
    resource_name_exclude_re:
        - "testvm12"
    metrics:
        - name: "memoryRssBytes"
        - name: "cpuUsageNanoCores"
```

```
- name: "cpuAllocatableNanoCores"
- name: "memoryAllocatableBytes"
- name: "cpuUsageNanoCores"
- name: "memoryCapacityBytes"
```

Step 20: To generate the azure_metrics_exporter executable file, execute the following inline command under the same directory; e.g., /home/prometheus/azure_metrics_exporter:

```
$ make build
```

Step 21: Create the Linux service for the azure_metrics_exporter executable. Create the azexporter.service file under the /etc/systemd/system directory and copy the following inline commands, as shown in Figure 4-51:

```
[Unit]
Description=azure-exporter
Wants=network-online.target
After=network-online.target
[Service]
Type=simple
ExecStart=/usr/local/bin/azure_metrics_exporter \
    --config.file /home/prometheus/azure_metrics_exporter/
azure.yml
Restart=always
RestartSec=1
[Install]
WantedBy=multi-user.target
```

```
[root@devops0087 azure_metrics_exporter]# cd /etc/systemd/system
[root@devops0087 system]# ll
total 16
-rw-r--r--  1 root root  301 Dec 12 11:02 azexporter.service
drwxr-xr-x. 2 root root   57 Feb 20  2019 basic.target.wants
```

Figure 4-51. *Create Linux service for Azure exporter*

Step 22: Start the service by executing the following command:

```
$ systemctl start azexporter
```

Verify whether the `azexporter` service has started by executing the following command, as shown in Figure 4-52:

```
$ systemctl status azexporter
```

```
[root@devops0087 system]# systemctl status azexporter
● azexporter.service - azure-exporter
   Loaded: loaded (/etc/systemd/system/azexporter.service; disabled; vendor preset: disabled)
   Active: active (running) since Thu 2019-12-12 11:03:19 IST; 19min ago
 Main PID: 1720 (azure_metrics_e)
    Tasks: 7
   Memory: 9.8M
   CGroup: /system.slice/azexporter.service
           └─1720 /usr/local/bin/azure_metrics_exporter --config.file /home/prometheus/azure_metrics_exporter/azure.yml
```

Figure 4-52. *Verification of Azure exporter*

Step 23: Copy the following content into the `config-map.yaml` file under the `scrape_configs:` section:

```
- job_name: 'azure-monitoring'
        static_configs:
          - targets: ['10.1.150.126:9276']
```

Under `targets`, give the IP address of the master node (10.1.150.126) and Azure Monitor port, which is 9276.

Step 24: Execute the following command to reflect the changes in Prometheus:

```
$ kubectl delete configmaps prometheus-server-conf
-n=monitoring
$ kubectl create -f config-map-new.yaml
```

```
$ kubectl delete deployment prometheus-deployment -n monitoring
$ kubectl apply -f prometheus-deployment.yaml -n monitoring
```

Step 25: Open the Prometheus GUI to get the status of the Azure exporter, as shown in Figure 4-53.

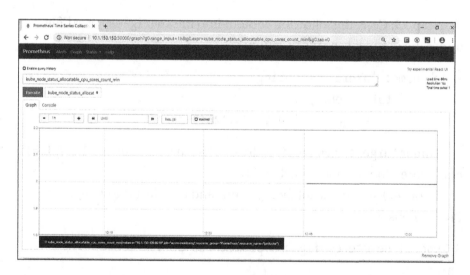

Figure 4-53. *Verification of Azure exporter on Prometheus console*

Step 26: Click on Graph tab and execute the following query to get the result (after configuring the exporter, please wait for at least twenty to thirty minutes to get the result), as shown in Figure 4-54.

```
kube_node_status_allocatable_cpu_cores_count_min
```

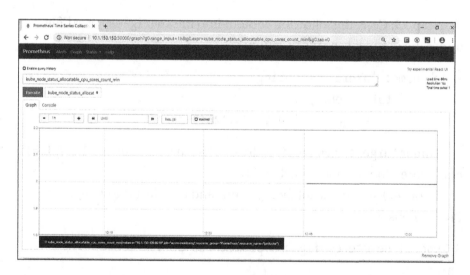

Figure 4-54. *Node status graph using Azure exporter*

Step 27: Click on the Graph tab and execute the following query to get the total amount of available memory in a managed cluster, as shown in Figure 4-55.

```
kube_node_status_allocatable_memory_bytes_bytes_average
```

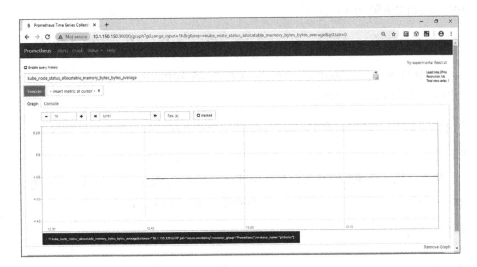

Figure 4-55. *Node allocated memory graph using Azure exporter*

Step 28: Click on the Graph tab and execute the following query to get the total number of ready pods:

```
kube_pod_status_ready_count_total
```

Step 29: Click on the Graph tab and execute the following query to get the maximum number of ready pods. See the result under the Console section of query.

```
kube_pod_status_ready_count_max
```

Kube Stat Metrics

The Kube-state-metrics exporter leverages the Kubernetes APIs to provide metrics for various Kubernetes objects. Let's configure Kube-state and see how we can fetch metrics using Prometheus. You will get more metrics at the following link:

https://github.com/kubernetes/kube-state-metrics/tree/master/docs

Step 1: Navigate to the /home/prometheus directory and execute the following inline command:

```
$ git clone https://github.com/kubernetes/kube-state-metrics.
git
```

Step 2: Verify whether the kube-state-metrics clone is successful by executing the following inline command, as shown in Figure 4-56:

```
$ ls -ltr
```

```
urwxr-xr-x    2 root root         24 Dec 24 17:15 kubestate
drwxr-xr-x   13 root root       4096 Dec 24 17:55 kube-state-metrics
```

Figure 4-56. *Kube-state-metrics clone from Git*

Step 3: Navigate to /home/prometheus/kube-state-metrics and execute the following command to install the kube-state exporter:

```
$ cd /home/prometheus/kube-state-metrics
$ kubectl apply -f examples/standard
```

Step 4: Execute the following command to get the kube-state service details, as shown in Figure 4-57:

```
$ kubectl get svc -n kube-system
```

```
[root@devops0087 prometheus]# kubectl get svc -n kube-system
NAME                    TYPE        CLUSTER-IP      EXTERNAL-IP     PORT(S)                    AGE
kube-dns                ClusterIP   10.96.0.10      <none>          53/UDP,53/TCP,9153/TCP     15d
kube-state-metrics      ClusterIP   None            <none>          8080/TCP,8081/TCP          39m
tiller-deploy           ClusterIP   10.106.148.3    <none>          44134/TCP                  14d
```

Figure 4-57. *Kube-state-metrics service status*

Step 5: Execute the following command to fetch the kube-state-metrics endpoint that needs to be set in Prometheus, as shown in Figure 4-58:

```
$kubectl describe svc kube-state-metrics -n kube-system
```

```
[root@devops0087 prometheus]# kubectl describe svc kube-state-metrics -n kube-system
Name:             kube-state-metrics
Namespace:        kube-system
Labels:           app.kubernetes.io/name=kube-state-metrics
                  app.kubernetes.io/version=v1.9.0
Annotations:      kubectl.kubernetes.io/last-applied-configuration:
                    {"apiVersion":"v1","kind":"Service","metadata":{"annotations":{},"labels":{"app
bernetes.i...
Selector:         app.kubernetes.io/name=kube-state-metrics
Type:             ClusterIP
IP:               None
Port:             http-metrics  8080/TCP
TargetPort:       http-metrics/TCP
Endpoints:        10.32.0.2:8080
Port:             telemetry  8081/TCP
TargetPort:       telemetry/TCP
Endpoints:        10.32.0.2:8081
Session Affinity: None
Events:           <none>
[root@devops0087 prometheus]# 
```

Figure 4-58. *Kube-state-metrics service endpoint details*

Copy the Endpoints value 10.32.0.2:8080, then update the config-map.yaml file and copy the following lines under the scrape_configs: section:

```
- job_name: 'kube-state-metrics'
  static_configs:
- targets: ['10.32.0.2:8080']
```

Step 6: Execute the following command to reflect the changes in Prometheus:

```
$kubectl delete configmaps prometheus-server-conf -n=monitoring
```

```
$kubectl create -f config-map.yaml
$kubectl delete deployment prometheus-deployment -n monitoring
$kubectl apply -f prometheus-deployment.yaml -n monitoring
```

Step 7: Log in to the Prometheus GUI (`http://master_ip:30000`) ➤ Targets to verify whether `kube-state-metrics` is up and running, as shown in Figure 4-59.

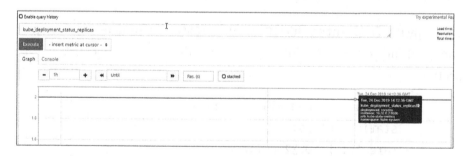

Figure 4-59. *Kube-state-metrics service verification on Prometheus console*

Step 8: Navigate to the Graph tab to execute the following query to analyze the Kubernetes deployment status to get the desired state of replicas. This helps in identifying the deployments that are having issues or facing errors, as shown in Figure 4-60.

```
kube_deployment_status_replicas
```

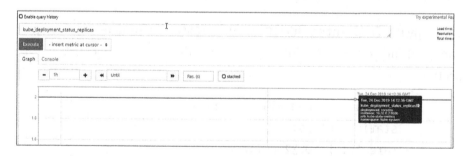

Figure 4-60. *Kube deployment status metrics graph using Kube-state-metrics*

Summary

In this chapter, we provided hands-on steps for setting up Helm and Tiller. We also provided information on various exporters' setup and their uses in Prometheus. We also guided readers in deploying exporters and viewing metrics for their containerized application. In the next chapter, we will start with an overview of Prometheus Query Language.

## CHAPTER 5

Working with Prometheus Query Language (PromQL)

PromQL (Prometheus Query Language) is a functional query language provided by Prometheus to enable the user to query data stored in real time and perform all sorts of analysis, aggregations, and operations. In this chapter, we will provide hands-on steps to the readers that will enable them to use PromQL.

Prior to getting started with PromQL, let's briefly understand the way data is stored in Prometheus.

Data in Prometheus

As we know by now, Prometheus monitors metrics and collects and stores time-series data.

Time-series data is defined as a series of data points ordered by time. Let's understand time-series data with an example. If we enable per-minute monitoring of the CPU in an environment comprising different types of Cis, such as servers, devices, networks, etc., then at every minute

© Navin Sabharwal, Piyush Pandey 2020
N. Sabharwal and P. Pandey, *Monitoring Microservices and Containerized Applications*,
https://doi.org/10.1007/978-1-4842-6216-0_5

a data point will be generated that depicts the CPU utilization at that point in time. If we represented the data collected as a table, the values collected would look like Table 5-1.

Table 5-1. *CPU Utilization example*

Timestamp	CPU Utilization (%)
1591709873808	67
1591709884270	66
1591709891811	67
1591709898278	68
1591709905225	67

In Prometheus, a time-series object is created for each metric monitored, in order to store the metric's data. The object is uniquely identified by the metric's name and primarily comprises a key–value pair, where the key is a millisecond-precision timestamp and the value is the measured data in Float format. Each key–value pair is termed as Sample; i.e., data at a given timestamp.

So, in Prometheus, the preceding data will become part of the time-series object uniquely identified by its metric name; i.e., cpu_util_perc. The hypothetical representation of the preceding data looks as follows:

```
cpu_util_perc:
(1591709873808, 67),
(1591709884270, 66),
(1591709891811, 67),
(1591709898278, 68),
(1591709905225, 67)
```

Though the preceding data provides information about the CPU utilization (%) against a timestamp, it doesn't provide any information related to which CI's data it is.

To cater to this, Prometheus enables us to define *labels*. Labels enable us to capture additional attributes of the data monitored. In the object, this is further stored as a key–value pair, where the key is the name of the attribute being captured and the value is the actual attribute data.

In the preceding example of object `cpu_util_perc` we can create a label named `CI` to capture details of the CI whose CPU utilization is being monitored.

With the labels in place, the samples—i.e., the time-series data—will be hypothetically represented as shown here:

```
cpu_util_perc {ci: "ci_1"}:
(1591709873808, 67),
(1591709884270, 66),
(1591709891811, 67),
(1591709898278, 68),
(1591709905225, 67)
cpu_util_perc {ci: "ci_2"}:
(1591709873808, 67),
(1591709884270, 66),
(1591709891811, 67),
(1591709898278, 68),
(1591709905225, 67)
```

. . . . . .

Multiple labels can be defined per metric to capture various information about the data being measured.

Getting Started

Now that we know the way data is stored in a Prometheus time-series database, let's begin querying the data.

We begin with selectors—different ways in which we can select data, aggregators, and functions. Finally, we will see the ways in which we can use operators (arithmetic and Boolean) to work with the result data.

Selectors

There are various options for selecting the data. In PromQL terminology, we will look at various selectors of the metrics data.

Please note for all the examples here we will refer to the data of metric jvm_memory_bytes_used. This metric stores the JVM memory area-wise bytes used by different jobs running across various instances.

Select Metric

We begin with simply typing the metric name into the query console, as follows:

```
jvm_memory_bytes_used
```

As mentioned earlier, all data related to the metric is stored in a time-series object identified by the metric name and its distinct labels. So, simply typing the metric name in the query console selects and displays data for all its distinct labels, as shown in Figure 5-1.

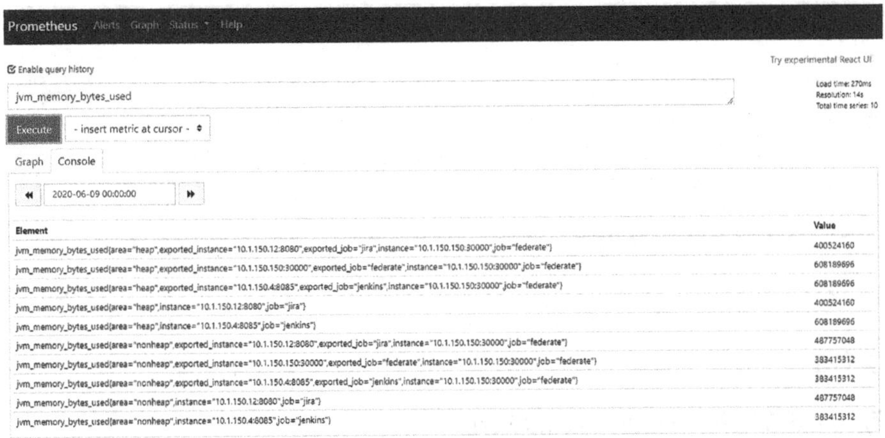

Figure 5-1. *Displaying data*

The data returned is a single sample value for all distinct labels timestamped at the same timestamp, which is probably the last timestamped value captured. This output is termed as an *instant* vector in PromQL.

Filter by Labels

As can be seen in the preceding output, the labels associated with the metric are area, job, instance, and so on. Let's next look at selectors with filters on labels.

Let's add a filter on the label "area" to select data where the value is heap. For this, we will simply mention the required label in the query, as shown here:

```
jvm_memory_bytes_used {area="heap"}
```

This returns data points where the label "area" has a value of heap, as shown in Figure 5-2.

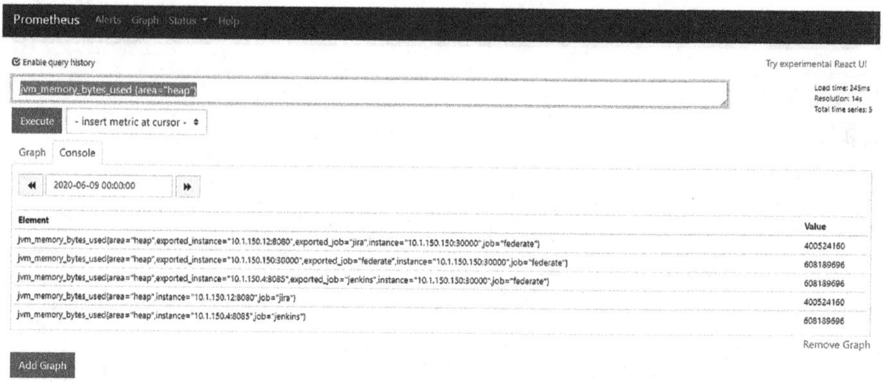

Figure 5-2. *Return values as heap*

In the preceding query we used the = operator to return matching data. Next, let's use the following query to display all data except the ones where "area" equals heap.

```
jvm_memory_bytes_used {area!="heap"}
```

Here, we have just replaced the = operator with the ! = operator. As we can see in Figure 5-3, the output instant vector comprises data where area! = "heap".

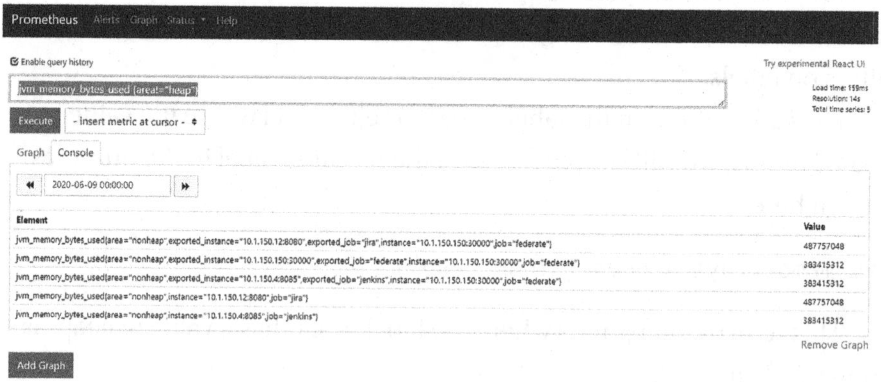

Figure 5-3. *Return values that are not heap*

The preceding were examples where we did exact matches of the values. Let's next look at regular expressions or searches where we will filter the data on the basis of a regular expression. The following query enables us to select all cases where the "job" label values begin with the characters fed.

```
jvm_memory_bytes_used {job=~"fed.+"}
```

As shown in the output in Figure 5-4, the instant vector–only data where the "Job" label values begin with fed are selected.

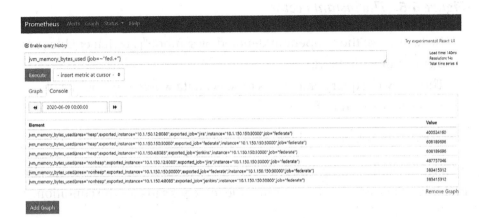

Figure 5-4. *The results of our query*

We can also filter the data by using a regular expression where we will fetch data *not* matching an expression. The following query fetches all data except those where the "Job" label value begins with fed:

```
jvm_memory_bytes_used {job!~"fed.+"}
```

Figure 5-5 depicts the instant vector returned.

Figure 5-5. The instant vector

Next, let's use the or operator denoted by symbol "|", which enables us to do either/or with the values.

The following query enables us to select data where the "Job" label values begin with either f or j.

```
jvm_memory_bytes_used {job=~"f.+|j.+"}
```

Figure 5-6 shows the data fetched. The | operator enables us to specify multiple values where either of the value matches satisfies the condition.

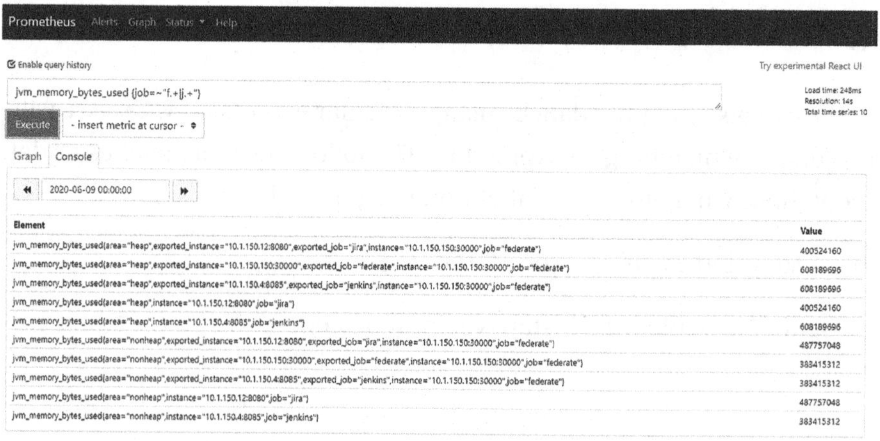

Figure 5-6. The fetched jobs

If we have exact values, we can use the values separated by the |
operator to select rows with either value, as shown in the following query,
where we fetch data where the "area" label value is either heap or nonheap.

```
jvm_memory_bytes_used {area=~"heap|nonheap"}
```

Figure 5-7 shows the vector returned.

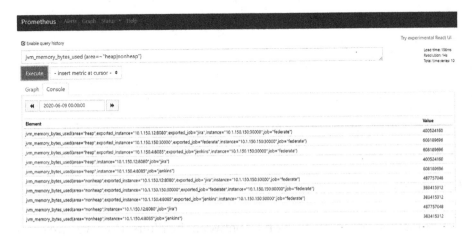

Figure 5-7. *The vector returned*

As can be seen, the data points were selected/fetched where the "area"
value is either heap or nonheap.

Filter by Multiple Labels

Let's next look at the way we can use multiple labels to filter the data.
The multiple filters are by default combined with an AND operator, which
implies that the data returns matches where all the filter criteria are
specified. Whatever operators and criteria we discussed previously can
be individually applied to each filter condition, and then we can combine
them.

Let's look at the following query:

```
jvm_memory_bytes_used {instance=~"10.1.150.12:8080",
area!~"heap", job=~'j.+'}
```

The query returns data where "instance" is `10.1.150.12:8080`, "area" is `not heap`, and "job" values start with j, as shown in Figure 5-8.

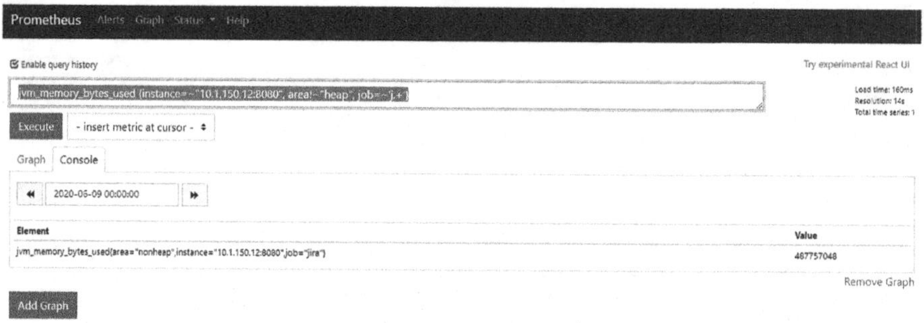

Figure 5-8. *Further filtering of the results*

Prometheus does not support `OR` between the filters. However, we can work around the requirement by using whatever selectors we have learned up until now.

For example, if we want to select data that matches the following criteria—"job" starts with `J` and "area" = `heap` or "area" = `nonheap`—we can use the following query:

```
jvm_memory_bytes_used {area=~"heap|nonheap", job=~'j.+'}
```

We will look at a few more examples toward the end of the section, where we will be talking about aggregation operations on the datasets.

Select to Return Range Vectors

The preceding query returned an instant vector, which we know returns a single sample value for each distinct labeled time series.

In addition, PromQL enables us to select a range of samples (timestamped data) for each distinct labeled time series from the current instant. We simply have to specify the range duration, as shown here in square brackets next to the selectors:

```
jvm_memory_bytes_used [1m]
```

It comprises the duration we want to look back at followed by one of the following units:

- s: seconds

- m: minutes

- h: hours

- d: days

- w: weeks

- y: years

In the preceding example query, we have specified to select data of the last one minute from the current instant. As shown in Figure 5-9, the range of all samples collected in the last one minute for each distinct labeled entry is selected.

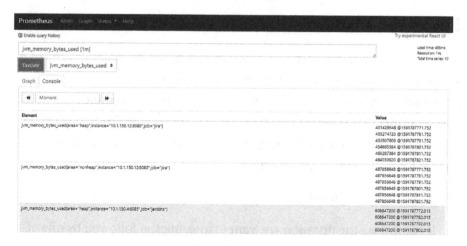

Figure 5-9. *The range of samples*

This data output is termed as a *range vector* in PromQL, as it returns a range of values per distinct labeled time-series object for the duration selected.

Note   The range vector cannot be directly graphed, but can be viewed in the console, as shown in Figure 5-9.

If square brackets do not specify the range, the default instant vector is returned, which is an instant single data sample for all distinct labeled time series objects.

The range operator can be combined with the other selection criteria we discussed previously.

In the following query, we return a range vector for data filtered by applying multiple filter criteria on different labels:

```
jvm_memory_bytes_used{area="heap", instance="10.1.150.150:30000",
job="federate",exported_job="federate"}[1m]
```

As shown in Figure 5-10, the output returns a range of data collected in the last one minute only for "instance" = 10.1.150.150:30000, "job" = federate, "exported_job" = federate, and "area" = heap.

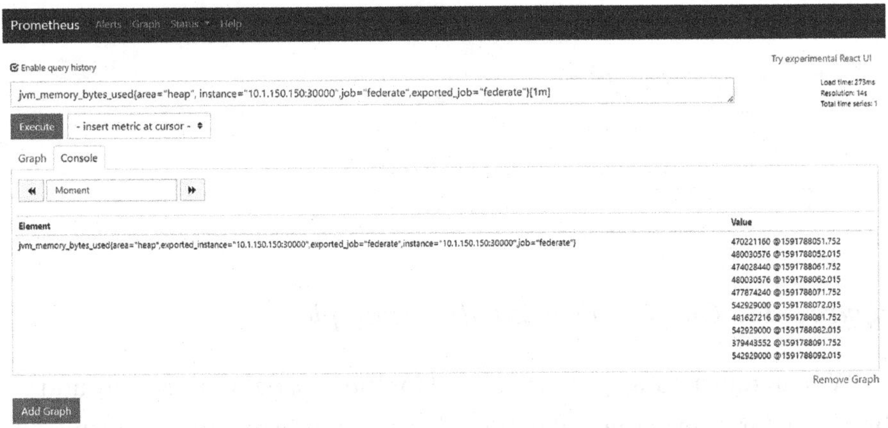

Figure 5-10. *Another range of samples*

So, in summary, to select a range vector we just need to append a range in square brackets at the end of the selector.

Select Past/Historical Data

Till now, we have looked at selecting the current data or data specified at a moment. PromQL also enables us to select data from the past. For this, we simply use Offset in the query, as in the following, followed by the duration and the units, which we covered earlier in the range section.

jvm_memory_bytes_used **Offset** 7d

As shown in Figure 5-11, the instant vector data returned is data that was collected seven days ago.

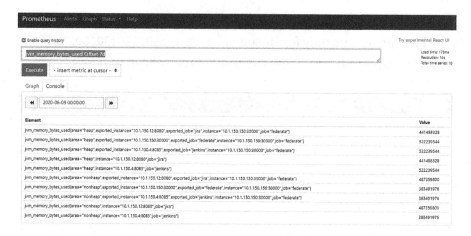

Figure 5-11. *Our first historical data example*

We can return range vectors as well for the past data. We simply add the range duration at the end of the selector, as shown in the following query. The query returns a range of all data collected in the last one minute seven days back.

```
jvm_memory_bytes_used[1m] Offset 7d
```

The output in Figure 5-12 shows the past timestamped range values.

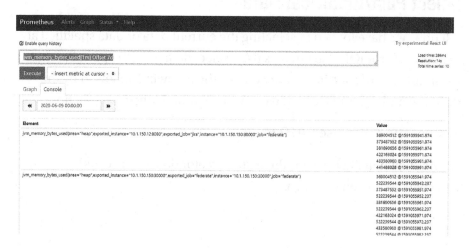

Figure 5-12. *Timestamped range values*

We can use the other selectors we discussed earlier and further combine offset to return historical data of the filtered lot. For example, the following query selects past range data only for instances starting with 10.1.150.150:

```
jvm_memory_bytes_used {instance =~ "10.1.150.150.*"}[1m] Offset 7d
```

The output in Figure 5-13 depicts the data returned.

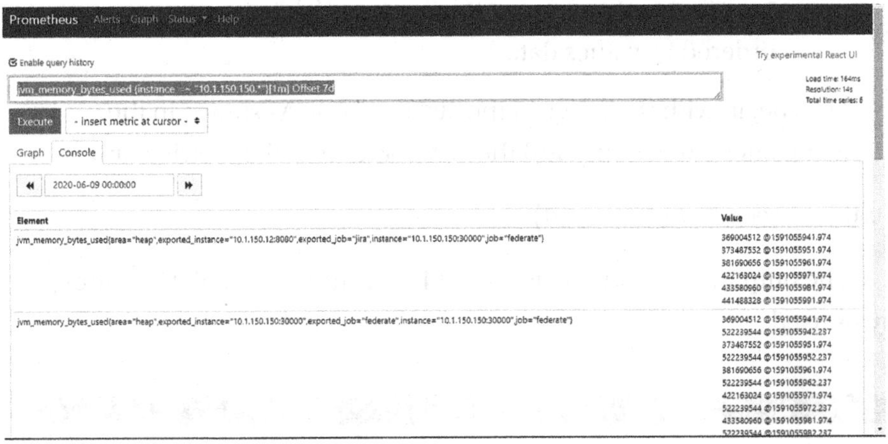

Figure 5-13. *The data returned from our query*

All the queries we just looked at enabled us to select the data from the Prometheus database using PromQL, and all are termed as part of the selector clause. We also looked at the different vectors returned; i.e., instant vector versus range vector.

Aggregation Example

Now that we have the data selected, let's apply aggregations to it to aggregate the data for meaningful analysis. PromQL supports multiple aggregation operators. Please refer to the official site for more details.[1] In the following examples, we refer to these operations:

- sum: to sum the values

- topk/bottomk: to return top/bottom K data points ordered by values data

Let's begin with the usage of the sum operator. As shown in the following query, we simply add the sum operator to the metric name.

sum(jvm_memory_bytes_used)

The output, as shown in Figure 5-14, returns the total JVM memory bytes used.

Figure 5-14. *Total memory bytes used*

---

[1]https://prometheus.io/docs/prometheus/latest/querying/operators/ #aggregation-operators

The preceding query gives overall consumption data. Let's next group the data by area using the by clause, as shown in the following query:

```
sum by (area) (jvm_memory_bytes_used)
```

The output, as shown in Figure 5-15, returns area-wise total memory bytes used.

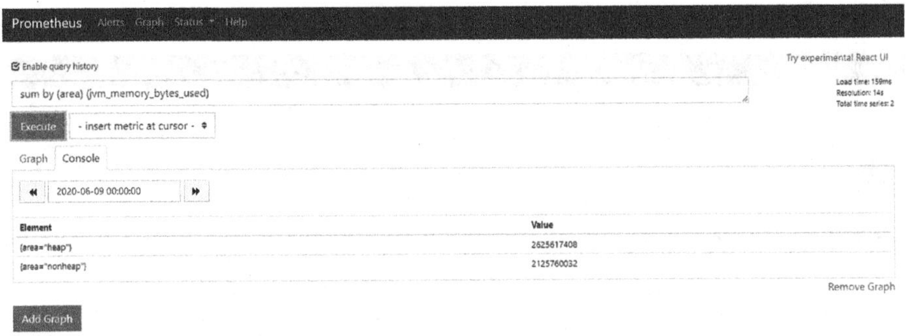

Figure 5-15. *Total memory bytes used per area*

Let's further group the data by job to view consumed memory by job:

```
sum by (job) (jvm_memory_bytes_used)
```

The output in Figure 5-16 shows job-wise memory consumed.

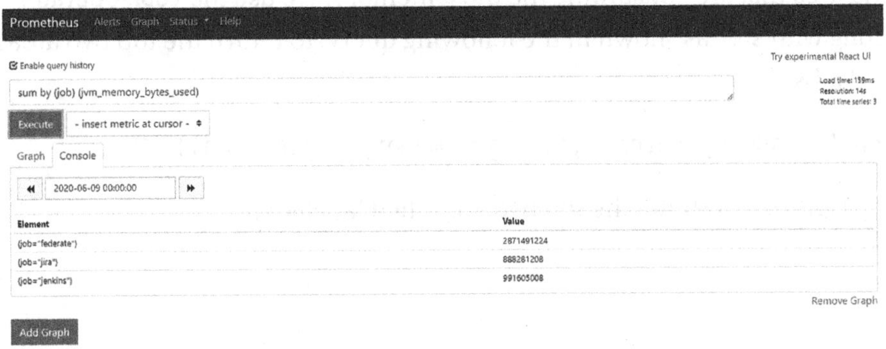

Figure 5-16. *Memory consumed per job*

We have individually grouped the data by different labels. Let's next use the following query to group the data by area and job so as to view job-wise each area-wise memory byte consumed.

```
sum by (area, job) (jvm_memory_bytes_used)
```

The output in Figure 5-17 shows the area-wise job-wise memory-consumed details.

Figure 5-17. *Memory used by area and job*

Now that we have grouped the data, let's next find out the top two jobs and area that are consuming the most memory. We use the topk operator along with sum, as shown in the following query, to return the top two areas and jobs:

```
topk(2, sum by (area, job) (jvm_memory_bytes_used))
```

Figure 5-18 shows the top two identified labeled data.

Figure 5-18. *The top two values*

If we need to find the bottom area and jobs consuming the least memory, we can use bottomk along with sum to return the data, as shown in the following query:

```
bottomk(2, sum by (area, job) (jvm_memory_bytes_used))
```

Figure 5-19 shows the bottom two identified labeled data.

Figure 5-19. *The bottom two results*

Until now, we have aggregated the instant vector, which actually aggregated the single latest timestamped value and did not take into consideration the range of data generated. Let's look at using the aggregation operators with the range vectors.

As we know, range vectors return a range of all data collected, so the vector cannot be directly used in the aggregation operators. We will first have to use the varied functions[2] offered by PromQL to fetch the most relevant data point from the range. Relevance depends on the characteristics of the data. In our examples, since we are looking at bytes consumed, we will be interested in looking at the average value in the range. To find the relevant data point from the range, we will use the `avg_over_time` function from the list.

Let's first look at the output of the function. We will use the following query to fetch all ranges of data generated in the last one min and then use the `avg_over_time` function on it.

```
avg_over_time(jvm_memory_bytes_used[1m])
```

As shown in Figure 5-20, the output returns the average value of each range.

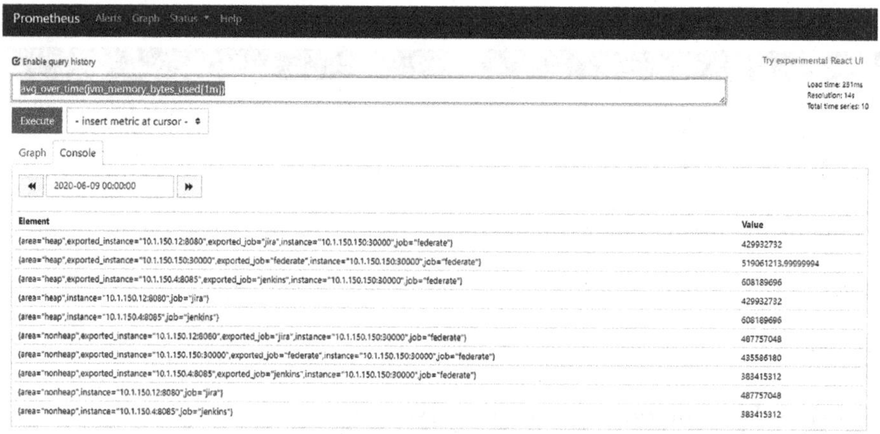

Figure 5-20. *The average value of each range*

---

[2]https://prometheus.io/docs/prometheus/latest/querying/functions/

As we can see, the Value field has single value for each distinct labeled data point and has been converted to an instant vector. The aggregation operator can now be used with the data, as we have done previously.

Let's continue with the preceding query. Let's expand the range selection to return all data in the last five minutes, average it per range, and then further use the AVG aggregation operator to find the average value of memory consumed grouped by area and job. Then we use topK to return the top five areas and jobs with maximum memory used. Use the following query to get the desired result:

```
TOPK(5, AVG by (area, job) (avg_over_time(jvm_memory_bytes_
used[5m])))
```

The output in Figure 5-21 shows the top five areas and jobs.

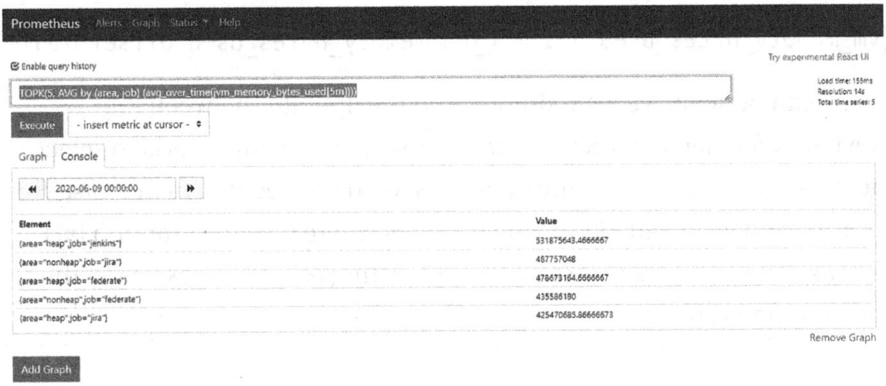

Figure 5-21. *Top five areas*

We know by now the way we can select data and group by and apply aggregation operators to aggregate the data. We have also looked at using the aggregation operators on range data.

Logical and Arithmetic Operators

With the data selected and aggregated, we can next look at operations that can be performed between the output data returned or on the metrics data. PromQL enables us to apply varied operators[3] on the result sets, allowing us to combine different datasets so as to compare and derive meaningful insights. In the examples in this section, we will use a few sample use cases.

Use Case 1: Let's begin with a use case wherein we compare current data with the historical data collected seven days back to identify any rise in memory consumed.

As shown in the following query, we use the comparison operator > between the two result sets to identify the labeled data where consumption is more than it was seven days before:

```
jvm_memory_bytes_used > 1 * (jvm_memory_bytes_used offset 7d)
```

As can be seen, we have simply used the operator between the previously fetched two vectors. We can use any selector criteria to select the data, and then can use the operators to do the needful; in this case we are comparing and identifying the ones where the consumption has increased. Figure 5-22 shows the output, listing only the ones where the consumption is high.

---

[3]https://prometheus.io/docs/prometheus/latest/querying/operators/

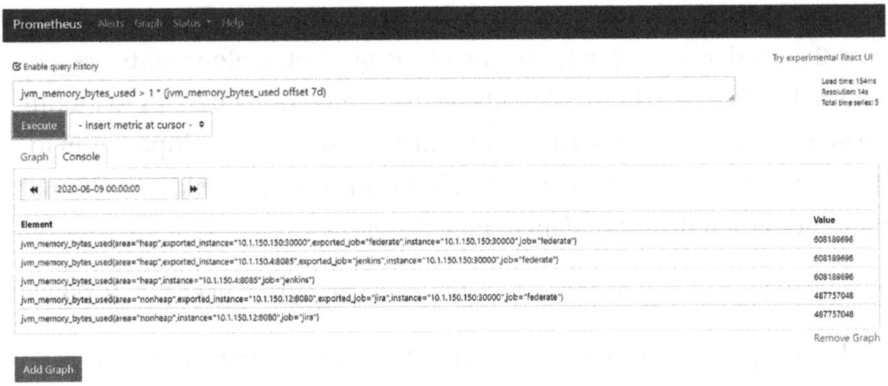

Figure 5-22. *High consumption*

Use Case 2: As we know, the data returned by the metric jvm_memory_bytes_used is in bytes. In this use case, we will use a scalar arithmetic operation to convert the value to megabytes. The following query uses the multiplication operator to multiply the value by 0.000001 to convert it to megabytes:

```
jvm_memory_bytes_used * 0.000001
```

The output returned is in megabytes, as shown in Figure 5-23.

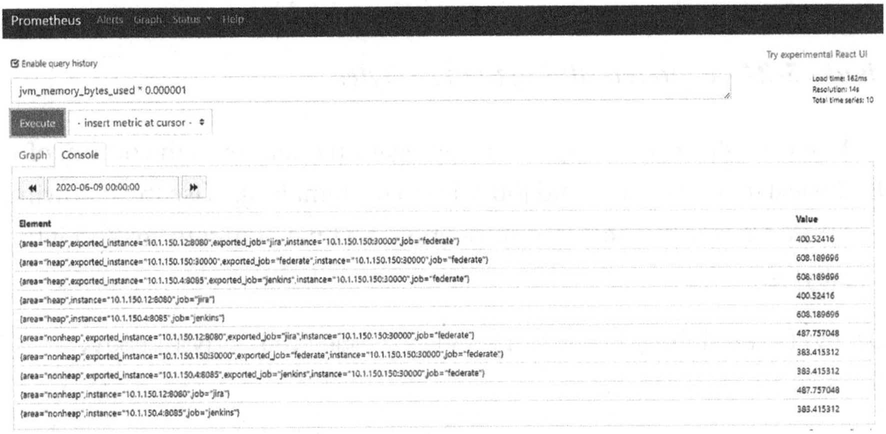

Figure 5-23. *Values in megabytes*

Use Case 3: Let's now use two different metrics' data. In this use case, we will consider the jvm_memory_bytes_usage metric along with jvm_memory_bytes_committed. We will use the subtraction operator to identify the bytes remaining to consume, and further use scalar multiplication to convert the data into megabytes. The following query enables us to find the difference and returns the data in megabytes:

```
(jvm_memory_bytes_committed - jvm_memory_bytes_used) * 0.000001
```

The output in Figure 5-24 shows per time-series object the data remaining in megabytes.

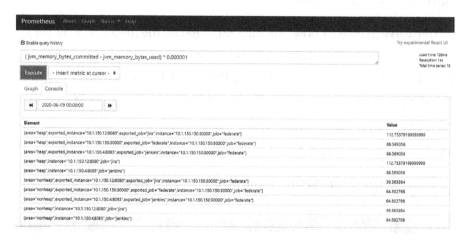

Figure 5-24. *Data remaining in megabytes*

Use Case 4: Next, let's apply an aggregation operator to the output of Use Case 3 to return area- and job-wise bytes remaining. Use the following query; we also use the scalar multiplier on the final output to convert it to megabytes:

```
sum by (area,job) (jvm_memory_bytes_committed - jvm_memory_
bytes_used) * 0.000001
```

Figure 5-25 shows the area- and job-wise remaining memory in megabytes.

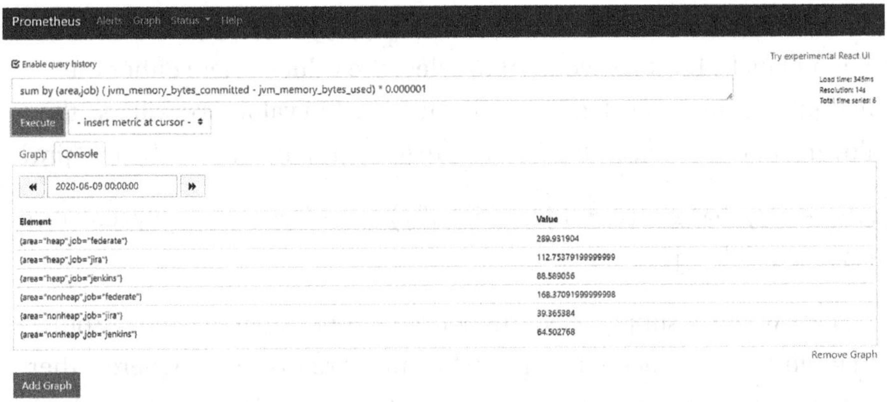

Figure 5-25. *Remaining megabytes, by area and job*

We can also apply topk to return the top two with maximum bytes remaining, as in the following query:

```
TOPK(2, sum by (job) (jvm_memory_bytes_committed - jvm_memory_
bytes_used) )* 0.000001
```

The output in Figure 5-26 shows the top two jobs.

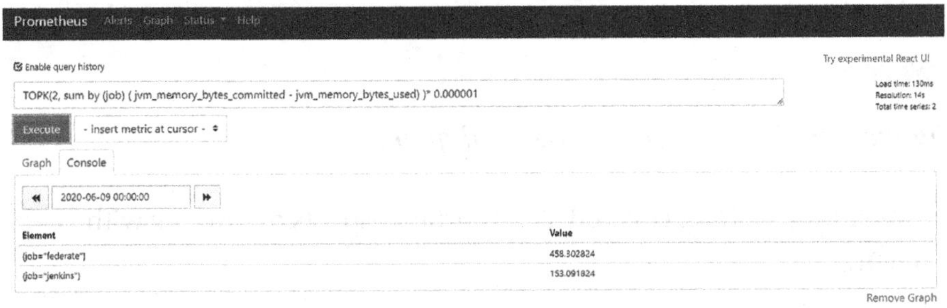

Figure 5-26. *Top two jobs*

Use Case 5: As we mentioned in the selector section, the filters when combined are joined by an AND operator. We looked at the way the | operator can be used to apply OR on values on the same label, so, prior to concluding, let's look at the way we can apply OR between filters on different labels. Let's say we want to select the values where either the label "job" or the "exported_job" label has the Jira value. We will use the following query to select the data where job="jira" or exported_job="jira".

```
(jvm_memory_bytes_used {job="jira"}) or (jvm_memory_bytes_used
{exported_job="jira"})
```

Here, we have simply used the OR operator between the two outputs, and it returns the expected output. The output returns rows where either the "job" value is jira or the "exported_job" value is jira, as shown in Figure 5-27.

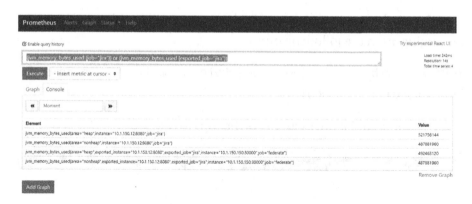

Figure 5-27. *The output of the final query*

With this, we have covered all important aspects of working with PromQL.

Summary

In this chapter, we have provided hands-on steps for using Prometheus Query Language (PromQL). In the next chapter, we will start with understanding the dashboard and reporting solutions by using Grafana as Prometheus; Grafana is a common combination of monitoring dashboard.

CHAPTER 6

Container Reporting & Dashboards

This chapter will provide hands-on steps for using container reporting and dashboard solutions. Grafana and Prometheus are commonly used by DevOps teams for storing and visualizing time-series data. Grafana supports querying Prometheus and being a data source for Prometheus. We will look at the following:

- Introduction to Container Reporting and Dashboards

- Working with Grafana

Introduction to Container Reporting and Dashboards

As we have seen so far, containers have become an integral part of modern application architectures, and as a result have changed the way software is deployed and operated. Once we have set up monitoring for the containers and applications, the next step from an operations visibility perspective is the dashboard and reporting. The dashboard and reporting solution will provide a graphical interface with which to visualize the container inventory, container metrics for availability and performance, and application metrics.

© Navin Sabharwal, Piyush Pandey 2020
N. Sabharwal and P. Pandey, *Monitoring Microservices and Containerized Applications*,
https://doi.org/10.1007/978-1-4842-6216-0_6

Dashboards also provide insight about the overall health of the container platform. From a security perspective, by leveraging container security and compliance solution integration, an operations team can also monitor the security posture of the container platform and any applications running on it.

There are various popular dashboard solutions available in the market for container dashboards and reporting. Let's look at a few of them.

Grafana: Grafana is a UI-based dashboard and reporting tool. It is used for data analysis and visualization that's generated by the various data sources in the form of metrics. Grafana has in-built support for time-series databases such as Prometheus and InfluxDB, and it also supports rational databases, such as MySQL, SQL Server, etc. Grafana also allows one to create alerts on a specific condition or set of conditions; e.g., CPU utilization more than 80 percent, or disk usage, etc.

Grafana is available as both an open source version and an enterprise version. In this chapter, we will use open source Grafana to demonstrate how to create the dashboard for a container monitoring ecosystem.

Sysdig: Sysdig is a container monitoring and security tool that also provides dashboard and reporting capabilities. Sysdig provides customized dashboard creation so as to display the most useful/relevant views and metrics for the infrastructure in a single location. Each dashboard comprises a series of panels configured to display specific data in a number of different formats.

Splunk: Splunk is a unified solution with which to analyze, search, and visualize the data gathered from the various applications, sensors , servers, and containers. Splunk does not need any databases to store the data, as it extensively makes use of its indexes to do so. In Splunk, one can analyze container ecosystem performance, do troubleshooting, and store/retrieve data for later use.

In the next section, we will focus on Grafana's features for container reporting and dashboards. We will do a hands-on exercise to set up Grafana and fetch reports leveraging metrics from Prometheus.

Grafana

Grafana uses the data source to connect with the system—e.g., Prometheus, MySQL, etc.—for collecting the data. Grafana has in-built support for time-series-based data sources like Prometheus or InfluxDB. Each data source has a specific query editor associated with it for executing the query to fetch the data; e.g., PromQL query editor for Prometheus. Grafana also supports mixed data sources, meaning the user can use multiple data sources in a single dashboard; e.g., user can map data from Elasticsearch along with data from Prometheus. Mixing different data sources can be done with custom data sources as well.

The following data sources are officially supported:

- CloudWatch

- Elasticsearch

- Graphite

- InfluxDB

- OpenTSDB

- Prometheus

Panel

In Grafana visualizations known as panels, users can create a dashboard containing panels for various data sources. Each panel is associated with the query editor to extract the metrics and display the result. Panels can be rearranged and resized on the dashboard.

The following are the available panel types:

- Alert list

- Dashboard list

- Graph

- Heatmap

- Logs

- Singlestat

- Table

- Text

Query Editor

The query editor allows the user to query the metrics. Each data source is associated with a different query editor that is used for creating the query; e.g., PromQL query editor is used to create any PromQL-based queries.

Dashboard

Grafana provides various types of pre-built dashboards—e.g., Prometheus, Kubernetes overview, etc.—to measure the data.[1] The user can also create customized dashboards based on various panels. Grafana supports templating to create a dynamic dashboard, and the user can share these dashboards among teams by publishing it.

Explore: Grafana Explore helps to analyze the metrics and logs to identify the cause of failure of the monitoring system. Since Grafana 6.0, Loki, a new data source introduced by Grafana, integrates with Explore to allow users to analyze metrics and correlated logs side-by-side to debug what went wrong.

Alerting: Grafana has a built-in alerting engine that allows the user to trigger alerts on the basis of the conditions/rules that apply on the panels. Grafana supports the following tools for notifying the user of the alerts: Slack, PagerDuty, VictorOps, and OpsGenie.

---

[1]Pre-built dashboard: https://grafana.com/grafana/dashboards

Now, let's start installing Grafana in the environment that we set up in earlier chapters. Figure 6-1 provides an overview of the task flows we will follow to deploy Grafana.

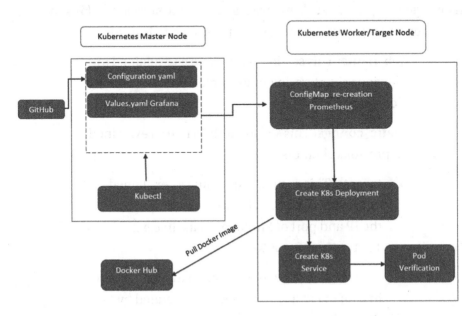

Figure 6-1. *Grafana deployment flow*

The following is the flow for the Grafana deployment that we will follow in this chapter:

- We will use the already cloned configuration files from GitHub. Additionally, we will pull a file from GitHub to be used for Grafana installation.

- We will recreate the config map and deploy Grafana as a pod.

- Finally, we will test the status of the Grafana deployment using command line and web browser access.

Step 1: Log in to the Kubernetes master node (10.1.150.126) and navigate to the /home/prometheus folder, and then append the following lines in config-map.yml in the scrape_configs: section. Search for the section named job - job_name: 'prometheus' under the scrape_configs: section in the config-map.yaml file and append as shown in Figure 6-2.

> **job_name:** This section is the same as explained in previous chapters. In our example case, we are using job_name as prometheus.
>
> **static_configs:** This section is the same as explained in previous chapters.
>
> • **targets:** This section is the same as explained in previous chapters. In targets, we specify the IP and port of Prometheus itself; e.g., 10.1.150.126:30000.
>
> This target will be used to set up the data source in Grafana to fetch the metrics generated by Prometheus itself.

```
    - job_name: 'prometheus'
      static_configs:
        - targets: ['10.1.150.150:30000']
```

Figure 6-2. *Config map file update*

Step 2: Execute the following in-line commands to reflect the changes in Prometheus:

```
$kubectl delete configmaps prometheus-server-conf -n=monitoring
$kubectl create -f config-map.yaml
$kubectl delete deployment prometheus-deployment -n monitoring
$kubectl apply -f prometheus-deployment.yaml -n monitoring
```

Step 3: Verify that all the components of Prometheus are running fine, as shown in Figure 6-3:

```
$ kubectl get all -n=monitoring
```

```
[root@k8s-master prometheus]# kubectl get all -n=monitoring
NAME                                         READY   STATUS    RESTARTS   AGE
pod/alertmanager-564d4884bd-mjjft            1/1     Running   0          20d
pod/prometheus-deployment-59b58c4594-xtpbg   1/1     Running   0          83m

NAME                         TYPE       CLUSTER-IP       EXTERNAL-IP   PORT(S)          AGE
service/alertmanager         NodePort   10.111.165.123   <none>        8080:32000/TCP   20d
service/prometheus-service   NodePort   10.97.107.57     <none>        8080:30000/TCP   20d

NAME                                    READY   UP-TO-DATE   AVAILABLE   AGE
deployment.apps/alertmanager            1/1     1            1           20d
deployment.apps/prometheus-deployment   1/1     1            1           83m

NAME                                              DESIRED   CURRENT   READY   AGE
replicaset.apps/alertmanager-564d4884bd           1         1         1       20d
replicaset.apps/prometheus-deployment-59b58c4594  1         1         1       83m
```

Figure 6-3. *Verifying Prometheus pod status*

Step 4: Open the Prometheus GUI (using the `http://kubernetes-master-node:30000` URL) and navigate to `targets` to review the Prometheus endpoint, as shown in Figure 6-4.

prometheus (1/1 up) show less					
Endpoint	State	Labels	Last Scrape	Scrape Duration	Error
http://10.1.150.126:30000/metrics	UP	instance="10.1.150.126:30000" job="prometheus"	1.663s ago	6.929ms	

Figure 6-4. *Verifying Prometheus pod status*

Step 5: Now, let's install the Grafana dashboard on the Kubernetes master node (10.1.150.126) by using Helm chart version 3.12.1 (GitHub URL: `https://github.com/helm/charts/tree/master/stable/grafana`)

Navigate to the `/home/prometheus` folder and execute the following command to clone the code from GitHub, as shown in Figure 6-5:

```
$ git clone https://github.com/dryice-devops/grafana.git
```

```
drwxr-xr-x. 2 root root        25 Nov 20 15:10 grafana
```

Figure 6-5. *Cloning file from GitHub*

Step 6: Navigate into the grafana folder by executing the following command:

```
$ cd grafana
```

Step 7: Open the values.yaml file and modify the following sections. Save the file before closing. Navigate to the section named service in values.yaml and add values to the following sections, as shown in Figure 6-6:

> **service:** This section represents Kubernetes service configuration for Grafana.
>
> **type:** This field provides information about the type of publishing services. Kubernetes service types allow you to specify what kind of service you want. The default is ClusterIP. In our example, we are using NodePort, which exposes the service on each node's IP at a static port (the NodePort).
>
> **port:** Inside the cluster, what port does the service expose? E.g., 9000.
>
> **targetPort:** This is the port at which the pod-based application will be listening on the network. We are using value 3000.
>
> **nodePort:** This is the port on the node, e.g., master_ node, on which the service will be available. We are using value 30007.

```
service:
  type: NodePort
  port: 9000
  targetPort: 3000
    # targetPort: 4181 To be used with a proxy extraContainer
  nodePort: 30007
  annotations: {}
  labels: {}
  portName: service
```

Figure 6-6. *Updating Value.yaml*

Step 8: Navigate into the /home/prometheus folder and execute the following Helm command to install Grafana, as shown in Figures 6-7 and 6-8:

```
$helm install -name Grafana-dashboard -f Grafana/values.yaml
stable/grafana --version 3.12.1
```

```
[root@k8s-master prometheus]# helm install --name grafana-dashboard -f grafana/values.yaml stable/grafana --version 3.12.1
NAME:   grafana-dashboard
LAST DEPLOYED: Wed Nov 20 13:40:54 2019
NAMESPACE: default
STATUS: DEPLOYED

RESOURCES:
==> v1/ClusterRole
NAME                             AGE
grafana-dashboard-clusterrole    <invalid>

==> v1/ClusterRoleBinding
NAME                                AGE
grafana-dashboard-clusterrolebinding  <invalid>

==> v1/ConfigMap
NAME                      AGE
grafana-dashboard         <invalid>
grafana-dashboard-test    <invalid>

==> v1/Deployment
NAME                 AGE
grafana-dashboard    <invalid>

==> v1/Pod(related)
NAME                                      AGE
grafana-dashboard-5856fb467b-5fp4w        <invalid>
```

Figure 6-7. *Installation of Grafana*

Figure 6-8. *Installation of Grafana*

Step 9: Execute the following command to get the secret password:

```
$kubectl get secret --namespace default grafana-dashboard -o
jsonpath="{.data.admin-password}" | base64 --decode ; echo
```

You will get the password—e.g., dom3BiALxXmM1Q2hAPuPVIFozxW
ID8yb7haMH6KU—which will be used to log in to the Grafana UI, as per
Figure 6-9.

```
[root@k8s-master prometheus]# kubectl get secret --namespace default grafana-dashboard -o jsonpath="{.data.admin-password}" | base64 --decode ; echo
dom3BiALxXmM1Q2hAPuPVIFozxWID8yb7haMH6KU
```

Figure 6-9. *Grafana temporary password fetch*

Step 10: Open the browser and enter the URL (http://master-node-
ip:30007), e.g., http://10.1.150.126:30007, and enter the username as
"admin" and password you got from step 9, as in Figure 6-10.

Figure 6-10. *Grafana login page*

Grafana Integration with Prometheus

Now, let's configure the Prometheus end point in Grafana.

Step 1: After entering the credentials, navigate to **Setting ➤ Data Source** as per Figure 6-11.

Figure 6-11. *Grafana data source configuration*

179

Step 2: Click "Add data source," as shown in Figure 6-12.

Figure 6-12. *Grafana data source configuration*

Step 3: Select Prometheus and enter the Prometheus URL `http://10.1.150.126:30000/` under the HTTP URL section and hit the Save & Test button, as shown in Figure 6-13.

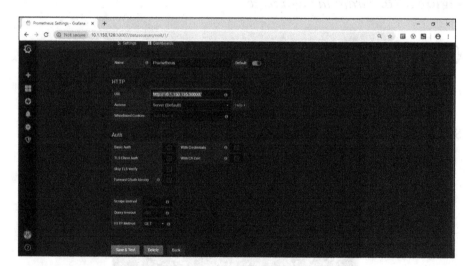

Figure 6-13. *Grafana data source configuration*

If the Prometheus end point has been configured successfully, you will get the message "Data source is working," as shown in Figure 6-14.

Figure 6-14. Grafana data source configuration validation

Step 4: Grafana provides one default dashboard. Click on Home to navigate to it, as shown in Figure 6-15.

Figure 6-15. Grafana default dashboard navigation

Click Prometheus 2.0 Stats, as shown in Figure 6-16.

Figure 6-16. Grafana default dashboard navigation

You can now view the Prometheus dashboard, as shown in Figure 6-17.

Figure 6-17. *Grafana default Prometheus dashboard navigation*

Summary

In this chapter, we have provided hands-on steps for using Grafana for container dashboard and reporting with Prometheus. In the next chapter, we will start with understanding how to leverage Dynatrace for container application monitoring, along with hands-on exercises.

CHAPTER 7

Container Application Monitoring Using Dynatrace

This chapter will provide hands-on steps for using Dynatrace for container application monitoring. We will look at the following:

- Introduction to Dynatrace

- Container Application Monitoring

- Working with Dynatrace for Container Application Monitoring

Introduction to Dynatrace

Dynatrace is a software-intelligence monitoring platform that simplifies enterprise cloud complexity and accelerates digital transformation. Dynatrace seamlessly brings infrastructure and cloud, application performance, and digital experience monitoring into an all-in-one automated solution that's powered by artificial intelligence named Davis.

© Navin Sabharwal, Piyush Pandey 2020   183
N. Sabharwal and P. Pandey, *Monitoring Microservices and Containerized Applications*,
https://doi.org/10.1007/978-1-4842-6216-0_7

The following are the key capabilities of Dynatrace:

Real User Monitoring: Dynatrace helps the support and development teams trace an interaction end-to-end from real users, whether it is from a desktop-based browser or from a mobile device. It covers the availability and response time of an application as seen by the end user. It also provides for verification of UI elements and third-party content, and analysis of the service-side application down to the code level, so it is easy to troubleshoot and analyze any issues that the users may face.

Server-side Service Monitoring: Web applications consist of web pages that are served by web servers which in turn interact with backend Application & Database servers depending upon incoming request type. Dynatrace OneAgent can provide details about which applications or services interact with which other services and which services or databases a specific service calls. We will cover this in detail using a hands-on lab exercise.

Network, Process, & Host Monitoring: Dynatrace enables monitoring of the entire infrastructure, including hosts, processes, and network.

Container Monitoring: Dynatrace seamlessly integrates with existing Docker environments and automatically monitors containerized applications and services. With Dynatrace, there is no need to modify Docker images, run commands, or create additional containers to enable Docker monitoring. Dynatrace has the ability to automatically detect the creation and termination of containers, and monitors the applications and services contained within those containers.

Architecture Overview

Dynatrace can be deployed either as an SaaS solution or within an on-premises deployment. The on-premises version is called Dynatrace Managed, while the SaaS version is known as Dynatrace SaaS. In this chapter, we will cover Dynatrace SaaS' capabilities for container monitoring.

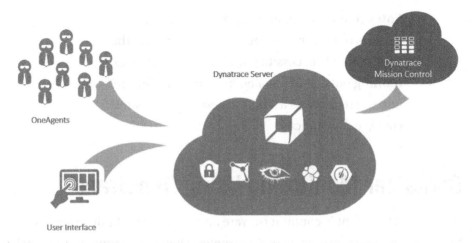

Figure 7-1. *Dynatrace SaaS architecture*

Dynatrace SaaS has a simplified architecture (Figure 7-1). Its core component comprises OneAgent and ActiveGate. SaaS customers only need to install OneAgent to enable monitoring for the target environment.

ActiveGate works as a proxy between Dynatrace OneAgent and Dynatrace SaaS/Managed versions. It can be installed on Windows or Linux. If you use Dynatrace SaaS, you only need to install an environment ActiveGate. The main functions of ActiveGate include the following:

> **Message routing:** ActiveGate knows about the runtime structure of the Dynatrace environment and routes messages from OneAgents to the correct server endpoints.

Buffering and compression: ActiveGate collects messages from OneAgent instances and builds bulks, which are then sent in compressed form to the Dynatrace server.

Authentication: ActiveGate authenticates OneAgent requests (SSL handshake and environment ID authentication).

Entry point for sealed networks: Dynatrace server clusters often run in protected environments that aren't directly accessible by OneAgent instances running outside of a sealed network. ActiveGate can be used to serve as a single access point for such OneAgent instances.

Container Monitoring Using Dynatrace

Dynatrace OneAgent is container-aware and comes with built-in support for out-of-the-box monitoring of Kubernetes. Dynatrace supports full-stack monitoring for Kubernetes; i.e., monitoring from the application down to the infrastructure layer.

For container monitoring, the Dynatrace OneAgent operator registers itself as a controller that watches for resources of type OneAgent, as defined by a custom resource definition. This allows you to define a configuration that describes your OneAgent deployment. By loading the configuration into Kubernetes, the configuration is automatically passed to the custom controller. Figure 7-2 outlines the involved components and objects.

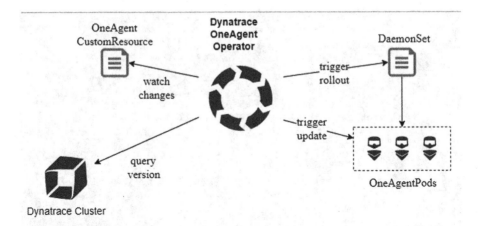

Figure 7-2. *Dynatrace container monitoring architecture*

By creating the OneAgent custom resource entity in Kubernetes, the object is automatically passed to the Dynatrace OneAgent operator. First, it determines if a corresponding DaemonSet already exists. If not, the Dynatrace OneAgent operator creates a new one. The DaemonSet is responsible for rolling out OneAgent to selected nodes. Dynatrace also automatically polls the pods to check for updated versions, and if the updated versions are not deployed then the latest version is automatically rolled out.

Now, let's begin with an exercise that uses Dynatrace for container monitoring. We will begin by requesting the evaluation version of Dynatrace SaaS.

Step 1: Navigate to the following URL to request a fifteen-day trial of Dynatrace SaaS. Click on the Free Trial button in the corner.

`https://www.dynatrace.com`

Step 2: Enter your email address and click on the Start Free Trial button.

Step 3: Add a valid password for your account and then click Continue.

Step 4: Add details regarding your account and click Continue.

Step 5: Select the region where you want to store your monitoring data, click on the radio button for "Yes, I agree to the above terms and conditions," and then click Create Account, as shown in Figure 7-3.

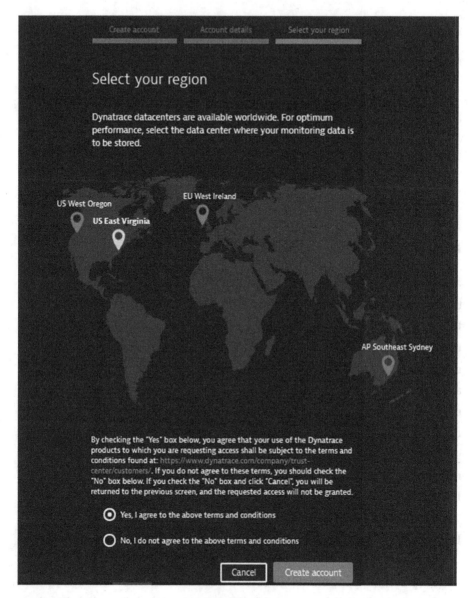

Figure 7-3. *Dynatrace SaaS region selection*

Step 6: After that, you will be redirected to the Dynatrace Welcome page. Click the Deploy Dynatrace button, as shown in Figure 7-4.

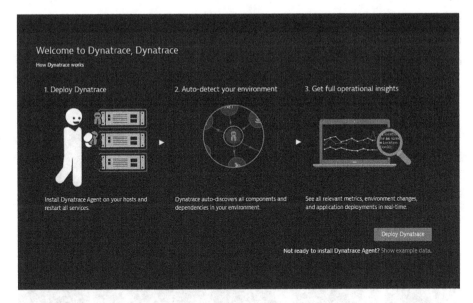

Figure 7-4. *Dynatrace SaaS Welcome page*

Step 7: You will be redirected to the Dynatrace console. Click on the Home icon at the top of the page, as highlighted in Figure 7-5, and it will take you to the Dynatrace home page dashboard.

Figure 7-5. *Dynatrace SaaS home page*

Step 8: On the home page you can see a default dashboard. As of now, since there are no agents reporting to this SAAS instance, there is no data reporting under any of the entities. Only sample data is provided by default. On the left-hand side, there are several tabs available for each entity that we monitor through Dynatrace. Once the data starts reporting to the console, the user can click on any of the tabs and look at the metrics of that entity, as shown in Figure 7-6.

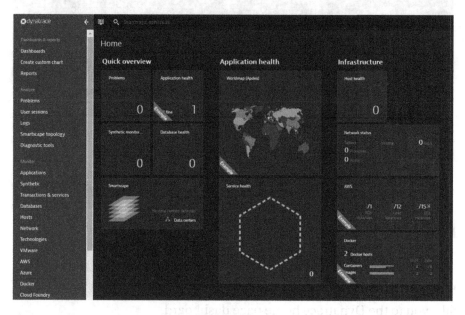

Figure 7-6. *Dynatrace SaaS tab navigation*

Now we will install a microservice application that will be monitored using Dynatrace. We will use easyTravel Application as the demo application. EasyTravel is a multi-tier application that uses microservice principles. We will use this application to simulate application issues such as high CPU load, database slowdown, or slow authentication. Figure 7-7 is the architecture diagram of the application. We have installed only the customer frontend part of the architecture, which includes nginx, frontend, backend, database, and a load generator.

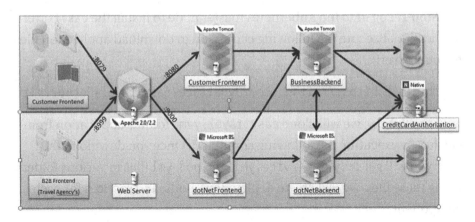

Figure 7-7. *Easy Travel Application architecture*

Please refer to Table 7-1 to get information about the components used by the travel application.

Table 7-1. *Application Components*

Component	Description
Mongodb	A pre-populated travel database (MongoDB)
Backend	The easyTravel business backend (Java)
Frontend	The easyTravel customer frontend (Java)
Nginx	A reverse proxy for the easyTravel customer frontend (NGINX)
Loadgen	A synthetic UEM load generator (Java)

Containerized Application Deployment

In this section, you will learn how to deploy the travel application on a Kubernetes cluster with kubectl commands. You can get the application code and its details from the following GitHub URL: https://github.com/Dynatrace/easyTravel-docker.

Step 1: Log in to the Kubernetes master node to install the easyTravel application. Execute the following command to download application files to your server:

```
$ git clone https://github.com/Dynatrace/easyTravel-Docker.git
```

Step 2: Now, we will clone easytravel.yaml for this application from GitHub by executing the following command. Once you download the repo you will get rc.yml, service.yml, and pod.yml files in various folders. Using these files, we will create deployment, pods, and services for each component.

```
$ git clone https://github.com/dryice-devops/dynatrace.git
```

Step 3: Copy the easytravel.yaml file into the Kubernetes folder / App/microservices-demo/deploy/kubernetes/. Now, let's create a namespace to run this application using Kubernetes by using the following command:

```
$ kubectl create namespace easytravel
```

To verify that the namespace has been created successfully, execute the following command, as shown in Figure 7-8:

```
$ kubectl get namespace
```

```
[root@devops0087 kubernetes]# kubectl get namespace
NAME               STATUS    AGE
default            Active    10d
dynatrace          Active    8d
easytravel         Active    14h
kube-node-lease    Active    10d
kube-public        Active    10d
kube-system        Active    10d
monitoring         Active    8d
```

Figure 7-8. *easyTravel application Kubernetes namespace creation*

Step 4: Now, execute the following command on the Kubernetes master node to create the deployment, services, and pods, as we specified in easytravel.yaml:

```
$ kubectl create -f easytravel.yaml
```

It will create all the components to run the application. Verify by using the following commands, as shown in Figure 7-9:

```
$ kubectl get deployment -n easytravel
```

```
[root@devops0087 easyTravel-Docker]# kubectl get deployment -n easytravel
NAME        READY   UP-TO-DATE   AVAILABLE    AGE
backend     1/1     1            1            13h
frontend    1/1     1            1            14h
loadgen     1/1     1            1            13h
mongodb     1/1     1            1            13h
nginx       1/1     1            1            13h
```

Figure 7-9. easyTravel application deployment using Kubernetes

Step 5: Now, execute the following command on the Kubernetes master node to fetch a list of pods for the easyTravel application, as shown in Figure 7-10:

```
$ kubectl get pod -n easytravel
```

```
[root@devops0087 easyTravel-Docker]# kubectl get pod -n easytravel
NAME                         READY   STATUS    RESTARTS   AGE
backend-794fc8bcf7-6tdgm     1/1     Running   0          13h
frontend-7d9969499f-2nxws    1/1     Running   0          14h
loadgen-68677457d6-1jds7     1/1     Running   0          13h
mongodb-5db656dd-mhfzb       1/1     Running   0          13h
nginx-68c4bb4ffd-h87zt       1/1     Running   0          13h
```

Figure 7-10. easyTravel application pod list

Step 6: Now, execute the following command on the Kubernetes master node to fetch a list of services for the easyTravel application, as shown in Figure 7-11:

```
$ kubectl get service -n easytravel
```

```
[root@devops0087 easyTravel-Docker]# kubectl get service -n easytravel
NAME       TYPE        CLUSTER-IP       EXTERNAL-IP   PORT(S)         AGE
backend    ClusterIP   10.104.148.186   <none>        8091/TCP        13h
frontend   NodePort    10.99.139.181    <none>        80:31012/TCP    14h
mongodb    ClusterIP   10.103.157.16    <none>        27017/TCP       13h
www        ClusterIP   10.106.198.252   <none>        80/TCP          13h
```

Figure 7-11. *easyTravel application service list*

Copy the `cluster IP` for the frontend service for application page access. Navigate to the following URL to access the easyTravel frontend application service:

```
http://< cluster IP >:port
```

In our case, the following is the URL, as shown in Figure 7-12: easyTravel URL: `http://10.99.139.181:31012/`

Figure 7-12. *easyTravel application frontend page, Dynatrace OneAgent installation*

Monitoring Application using Dynatrace

In this section, you will learn how to install Dynatrace OneAgent on the Kubernetes cluster to enable the monitoring for the easyTravel application.

Step 1: Log in to the Kubernetes master server and create the namespace Dynatrace using the following command:

```
$ kubectl create namespace Dynatrace
```

Step 2: Create a LATEST_RELEASE variable, which will contain the URI for the latest image of the OneAgent operator. Execute the following command:

```
$LATEST_RELEASE=$(curl -s https://api.github.com/repos/
dynatrace/dynatrace-oneagent-operator/releases/latest | grep
tag_name | cut -d '"' -f 4)
```

Step 3: Once the variable is created, run the following command to create Dynatrace entities:

```
$kubectl create -f https://raw.githubusercontent.com/Dynatrace/
dynatrace-oneagent-operator/$LATEST_RELEASE/deploy/kubernetes.
yaml
```

Step 4: Now we check the logs of the OneAgent operator to verify that it is successfully installed on the Kubernetes cluster; we do so by executing the following command:

```
$kubectl -n dynatrace logs -f deployment/dynatrace-oneagent-
operator
```

Step 5: We will now create the secret holding API and PaaS tokens for authenticating the Dynatrace SaaS setup. To generate and manage API tokens, log in to your Dynatrace environment, and from the navigation menu click Settings ➤ Integration. Select Dynatrace API, Platform as a Service, or Dynatrace modules to generate a token for the Dynatrace API, a token for PaaS, or a token for DCRUM or Synthetic, as shown in Figure 7-13.

195

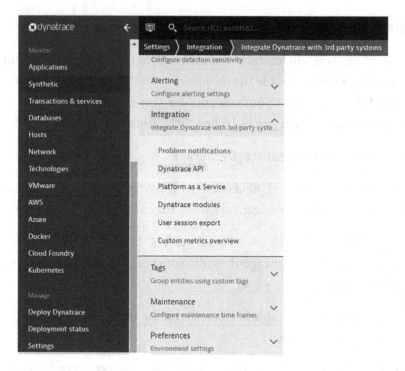

Figure 7-13. *Dynatrace API token generation*

Step 6: Click the Generate Token button as shown in Figure 7-14, and then type a meaningful token name in the text field, as shown in Figure 7-15.

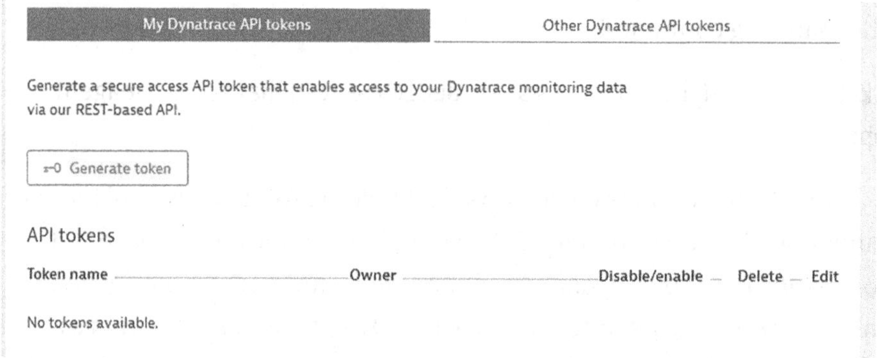

My Dynatrace API tokens   Other Dynatrace API tokens

Generate a secure access API token that enables access to your Dynatrace monitoring data via our REST-based API.

`⊢O  Generate token`

API tokens

Token name _____Owner _____Disable/enable __ Delete __ Edit

No tokens available.

Figure 7-14. *Dynatrace API token generation*

196

Step 7: To create Dynatrace API tokens, select or clear the access switches as needed to set the access scope of the API token. For example, to create an API authentication token to access Dynatrace monitoring data for user session queries, select "User session" as shown in Figure 7-15.

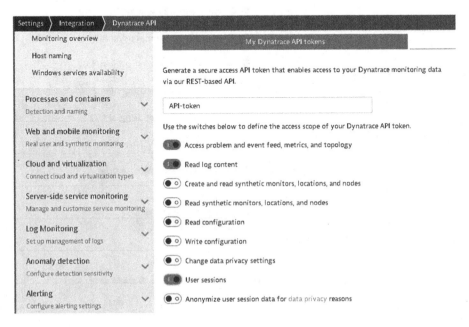

Figure 7-15. *Dynatrace API token generation*

Step 8: Click the Generate button. The token will appear in the My Dynatrace Tokens list, as shown in Figure 7-16.

Settings 〉 Integration 〉 Dynatrace API

User session export

Remote environments

Tags
Group entities using custom tags

Maintenance
Configure maintenance time frames

Preferences
Environment settings

Accounting
Verify consumption

Read audit logs

Fetch data from a remote environment

Read entities using API V2

Write entities using API V2

Read network zones using API V2

Write network zones using API V2

Read ActiveGates using API V2

Write ActiveGates using API V2

Read Credential Vault entries

Write Credential Vault entries

Generate   Cancel

API tokens

Token name	Owner	Disable/enable	Delete	Edit
API-token	hcl.demo.dynatrace@gmail.com		✖	⌃

Generated token

V4l5p4fzT3iYWwP5dMmrQ   Copy

Token name

API-token

Figure 7-16. *Dynatrace API token generation*

Step 9: Now, we will create a PaaS token by enacting the following steps. Log in with your Dynatrace account and select "Deploy Dynatrace" from the navigation menu. Click the Set up PaaS Integration button, as shown in Figure 7-17.

Figure 7-17. *Dynatrace PaaS token generation*

Step 10: Your environment ID appears in the Environment ID text box. You'll need this ID to link your Dynatrace account with your PaaS environment. Click Copy to copy the ID to the clipboard. You can do this at any time by revisiting this page, as shown in Figure 7-18.

Figure 7-18. *Dynatrace PaaS token generation*

Step 11: To generate a PaaS token, click the Generate New Token button. The PaaS token is essentially an API token that's used in combination with your environment ID to download Dynatrace OneAgent.

As you'll see, there's also a default InstallerDownload token available that you can alternatively use. However, for security reasons, it's recommended that you create several discrete tokens for each environment you have, as shown in Figure 7-19.

Figure 7-19. *Dynatrace PaaS token generation*

Step 12: Type in a meaningful name for your PaaS token. A meaningful token name might be the name of the PaaS platform you want to monitor (for example, azure, cloud-foundry, or openshift). To view and manage your existing PaaS tokens, go to Settings ➤ Integration ➤ Platform as a Service.

Click Generate to create the PaaS token. The newly created PaaS token will appear in the list below. Click Copy to copy the generated token to the clipboard. You can do this at any time by revisiting this page and clicking Show Token next to the relevant PaaS token.

Step 13: Set up API and PaaS tokens using the following command:

```
$kubectl -n dynatrace create secret generic oneagent --from-
literal="apiToken=D62yuwExSpOUeOM1d7_gE" --from-   literal=
"paasToken=r_6pQgOzSwivPXym3dTKp"
```

Step 14: Now, let's create a custom resource for OneAgent. Navigate to the Kubernetes folder /App/microservices-demo/deploy/kubernetes/ and run the following command. This will download the cr.yaml file to your Kubernetes master node.

```
$curl -o cr.yaml https://raw.githubusercontent.com/Dynatrace/
dynatrace-oneagent-operator/$LATEST_RELEASE/deploy/cr.yaml
```

Step 15: Edit cr.yml and modify the values of the custom resource as indicated below. You need to update the API URL, tokens, and APP_LOG_CONTENT variable:

Before making changes, follow the code in Listing 7-1.

Listing 7-1. Dynatrace OneAgent custom resource cr.yml sample

```
apiVersion: dynatrace.com/v1alpha1
kind: OneAgent
metadata:
  # a descriptive name for this object.
  # all created child objects will be based on it.
  name: oneagent
  namespace: dynatrace
spec:
  # dynatrace api url including `/api` path at the end
  # either set ENVIRONMENTID to the proper tenant id or change
  the apiUrl as a whole, e.q. for Managed
  apiUrl: https://ENVIRONMENTID.live.dynatrace.com/api
  # disable certificate validation checks for installer
  download and API communication
  skipCertCheck: false
  # name of secret holding `apiToken` and `paasToken`
  # if unset, name of custom resource is used
  tokens: ""
```

```
# node selector to control the selection of nodes (optional)
nodeSelector: {}
# https://kubernetes.io/docs/concepts/configuration/taint-
and-toleration/ (optional)
tolerations:
- effect: NoSchedule
  key: node-role.kubernetes.io/master
  operator: Exists
# oneagent installer image (optional)
# certified image from RedHat Container Catalog for use on
OpenShift: registry.connect.redhat.com/dynatrace/oneagent
# for kubernetes it defaults to docker.io/dynatrace/oneagent
image: ""
# arguments to oneagent installer (optional)
# https://www.dynatrace.com/support/help/shortlink/oneagent-
docker#limitations
args:
- APP_LOG_CONTENT_ACCESS=1
# environment variables for oneagent (optional)
env: []
# resource settings for oneagent pods (optional)
# consumption of oneagent heavily depends on the workload to
monitor
# please adjust values accordingly
#resources:
#  requests:
#    cpu: 100m
#    memory: 512Mi
#  limits:
#    cpu: 300m
#    memory: 1.5Gi
```

```
# priority class to assign to oneagent pods (optional)
# https://kubernetes.io/docs/concepts/configuration/pod-
priority-preemption/
#priorityClassName: PRIORITYCLASS
# disables automatic restarts of oneagent pods in case a new
version is available
#disableAgentUpdate: false
# when enabled, and if Istio is installed on the Kubernetes
environment, then the Operator will create the corresponding
# VirtualService and ServiceEntries objects to allow access
to the Dynatrace cluster from the agent.
#enableIstio: false
# DNS Policy for OneAgent pods (optional.) Empty for default
(ClusterFirst), more at
# https://kubernetes.io/docs/concepts/services-networking/
dns-pod-service/#pod-s-dns-policy
#dnsPolicy: ""
# Labels are customer-defined labels for oneagent pods to
structure workloads as desired
#labels:
#   custom: label
# Name of the service account for the OneAgent (optional)
#serviceAccountName: "dynatrace-oneagent"
# Configures a proxy for the Agent, AgentDownload, and the
Operator (optional)
# Either provide the proxy URL directly at 'value' or create
a secret with a field 'proxy' which holds your encrypted
proxy URL
#proxy:
#   value: https://my-proxy-url.com
#   valueFrom: name-of-my-proxy-secret
```

```
# Adds the provided CA certficates to the Operator and the
OneAgent (optional)
# Provide the name of the configmap which holds your .pem in
a field called 'certs'
# If this is not set the default embedded certificates on the
images will be used
#trustedCAs: name-of-my-ca-configmap
# Sets a NetworkZone for the OneAgent (optional)
# Note: This feature requires OneAgent version 1.195 or
higher
#networkZone: name-of-my-network-zone
```

Edit ENVIRONMENTID to be the environment ID of your SaaS instance. For example, in our case it's euz01562. You can navigate to your Dynatrace SaaS instance and get the environment ID from its URL, as highlighted in Figure 7-20.

Figure 7-20. *Dynatrace environment ID*

For tokens, set the value to the name of the secret that we have created: oneagent. Set APP_LOG_CONTENT_ACCESS=1 and env: [].

After making required changes, Listing 7-2 will be the contents of the cr.yml file.

Listing 7-2. Dynatrace oneagent custom resource cr.yml

```
apiVersion: dynatrace.com/v1alpha1
kind: OneAgent
metadata:
  # a descriptive name for this object.
  # all created child objects will be based on it.
  name: oneagent
  namespace: dynatrace
spec:
  # dynatrace api url including `/api` path at the end
  # either set ENVIRONMENTID to the proper tenant id or change
  the apiUrl as a whole, e.q. for Managed
  apiUrl: https://euz01562.live.dynatrace.com/api
  # disable certificate validation checks for installer
  download and API communication
  skipCertCheck: false
  # name of secret holding `apiToken` and `paasToken`
  # if unset, name of custom resource is used
  tokens: "oneagent"
  # node selector to control the selection of nodes (optional)
  nodeSelector: {}
  # https://kubernetes.io/docs/concepts/configuration/taint-
  and-toleration/ (optional)
  tolerations:
  - effect: NoSchedule
    key: node-role.kubernetes.io/master
    operator: Exists
  # oneagent installer image (optional)
  # certified image from RedHat Container Catalog for use on
  OpenShift: registry.connect.redhat.com/dynatrace/oneagent
  # for kubernetes it defaults to docker.io/dynatrace/oneagent
```

```
image: ""
# arguments to oneagent installer (optional)
# https://www.dynatrace.com/support/help/shortlink/oneagent-
docker#limitations
args:
- APP_LOG_CONTENT_ACCESS=1
# environment variables for oneagent (optional)
env: []
# resource settings for oneagent pods (optional)
# consumption of oneagent heavily depends on the workload to
monitor
# please adjust values accordingly
#resources:
#   requests:
#     cpu: 100m
#     memory: 512Mi
#   limits:
#     cpu: 300m
#     memory: 1.5Gi
# priority class to assign to oneagent pods (optional)
# https://kubernetes.io/docs/concepts/configuration/pod-
priority-preemption/
#priorityClassName: PRIORITYCLASS
# disables automatic restarts of oneagent pods in case a new
version is available
#disableAgentUpdate: false
# when enabled, and if Istio is installed on the Kubernetes
environment, then the Operator will create the corresponding
# VirtualService and ServiceEntries objects to allow access
to the Dynatrace cluster from the agent.
#enableIstio: false
```

```
# DNS Policy for OneAgent pods (optional.) Empty for default
(ClusterFirst), more at
# https://kubernetes.io/docs/concepts/services-networking/
dns-pod-service/#pod-s-dns-policy
#dnsPolicy: ""
# Labels are customer defined labels for oneagent pods to
structure workloads as desired
#labels:
#   custom: label
# Name of the service account for the OneAgent (optional)
#serviceAccountName: "dynatrace-oneagent"
# Configures a proxy for the Agent, AgentDownload, and the
Operator (optional)
# Either provide the proxy URL directly at 'value' or create
a secret with a field 'proxy' which holds your encrypted
proxy URL
#proxy:
#   value: https://my-proxy-url.com
#   valueFrom: name-of-my-proxy-secret
# Adds the provided CA certficates to the Operator and the
OneAgent (optional)
# Provide the name of the config map which holds your .pem in
a field called 'certs'
# If this is not set the default embedded certificates on the
images will be used
#trustedCAs: name-of-my-ca-configmap
# Sets a NetworkZone for the OneAgent (optional)
# Note: This feature requires OneAgent version 1.195 or
higher
#networkZone: name-of-my-network-zone
```

Step 15: Create the custom resource by executing the following command:

```
$ kubectl create -f cr.yaml
```

Step 16: Now, we will install an ActiveGate component to connect our Kubernetes cluster with Dynatrace SaaS. Log in to the Dynatrace console and select "Deploy Dynatrace." Then, click on Install ActiveGate, as shown in Figure 7-21.

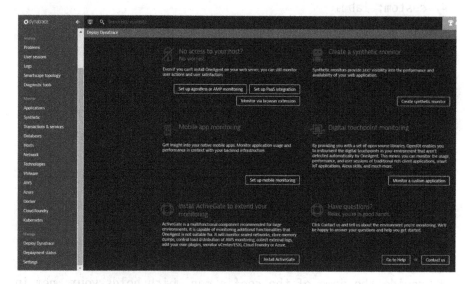

Figure 7-21. Dynatrace ActiveGate installation

Step 17: Select "Linux" and click Copy underneath "Run this command on the target host to download the installer"; run it onto the server where we are installing the OneAgent operator. It will download the installer as shown in Figure 7-22.

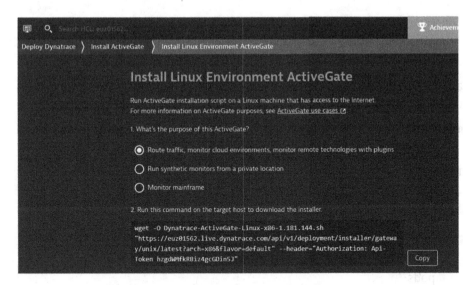

Figure 7-22. *Dynatrace ActiveGate installation*

```
$wget -O Dynatrace-ActiveGate-Linux-x86-1.181.144.sh
"https://euz01562.live.dynatrace.com/api/v1/deployment/
installer/gateway/unix/latest?arch=x86&flavor=default"
--header="Authorization: Api-Token hzgdWMfkRBiz4gcGDin5J"
```

Step 18: Execute the installer to install ActiveGate. After this, we can proceed to further Kubernetes-related configuration.

```
$./Dynatrace-ActiveGate-Linux-x86-1.181.144.sh
```

Step 19: In previous steps, we have cloned a file named kubernetes-monitoring-service-account.yaml. Readers can review the content of this file in Listing 7-3, as we will use this file in the next step.

Listing 7-3. Dynatrace Kubernetes monitoring configuration file

```
apiVersion: v1
kind: ServiceAccount
metadata:
```

```
  name: dynatrace-monitoring
  namespace: dynatrace
---
apiVersion: rbac.authorization.k8s.io/v1
kind: ClusterRole
metadata:
  name: dynatrace-monitoring-cluster
rules:
- apiGroups:
  - ""
  resources:
  - nodes
  - pods
  verbs:
  - list
---
apiVersion: rbac.authorization.k8s.io/v1
kind: ClusterRoleBinding
metadata:
  name: dynatrace-monitoring-cluster
roleRef:
  apiGroup: rbac.authorization.k8s.io
  kind: ClusterRole
  name: dynatrace-monitoring-cluster
subjects:
- kind: ServiceAccount
  name: dynatrace-monitoring
  namespace: dynatrace
```

Step 20: Create a service account and cluster role for accessing the Kubernetes API with the following snippet:

```
$ kubectl apply -f kubernetes-monitoring-service-account.yaml
```

Step 21: Get the Kubernetes API URL for later use using the following command:

```
$ kubectl config view --minify -o jsonpath='{.clusters[0].
cluster.server}'
```

Step 22: Get the Bearer token for later use using the following command:

```
$ kubectl get secret $(kubectl get sa dynatrace-monitoring -o
jsonpath='{.secrets[0].name}' -n dynatrace) -o jsonpath='{.
data.token}' -n dynatrace | base64 –decode
```

Step 23: Now, let's connect the Kubernetes cluster through Dynatrace settings. Log in to Dynatrace and navigate to Settings ➤ Cloud. Go to Virtualization ➤ Kubernetes. Click Connect New Cluster. Provide a name, Kubernetes API URL, and the Bearer token for the Kubernetes cluster, as shown in Figure 7-23.

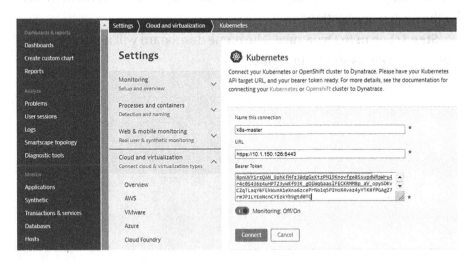

Figure 7-23. *Dynatrace and Kubernetes integration*

Step 24: Once the cluster is added successfully, it will be listed like in Figure 7-24.

Figure 7-24. *Dynatrace and Kubernetes integration*

Container Metrics on Dynatrace

Now that we have integrated Dynatrace with our Kubernetes setup and deployed the easyTravel application, let's navigate the console to view the container application monitoring metrics. OneAgent will do full-stack monitoring, including infrastructure, Docker, and code-level monitoring, for the hosted applications.

Step 1: Log in to Dynatrace. The home dashboard will now report additional data, as shown in Figure 7-25.

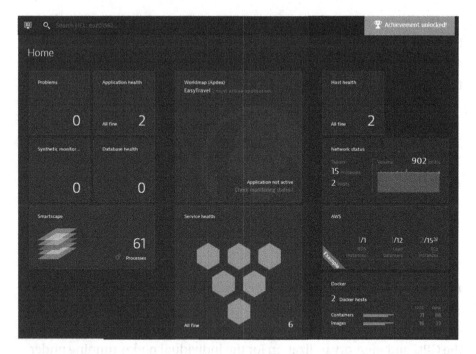

Figure 7-25. *Dynatrace dashboard after Kubernetes integration*

Step 2: To view the Kubernetes cluster status, navigate to the Kubernetes tab at the left-hand side and then click on the cluster, as shown in Figure 7-26.

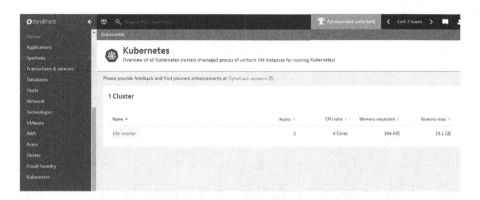

Figure 7-26. *Dynatrace Kubernetes cluster metrics*

213

By clicking on the cluster, we can look at cluster utilization. It will show the CPU and memory utilization based on usage, requests, limits, and availability. The same pane will show the number of nodes running under that cluster, as shown in Figure 7-27.

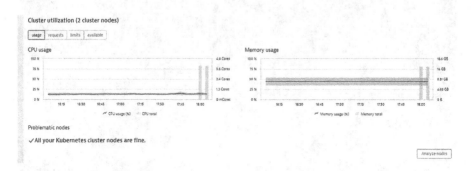

Figure 7-27. *Dynatrace Kubernetes cluster metrics*

Step 3: By clicking the Analyze Nodes button, the page will showcase the CPU and memory utilization for the individual nodes running under this Kubernetes cluster, as shown in Figure 7-28.

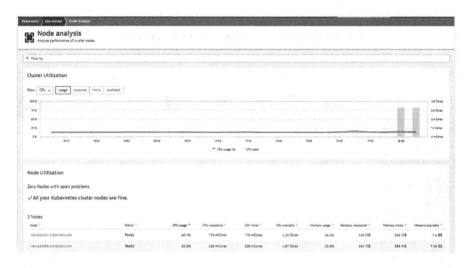

Figure 7-28. *Dynatrace Kubernetes cluster node metrics*

214

Step 4: To take a closer look at these nodes, we can go to the Hosts tab from the navigation menu. Here, the nodes are listed out as hosts, as shown in Figure 7-29.

Figure 7-29. *Dynatrace Kubernetes Host view*

Individual Host pages show problem history, event history, and related processes for each host. To assess health, the following performance metrics are captured for each host and presented on each Host overview page, as shown in Figure 7-30:

> CPU
>
> Memory
>
> Disk (storage health)
>
> NIC (network health)

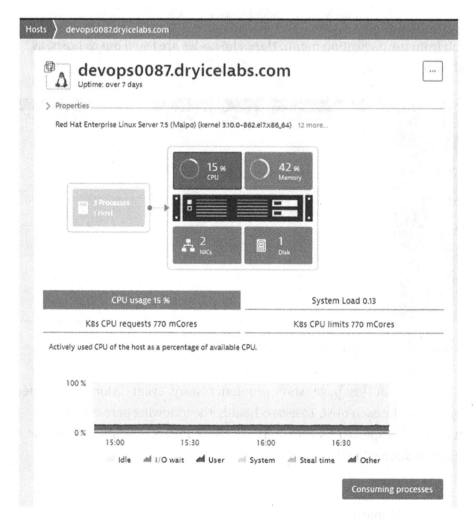

Figure 7-30. *Dynatrace Kubernetes Host view*

On the same page, we can see if there is any connectivity from this host to any another host, as shown in Figure 7-31.

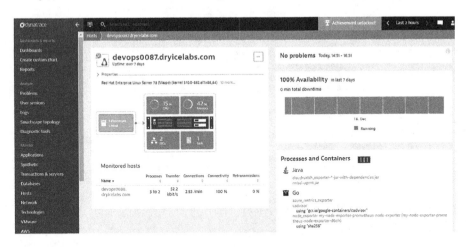

Figure 7-31. *Dynatrace Kubernetes Host view*

Step 5: On the same page, at the right-hand side, a complete list of processes and containers running on this host can be seen. We can view easyTravel processes and containers on this page, as shown in Figure 7-32.

Figure 7-32. *Dynatrace Kubernetes Processes and Containers view*

On the same page, by clicking on View Container, we can see the containers grouped by image type, as shown in Figure 7-33.

III Containers grouped by image name

Name ⇕	CPU ⇕	Memory ▾	Traffic ⇕	CPU throttling ⇕	Details
dynatrace/easytravel-backend	0.92 %	2 GB	22.5 kbit/s	0 ms	⌄
sha256	0.23 %	622 MB	-	0 ms	⌄
weaveworksdemos/queue-master	0.28 %	492 MB	5.14 kbit/s	0 ms	⌄
dynatrace/easytravel-frontend	1.19 %	484 MB	39.6 kbit/s	0 ms	⌄
dynatrace/easytravel-loadgen	0.76 %	393 MB	13.5 kbit/s	0 ms	⌄
dynatrace/oneagent	24 %	315 MB	-	0 ms	⌄
weaveworksdemos/carts	0.06 %	259 MB	368 bit/s	0 ms	⌄
weaveworksdemos/orders	0.05 %	247 MB	368 bit/s	0 ms	⌄
weaveworksdemos/shipping	0.07 %	247 MB	0 bit/s	0 ms	⌄
weaveworksdemos/catalogue-db	0.04 %	191 MB	0 bit/s	0 ms	⌄

Figure 7-33. *Dynatrace Containers Grouped by Image Name view*

Step 6: Expand one of the images to view the details regarding those containers running using this image. In this view, the following details are available, as shown in Figure 7-34.

CPU: CPU user divided by CPU system, expressed as a percentage.

Memory: Resident Set Size (RSS) and cache memory. RSS reflects data belonging to processes, while cache memory represents the data stored on disk that is currently cached in memory.

Traffic: Both incoming and outgoing network traffic

Throttling: Total time that a container's CPU usage was throttled

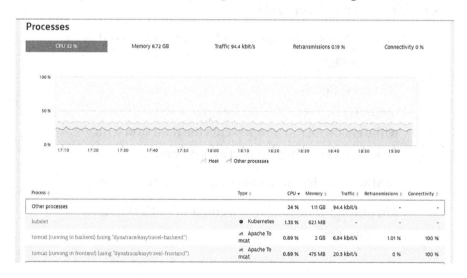

Figure 7-34. Dynatrace container metrics

For the processes, details are captured as shown in Figure 7-35.

Processes

Process	Type	CPU ▾	Memory	Traffic	Retransmissions	Connectivity
Other processes		24 %	1.11 GB	94.4 kbit/s	-	-
kubelet	● Kubernetes	1.33 %	62.1 MB	-	-	-
tomcat (running in backend) (using "dynatrace/easytravel-backend")	⚙ Apache Tomcat	0.89 %	2 GB	6.84 kbit/s	1.01 %	100 %
tomcat (running in frontend) (using "dynatrace/easytravel-frontend")	⚙ Apache Tomcat	0.89 %	475 MB	20.5 kbit/s	0 %	100 %

Figure 7-35. Dynatrace Kubernetes process metrics

Step 7: On the navigation menu, we can see a summary of the most relevant details of the Docker, as shown in Figure 7-36. The graphical view at the top of the page displays the following:

> Number of running containers
>
> Number of Docker images
>
> Top three containers consuming the most memory
>
> Most recently started container
>
> Most frequently used images

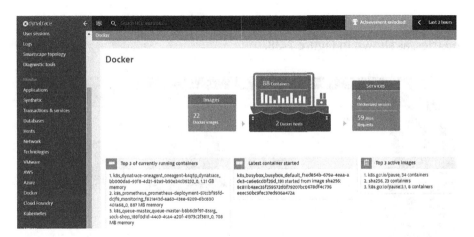

Figure 7-36. *Dynatrace Docker dashboard view*

The Docker Hosts section at the bottom of the page shows the resource usage of individual Docker hosts, including number of containers running, as shown in Figure 7-37.

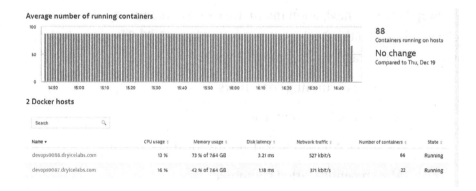

Figure 7-37. *Dynatrace Docker view*

Step 8: Click on the Application tab to view application monitoring metrics, as shown in Figure 7-38.

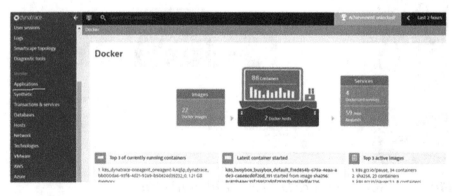

Figure 7-38. *Dynatrace application monitoring*

By default, there will be an application created called "My web application." All the traffic will report to this application at first. Now, let's create a new application using the following steps. Navigate to Settings ➤ Web & mobile Monitoring ➤ Application Detection and run as shown in Figure 7-39.

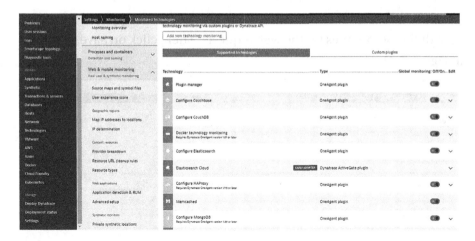

Figure 7-39. *Dynatrace easyTravel application onboarding*

Click on Create Application Detection Rule, as shown in Figure 7-40.

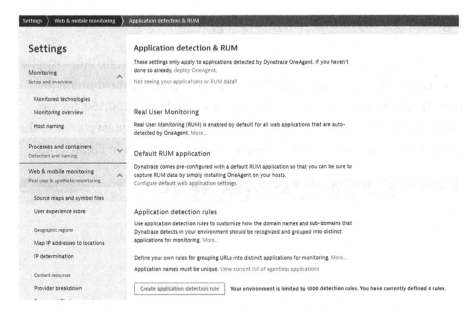

Figure 7-40. *Dynatrace easyTravel application onboarding*

Now click on New Application. Give a name for the application and then define some rules for the web requests. Then, click on Save, as shown in Figure 7-41.

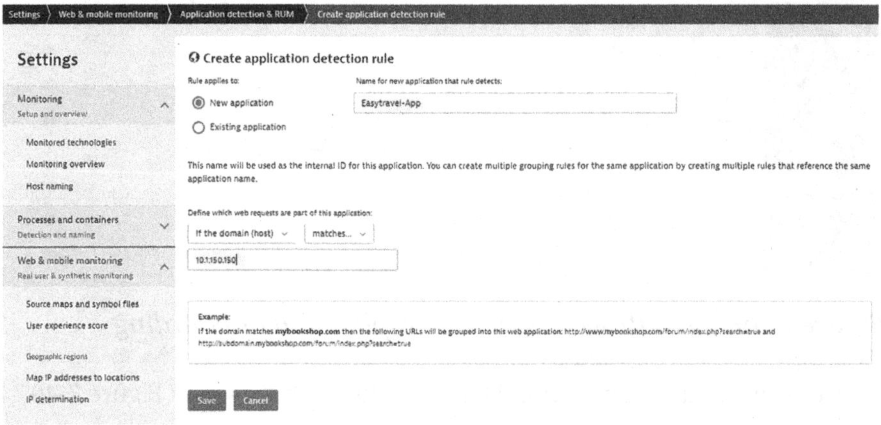

Figure 7-41. *Dynatrace easyTravel application onboarding*

This will create an application under the Application tab. Rules can be defined based on domain and URLs. Here, we are using the domain for detecting web requests. Our application domain is 10.1.150.150. So, we have specified the same in the rule. Now, whenever a request comes to this domain, it will get registered under easyTravel, as shown in Figure 7-42.

Figure 7-42. *Dynatrace easyTravel application onboarding*

Step 9: To view the easyTravel application, we navigate to Applications and click on easyTravel, as shown in Figure 7-43.

Figure 7-43. *Dynatrace easyTravel application metrics*

We will view the application as seen in Figure 7-44.

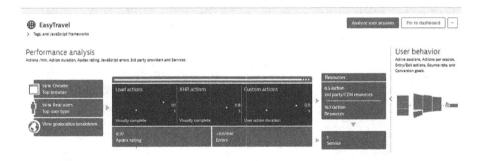

Figure 7-44. *Dynatrace easyTravel application metrics*

By clicking on User Behavior, we will see the screen in Figure 7-45.

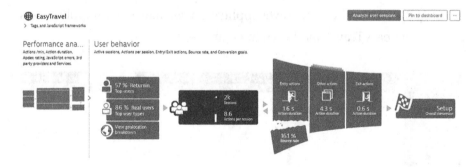

Figure 7-45. *Dynatrace easyTravel application metrics*

On the same page, we can see the user actions and errors, as shown in Figure 7-46.

Figure 7-46. *Dynatrace easyTravel application metrics*

By clicking on any of the errors, we can see the details of the errors captured, as shown in Figure 7-47.

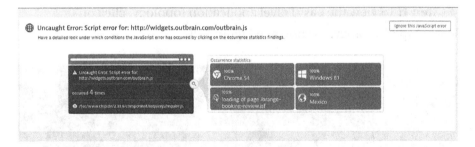

Figure 7-47. *Dynatrace easyTravel application metrics*

Here, we can see the occurrences of the error, browser, OS, and location-specific details. Below that we can see a detailed description of the error, as shown in Figure 7-48.

Error details

View details for   Chrome ⌄

Script file	⊖require.js ⏷	Occurring domains	easytravel-frontend
Script origin	www.chip.de	Count	4
Browser	⊕ Chrome	Message	Uncaught Error: Script error for: http://widgets.outbrain.com/outbrain.js
User actions	loading of page /orange-booking-review.jsf		
Info	⚠		

"Script error" is usually reported when an exception violates the browsers same-origin-policy i.e. when the error occurs in a script that is hosted on a domain other than the domain of the current page.
If the script is received with the CORS HTTP headers set, it is possible to get the full error details for most browsers by adding the attribute crossorigin="anonymous" to the script tag. Unfortunately Internet Explorer 11 and Edge do not currently support the crossorigin attribute. Care is also required to only set the crossorigin attribute for scripts with CORS headers present as otherwise the script will not be executed anymore.

Figure 7-48. *Dynatrace easyTravel application metrics*

So, by using the preceding drill-down, we can identify the root cause of all the errors in our container application.

Application Topology

In Dynatrace there is a feature called Smartscape. Smartscape auto-discovery delivers a quick and efficient overview of all the topological dependencies in your infrastructure, processes, and services, both on the vertical axis (where full-stack dependencies across all tiers are displayed) as well as on the horizontal axis (where all ingoing and outgoing call relationships within each tier are visualized). Let's view the Smartscape topology for our easyTravel application.

Step 1: To view the easyTravel application topology, click on Smartscape Topology, as shown in Figure 7-49.

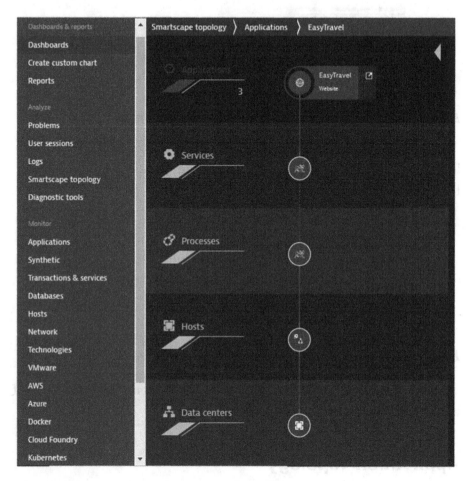

***Figure 7-49.** Dynatrace easyTravel application topology*

To see a detailed description of the easyTravel processes, click on Host and select the target node host. Under Processes and Containers, click any process to explore that process in detail on a dedicated process page.

On each process page, you'll find process-specific statistics related to CPU consumption, memory consumption, network utilization (see

Figure 7-50), and other infrastructure measurements. You'll also find details regarding related events, problems, and dependencies (including called and calling process).

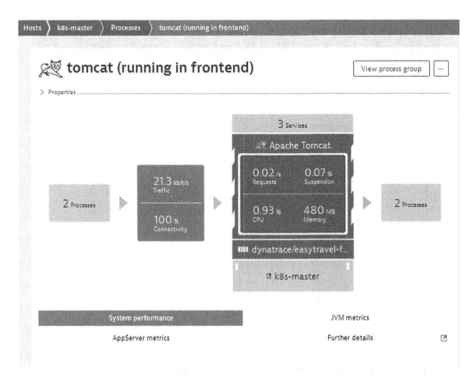

Figure 7-50. *Dynatrace easyTravel application processes*

At the top of this process page, we can also see provided services, as shown in Figure 7-50.

In this Figure 7-51, a topology is created for every process, and we can see its caller and called processes as well by clicking on the Process tab at the left and right-hand side, as shown in Figure 7-50.

Figure 7-51. *Dynatrace easyTravel application processes*

Transactions and Services

We can check the availability of the processes, and in the graph itself we can see if a process was shut down at any point in time. Below that there will be a list of events for this process. If any changes have been made in the process deployment, there will be an event listed for this. If the process was restarted, there will be an event for this as well.

Step 1: When you look at processes, you're seeing topology information, whereas services give you code-level insight. To view service-specific details in Dynatrace, go to Transactions & Services and click on one of the services, as shown in Figure 7-52.

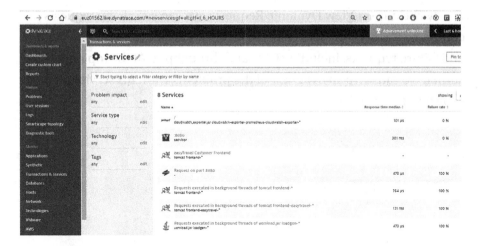

Figure 7-52. *Dynatrace easyTravel application transaction metrics*

For every service, we can see the caller and calling requests, number of requests, and response time, including dynamic web requests and resource requests, as shown in Figure 7-53.

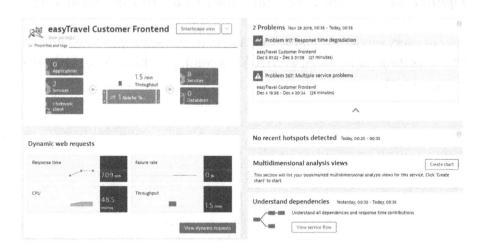

Figure 7-53. *Dynatrace easyTravel application transaction metrics*

By clicking on View Dynamic Requests, we can see all the requests coming to this service. On the same page, we can see the response time and failure requests, including CPU and throughput. At the top right corner, we can have an overview of the problems with this service, as shown in Figure 7-54.

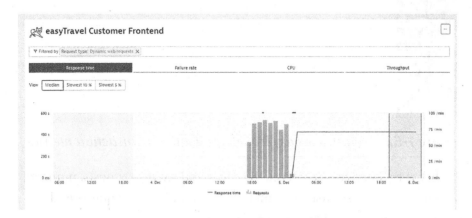

Figure 7-54. *Dynatrace easyTravel application transaction metrics*

For every service, we can see a graph of response time, failure rate, CPU, and throughput for all web requests coming to this service, as shown in Figure 7-55.

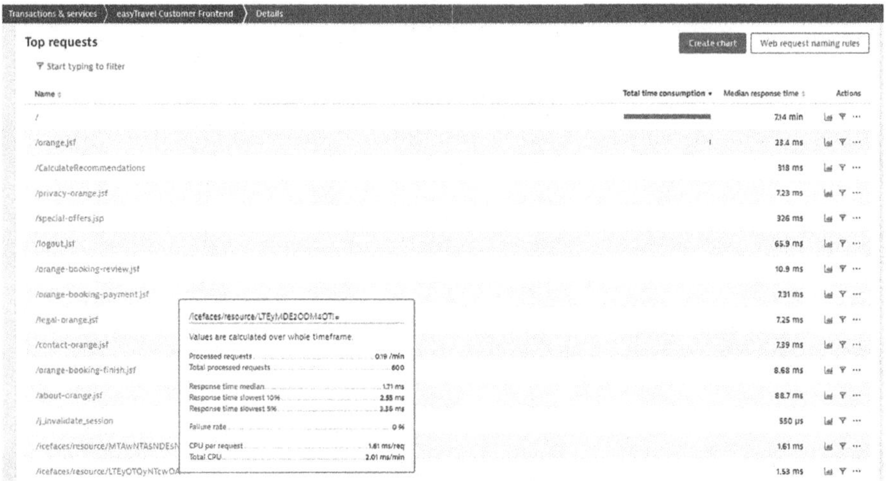

Figure 7-55. *Dynatrace easyTravel application transaction metrics*

Summary

In this chapter, we have provided an overview of Dynatrace and its capabilities, along with hands-on steps for using Dynatrace for container application monitoring. In the next chapter, we will provide overview of Sysdig and look at its capabilities for monitoring Container ecosystem. We will also provide hands-on steps for using Sysdig for container application monitoring.

CHAPTER 8

Container Application Monitoring Using Sysdig

This chapter will provide hands-on steps for doing container application monitoring using Sysdig. We will look at the following:

- Introduction to Sysdig

- Container Application Monitoring

- Working with Sysdig for Container Application Monitoring

Introduction to Sysdig

Sysdig Monitor is a powerful container-native monitoring and troubleshooting solution that provides comprehensive observability. It comes out of the box with unmatched container visibility and deep orchestrator integrations, including Kubernetes, Docker Swarm, AWS

© Navin Sabharwal, Piyush Pandey 2020
N. Sabharwal and P. Pandey, *Monitoring Microservices and Containerized Applications*,
https://doi.org/10.1007/978-1-4842-6216-0_8

EKS, Azure AKS, and Google GKE. It is available as both a cloud and an on-premises software offering. The following are the key features of Sysdig Monitor:

- **Simplifies discovery and metric collection:** Sysdig provides transparent instrumentation that dynamically discovers applications, containers, hosts, networks, and custom metrics, like Prometheus, JMX, and statsD, for deep insight into complex environments.

- **Visualizes service reliability:** Sysdig provides a consolidated overview of your service performance, capacity, and risk profile, which helps developers and DevOps quickly identify application issues and take action.

- **Monitors infrastructure and applications:** By leveraging deep integrations with Kubernetes, OpenShift, Docker, Mesos, DC/OS, AWS, Google, IBM, Azure, etc., Sysdig lets you see beyond infrastructure into how your apps and services are performing.

- **Builds robust dashboards:** Sysdig provides out-of-the-box and customizable dashboards that enable at-a-glance views of your infrastructure, applications, compliance, and metrics and let you visualize your environment the way you want.

- **Simplifies and scales Prometheus monitoring:** Using turn-key, horizontal scalability, enterprise access control and security, Prometheus metrics correlation, and PromQL queries with any event or metric, Sysdig helps you keep pace with large, complex environments.

- **Allows you to explore your entire infrastructure:**
  Sysdig provides automatic correlation of data from
  across your infrastructure, including custom metrics
  from statsD, JMX, and Prometheus, providing deep
  insight into complex environments.

- **Proactively alert for faster response:** Sysdig provides
  configurable alerts to enable proactive notification
  of any condition, including events, downtime, and
  anomalies, to help you get a handle on issues before
  they impact operations.

- **Accelerates troubleshooting:** Sysdig provides deep
  container visibility, service-oriented views, and
  comprehensive metrics that help you hunt threats and
  eliminate issues faster.

Sysdig's functional architecture is shown in Figure 8-1.

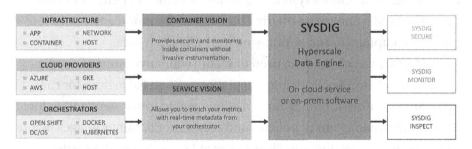

Figure 8-1. *Sysdig functional architecture*

Container Application Monitoring

Sysdig's commercial offering unifies all operational data and turns it
into insights. Starting with thousands of metrics and events for every
application, container, and host, the Sysdig platform enriches the data to

give you precise, in-context views of your applications and microservices. Sysdig then provides you with apps that deliver key visualizations to help you achieve your specific workflows.

Sysdig gets its data from the kernel by subscribing to trace-points that many system kernels are already processing and publishing; this is called Container Vision. This makes the data capture a very lightweight exercise (typically 1–3% CPU resource and 500 MB system memory). Sysdig is based on the open source Linux troubleshooting and forensics project by the same name (Sysdig). The open source project allows you to see every single system call, down to process, arguments, payload, and connection, on a single host. This data is dynamically mapped to containers, microservices, clouds, and orchestrators in a way that is at once powerful and simple to use.

To further leverage the unique visibility created by the original Sysdig project, the developers built an open source security tool called Falco . Falco combines the visibility of open source Sysdig with a rules engine that constantly monitors system events for violations of policies at run-time. The Sysdig enterprise offering then allows for enforcement of these policies, compliance, and auditing on top of this rich data.

To further enrich the data used to secure your environment, Sysdig has also integrated Anchore into the platform. What Falco does for run-time, Anchore does for build-time: it allows you to implement and enforce vulnerability management policies and scan your container images before they ever go into production. Please refer to Figure 8-2 for the Sysdig container monitoring system architecture components.

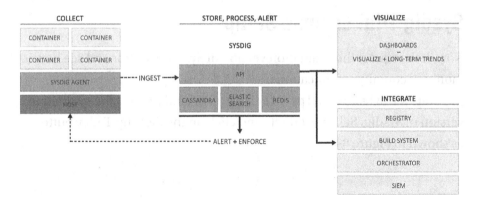

Figure 8-2. *Sysdig container monitoring architecture*

Sysdig's architecture is very similar to those of tcpdump and Wireshark, as events are first captured at the kernel level by a small driver called sysdig-probe, which leverages a kernel facility called tracepoints.

Sysdig also now supports eBPF, shown in Figure 8-3, as an alternative to the kernel module-based architecture just described. eBPF—extended Berkeley Packet Filter—is a Linux-native in-kernel virtual machine that enables secure, low-overhead tracing for application performance and event observability and analysis.

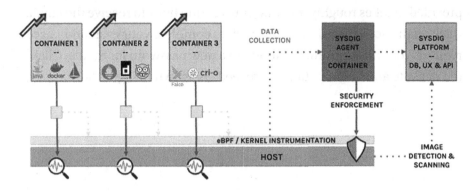

Figure 8-3. *Sysdig container monitoring architecture*

Sysdig Trial License Setup

Now, let's request the evaluation version of Sysdig Monitor and see how it monitors container applications.

Step 1: Navigate to https://sysdig.com/ and request the evaluation version of Sysdig. Select Products and click on the Sign-up Today button, as shown in Figure 8-4.

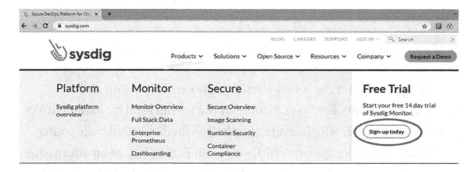

Figure 8-4. *Sysdig evaluation request*

Step 2: Fill in the required details and click the Submit button.

Step 3: You will receive an activation link at the email address you provided. It takes roughly thirty minutes to one hour to receive the email. Click on the activation link in the email to complete your evaluation access request. You will be prompted to set up a new password for Sysdig. Click the Activate and Login button to proceed, as shown in Figure 8-5.

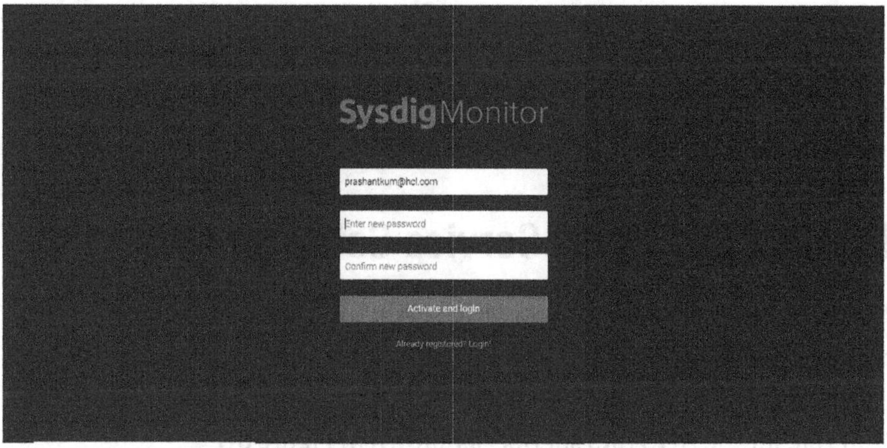

Figure 8-5. *Sysdig evaluation account password setup*

Step 4: On the next screen, you will be prompted to go to the Sysdig Welcome screen. Click on Next to proceed.

Step 5: We are using Sysdig to monitor our Kubernetes cluster, so please select "Kubernetes | GKE | OpenShift" on the next screen. On selection, you will view a key, as shown in Figure 8-6. Copy the key. We will use this later in the chapter.

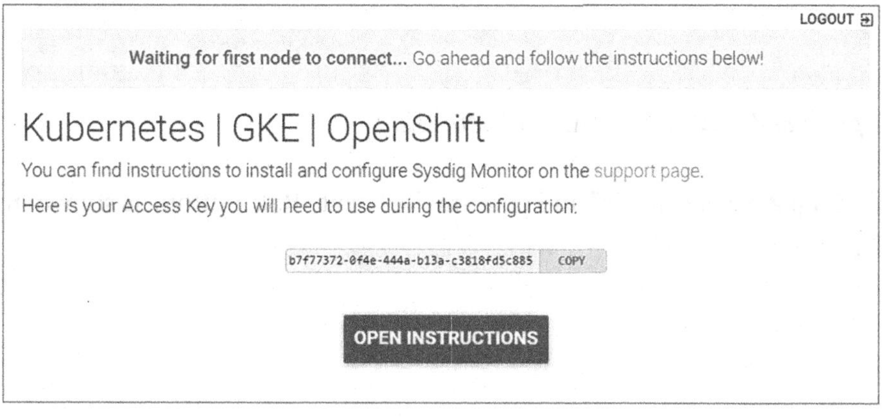

Figure 8-6. *Sysdig evaluation account Kubernetes integration key*

Now, we will set up a cluster on AWS using Amazon Elastic Kubernetes Services (EKS), and then integrate Sysdig Monitor for container application monitoring. We will assume the reader has knowledge of working with AWS and has an AWS account.

Elastic Kubernetes Service Setup on AWS

Please perform the following steps to set up the Elastic Kubernetes Services on AWS.

Step 1: Log in to your AWS account and navigate to IAM to create the IAM role for the AWS EKS service, as shown in Figure 8-7.

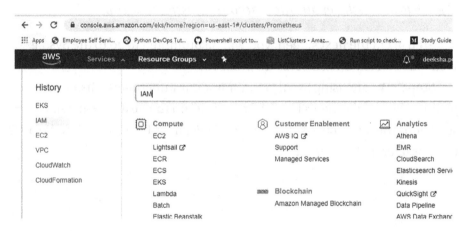

Figure 8-7. *AWS EKS IAM role creation*

Step 2: Select "Roles" and click on the Create Role button, as shown in Figure 8-8.

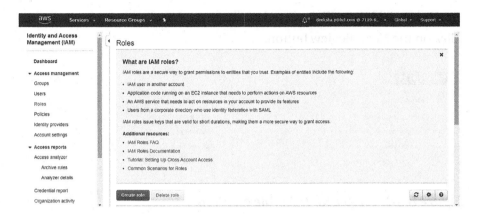

Figure 8-8. *AWS EKS IAM role creation*

Step 3: Select "AWS EKS Service" from the services list and select the use case of EKS for managing the cluster on the user's behalf. Provide role name and description. Click the Next: Permissions button, as shown in Figure 8-9.

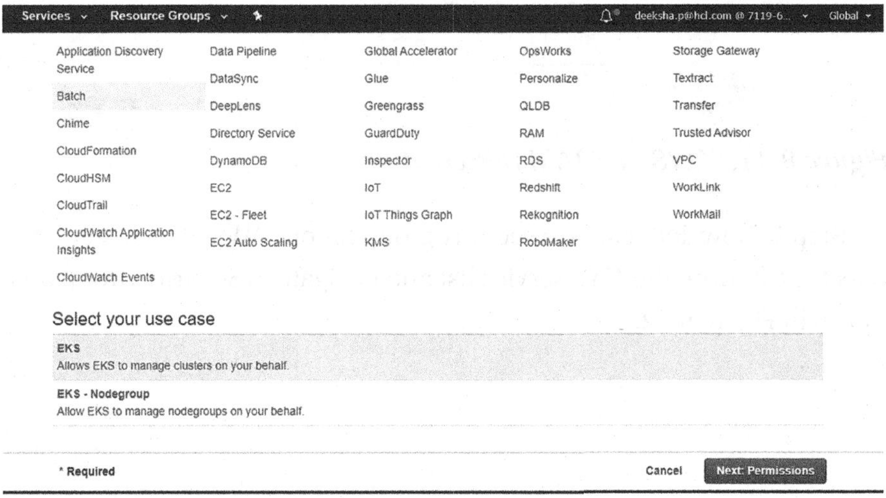

Figure 8-9. *AWS EKS IAM role creation*

Step 4: Add the policies listed in Figure 8-10 and add tags (optional). Click on the Next: Review button.

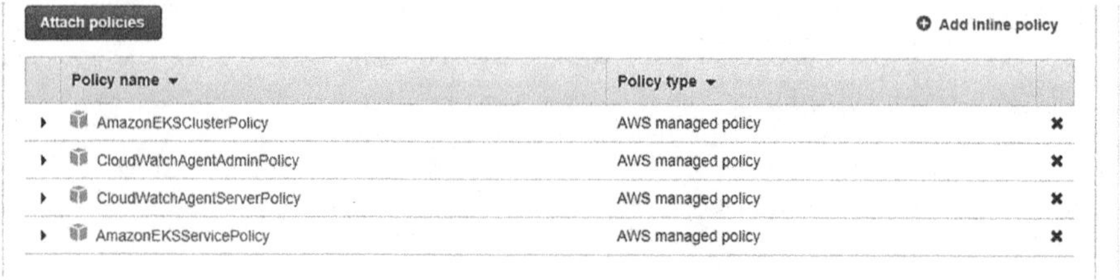

Figure 8-10. *AWS EKS IAM role creation*

Step 5: Review and click the Create Role button, as shown in Figure 8-11. Review after the role has been created.

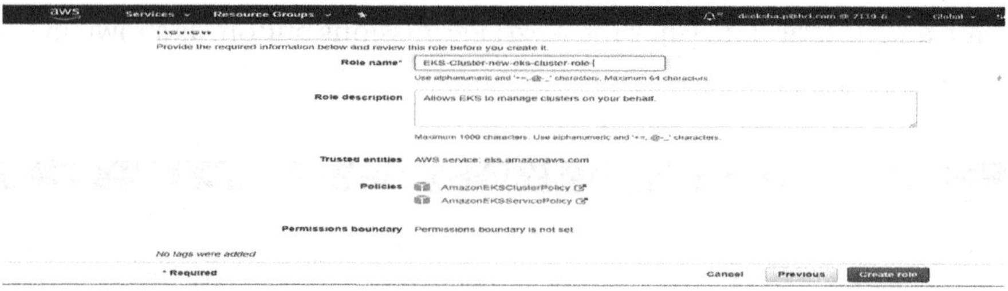

Figure 8-11. *AWS EKS IAM role creation*

Step 6: Now, let's create a security group for our AWS EKS cluster. Select "EC2" from the AWS service list and navigate to Security Groups, as shown in Figure 8-12.

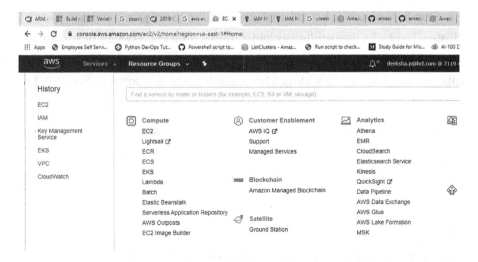

Figure 8-12. *AWS EKS security group creation*

Step 7: Click on Create Security Group. Provide a name for the security group and add a description (optional). Select a pre-built VPC. Click on the Create button to set up a security group for the AWS EKS cluster, as shown in Figure 8-13.

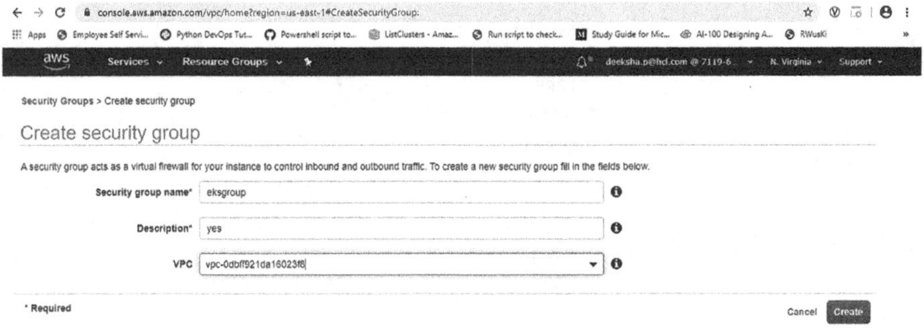

Figure 8-13. *AWS EKS security group creation*

Step 8: Now add inbound and outbound security group ports to your \
cluster. Typically, users follow organizational policies, AWS architecture, and
security best practices to allow selective ports for their AWS EKS cluster. For
this lab exercise, we are adding a few default ports, as shown in Figure 8-14.

Security Group: sg-0b28ea220f42e8ca3

| Description | Inbound | Outbound | Tags |

Edit

Type ⓘ	Protocol ⓘ	Port Range ⓘ	Source ⓘ	Description ⓘ
All TCP	TCP	0 - 65535	0.0.0.0/0	
HTTPS	TCP	443	0.0.0.0/0	
HTTPS	TCP	443	::/0	

Figure 8-14. AWS EKS security group inbound port

Step 9: Now, let's create an SSH key pair for the AWS EKS cluster. Select
"EC2" from the service list and navigate to Key Pairs, as shown in Figure 8-15.

Figure 8-15. AWS EKS SSH key pair creation

Step 10: Click on Create Key Pair. Provide key pair name and click the Create button, as shown in Figure 8-16.

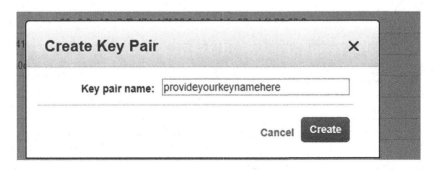

Figure 8-16. *AWS EKS SSH key pair creation*

Step 11: Now, let's create the AWS EKS cluster. Select "EKS" from the services list. Click the Create Cluster button, as shown in Figure 8-17.

Figure 8-17. *AWS EKS creation*

Provide a cluster name and select Kubernetes version 1.14. Select the IAM role created in previous steps, as shown in Figure 8-18.

EKS > Clusters > Create EKS cluster

Create cluster

General configuration

Cluster name
Enter a unique name for your Amazon EKS cluster.

```
Prometheus
```

Kubernetes version
Select the Kubernetes version to install.

```
1.14                                                    ▼
```

Role name ☑ Info
Select the IAM Role that will be used by the nodes.

```
EKS-Cluster-1-eks-cluster-role                          ▼
```

Figure 8-18. *AWS EKS creation*

Step 12: Select the pre-built VPC and subnet, as shown in Figure 8-19.

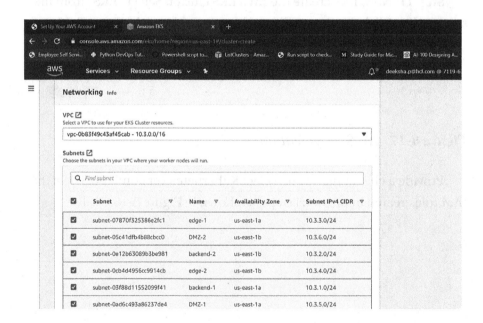

Figure 8-19. *AWS EKS creation*

Select the security group created in a previous step, as shown in Figure 8-20.

Figure 8-20. *AWS EKS creation*

Step 13: Enable public access for AWS EKS APIs, as shown in Figure 8-21.

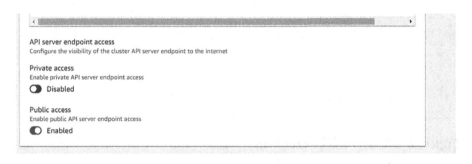

Figure 8-21. *AWS EKS creation*

Also enable all logging options, as shown in Figure 8-22.

Figure 8-22. *AWS EKS creation*

Step 14: Add tag values (optional) and click the Create button, as shown in Figure 8-23.

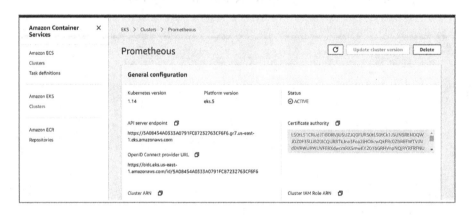

Figure 8-23. *AWS EKS creation*

Step 15: Validate your EKS cluster after setup. You can view if status is ACTIVE on the AWS console, as shown in Figure 8-24.

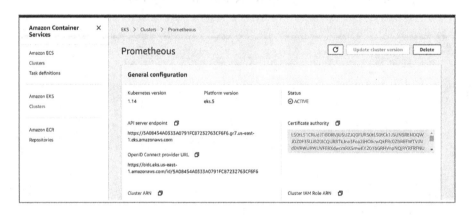

Figure 8-24. *AWS EKS creation validation*

Step 16: Now, let's create a node group in the AWS EKS cluster. Click the Add Node Group button on the newly created AWS EKS cluster's page, as shown in Figure 8-25.

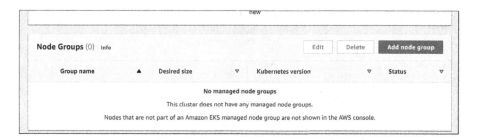

Figure 8-25. *AWS EKS node group creation*

Provide the name of the node group, then select subnets and the IAM role created in previous steps. Click the Next button.

Step 17: Select "Amazon Linux 2" for AMI type, select instance type as "t3.xlarge," and set the disk size to "20," as shown in Figure 8-26.

Figure 8-26. *AWS EKS node group creation*

Step 18: Select the SSH key pair created in previous steps. Select "Allow remote access from All." Click the Next button.

Step 19: Provide cluster scaling configuration of minimum, maximum, and desired size as 1. Click the Next button, as shown in Figure 8-27.

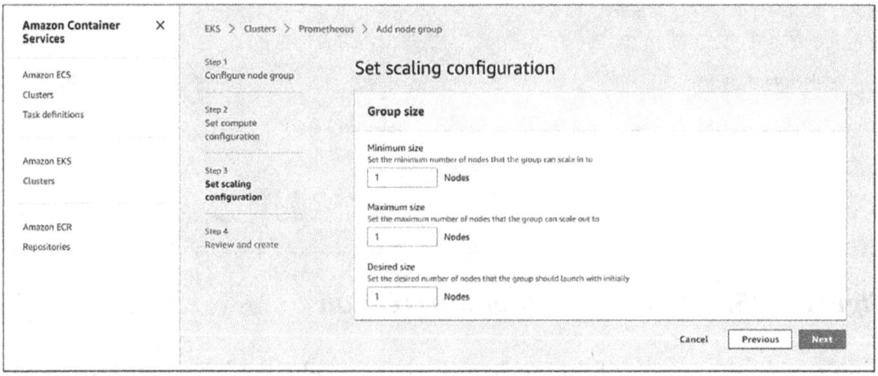

Figure 8-27. AWS EKS node group creation

Step 20: Review and click the Create button as shown in Figure 8-28. After creation, you can view whether the node group is in an active state on the AWS EKS cluster home page, as shown in Figure 8-24.

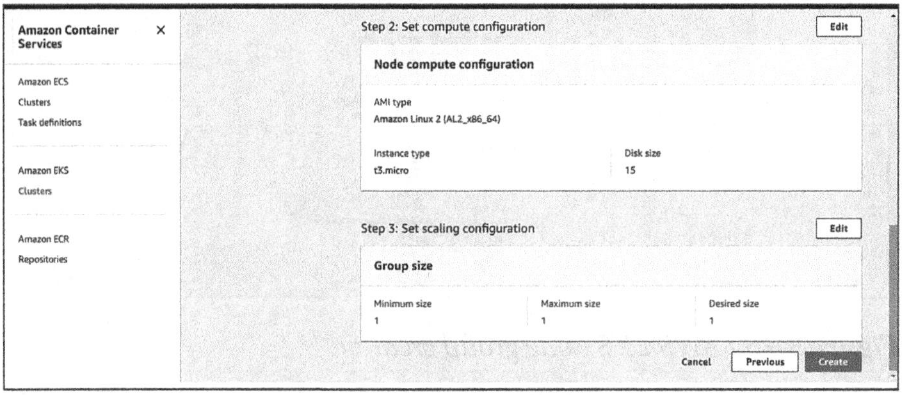

Figure 8-28. AWS EKS node group creation

Step 21: Now we will set up the AWS cli tool on our Kubernetes master node server. Execute the following command to install Python36 on your system:

```
$sudo yum install python36
```

Step 22: Verify the Python version by executing the following command:

```
$Python3 -version
```

Step 23: Install AWS cli by executing the following command:

```
$Pip3 install awscli -upgrade -user
```

Step 24: Verify AWS cli version by executing the following command:

```
$aws --version
```

Step 25: Configure your AWS account credentials (access and secret key) by executing the following command. Add the secret key, access key, and region where the AWS EKS cluster was created. Select "json" as the output format, as shown in Figure 8-29.

```
$aws configure
```

```
[saurabht@dryicelabs.com@devops0088 ~]$
[saurabht@dryicelabs.com@devops0088 ~]$ aws configure
AWS Access Key ID [*****************YWKP]:
AWS Secret Access Key [****************H64g]:
Default region name [None]: us-east-1
Default output format [None]: json
```

Figure 8-29. *AWS cli tool configuration*

Step 26: Execute the following command to fetch the AWS EKS cluster kubeconfig details (which we created in a previous step) from our master Kubernetes node:

```
$aws eks --region "us-east-1" update-kubeconfig --name "Prometheus"
```

Step 27: Fetch the kernel details of the AWS EKS cluster by executing the following command, as shown in Figure 8-30:

```
$kubectl describe nodes
```

```
pods:                      58
System Info:
  Machine ID:              ec2e9243dde353f5e947ac1cdff26ad0
  System UUID:             EC2E9243-DDE3-53F5-E947-AC1CDFF26AD0
  Boot ID:                 5a2a4007-2b54-4d50-90b3-04c878c52879
  Kernel Version:          4.14.146-119.123.amzn2.x86_64
  OS Image:                Amazon Linux 2
  Operating System:        linux
  Architecture:            amd64
  Container Runtime Version: docker://18.6.1
```

Figure 8-30. *AWS EKS cluster kernel version*

Sysdig Agent Installation

So far we have created an evaluation account for Sysdig, created an AWS EKS cluster, and connected our Kubernetes master node with AWS EKS. Now, we will install a Sysdig agent on the AWS EKS cluster.

Step 1: Execute the following command to download and install dependencies for the Sysdig agent:

```
$yum -y install kernel-devel-$(uname -r)
```

Step 2: Navigate to the /home/Prometheus directory and execute the following command to clone the file from GitHub:

```
$cd /home/promethues
$ git clone https://github.com/dryice-devops/sysdig.git
```

Step 3: Under the cloned Sysdig directory, you will find sysdig-agent-clusterrole.yaml, sysdig-agent-configmap.yaml, and sysdig-agent-daemonset-v2.yaml files. You can get sample files from this GitHub link:

```
https://github.com/draios/sysdig-cloud-scripts/tree/master/
agent_deploy/kubernetes.
```

You don't need to modify anything in the sysdig-agent-clusterrole. yaml or sysdig-agent-daemonset-v2.yaml files. In the sysdig-agent-configmap.yaml file, you need to update the k8s_cluster_name field with the name of the AWS EKS cluster (Prometheus, in our case). Also set Prometheus monitoring to true, as shown in Figure 8-31.

254

```
new_k8s: true
    k8s_cluster_name: "Prometheus"
prometheus:
    enabled: true
```

Figure 8-31. *Sysdig agent config files update*

Step 4: Create a namespace for the Sysdig agent using the non-root user, as follows:

```
$kubectl create ns sysdig-agent
```

Step 5: Create secrets for the Sysdig agent by executing the following command. This will use the key (highlighted) we got when we created the evaluation account for Sysdig (while selecting Kubernetes on the Welcome screen).

```
$kubectl create secret generic sysdig-agent --from-
literal=access-key=b7f77372-0f4e-444a-b13a-c3818fd5c885 -n
sysdig-agent
```

Step 6: Execute the following command to deploy the Sysdig agent cluster role. Here, the cluster role file is the same one we created in previous steps.

```
$ kubectl apply -f sysdig-agent-clusterrole.yaml -n sysdig-
agent
```

Step 7: Execute the following command to create a service account in the Sysdig agent namespace:

```
$ kubectl create serviceaccount sysdig-agent -n sysdig-agent
```

Step 8: Execute the following command to create cluster role binding in the Sysdig namespace:

```
$ kubectl create clusterrolebinding sysdig-agent --clusterrole=
sysdig-agent --serviceaccount=sysdig-agent:sysdig-agent
```

Step 9: Execute the following commands to complete installation of the Sysdig agent:

```
$ kubectl apply -f sysdig-agent-configmap.yaml -n sysdig-agent
$kubectl apply -f sysdig-agent-daemonset-v2.yaml -n sysdig-
agent
```

Deploy Sock Shop Application on EKS

Before starting to use Sysdig, let's deploy an application on our AWS EKS cluster. We will use the Sock Shop application in this example. The application is the user-facing part of an online shop that sells socks. It is intended to aid the demonstration and testing of microservice and cloud-native technologies. We will use this application to demonstrate Sysdig's container application monitoring capability. Figure 8-32 shows the architecture of the application.

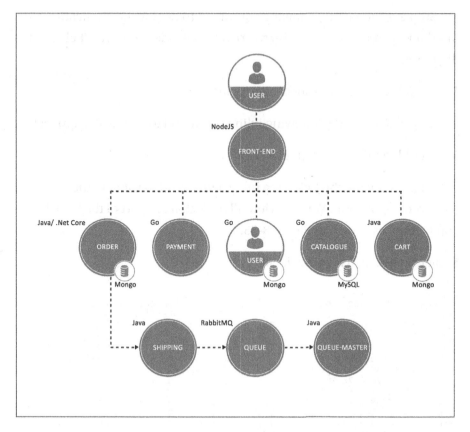

Figure 8-32. *Sock Shop application architecture*

Step 1: Execute the following command to download the Sock Shop application's yaml file to the /home/prometheus/sysdig directory. This file contains the configuration information related to Kubernetes deployments, pods, Docker images, and services required to deploy the Sock Shop application on the AWS EKS cluster.

```
$ git clone https://github.com/dryice-devops/microservices-
demo.git
```

Step 2: Execute the following command to deploy the application to the /home/prometheus/sysdig/microservices-demo/deploy/Kubernetes directory:

```
$ kubectl create namespace sock-shop
```

Step 3: Execute the following inline command to deploy the application:

```
$ kubectl apply -f complete-demo.yaml
```

Step 4: Execute the following inline command to validate the deployed application. You can view all pods that are part of the Sock Shop application, as shown in Figure 8-33.

```
$kubectl get pods -n sock-shop
```

```
[saurabht@dryicelabs.com@devops0087 kubernetes]$ kubectl get pods -n sock-shop
NAME                             READY   STATUS    RESTARTS   AGE
carts-668ff7f449-wbxc6           1/1     Running   0          112s
carts-db-d6475f9b8-sdj2t         1/1     Running   0          113s
catalogue-6fbf7d5588-5vmfw       1/1     Running   0          109s
catalogue-db-bdf476f4c-cjmwh     1/1     Running   0          110s
front-end-6fd4d97c75-dgd88       1/1     Running   0          107s
orders-78f5667b66-78vxn          1/1     Running   0          105s
orders-db-fb97f74c8-s9t4v        1/1     Running   0          106s
payment-7b968b8688-tt9h9         1/1     Running   0          103s
queue-master-6494b9f944-gc7wg    1/1     Running   0          102s
rabbitmq-774977d74-9w6dj         1/1     Running   0          101s
shipping-5bd79d96dd-1jpcx        1/1     Running   0          99s
user-6dbd855f5-g8kx5             1/1     Running   0          97s
user-db-78b67dfd4c-q8d6p         1/1     Running   0          98s
[saurabht@dryicelabs.com@devops0087 kubernetes]$
```

Figure 8-33. *Sock Shop application deployment validation*

EKS Metrics on Sysdig

Now we will navigate to the Sysdig console for reviewing monitoring metrics.

Step 1: Navigate to https://sysdig.com/ and click the Login button, then select "Monitor." Log in using the username/password used at the registration stage.

Step 2: After login, you will view the Welcome to Sysdig page. You will also see a "You have 1 agent connected" notification. Click on Next to navigate to the next screen, as shown in Figure 8-34.

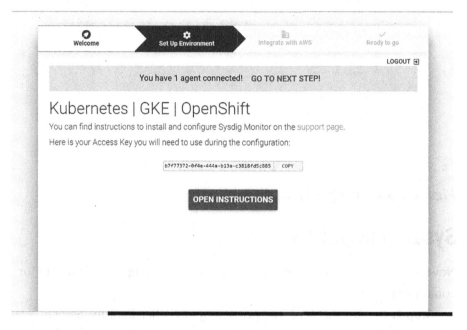

Figure 8-34. *Sysdig welcome page*

Step 3: Add the AWS access and secret key on the screen. Enable Cloudwatch and click the Next button. You will see the "setup complete" message on the screen, as shown in Figure 8-35.

To enable the integration, you just need to provide Sysdig Monitor with read-only access to your account. See here for specific instructions on how to generate the necessary keys.

Access Key ID: AKIA2LRC63BIHS7YYWKP

Secret Access Key: •••••••••••••••••••••••••••••••••|

CloudWatch Integration Status
Disabled ⬤ Enabled

Note: Once you provide the necessary keys, CloudWatch integration will be enabled by default. When this feature is enabled, Sysdig Monitor will poll the CloudWatch API every 5 minutes, which will generate a small additional charge from AWS (see Amazon CloudWatch Pricing).

You're not using a cloud provider? Don't worry, Sysdig Monitor will still work well for your infrastructure.

BACK   SKIP   NEXT

Figure 8-35.   Sysdig adding AWS account

Sysdig Navigation

Now, let's navigate across various reports on the Sysdig console useful for container monitoring.

Step 1: To view the deployed pods in Sysdig, click Explore. Select "Hosts & Containers" from the drop-down menu. On the other node, select "Kubernetes Health Overview" under the Kubernetes category (subcategory of Default Dashboards), as shown in Figure 8-36.

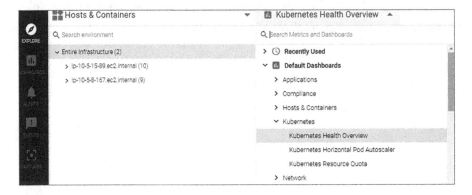

Figure 8-36.   Sysdig Kubernetes health dashboard

Step 2: You will view rich metrics regarding the entire Kubernetes environment, including top namespace (by container), CPU/memory/file system usage, and network in/out, as shown in Figure 8-37.

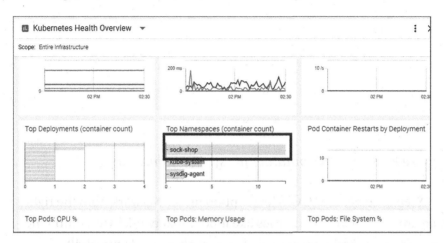

Figure 8-37. *Sysdig Kubernetes health dashboard*

Step 3: Select "Container Limits" from the right-side drop-down (Figure 8-38) to view CPU/memory share and quotas.

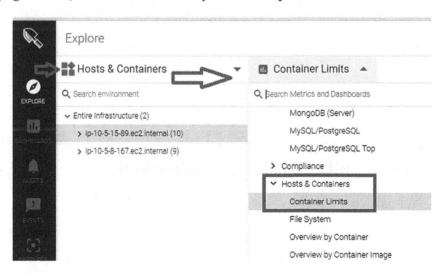

Figure 8-38. *Sysdig container limit monitoring*

Step 4: Select "File system" from the right-side drop-down to view the number of bytes free/bytes used, number of nodes in the file system, etc., as shown in Figure 8-39.

File System							
Scope: Entire Infrastructure							
File System							
fs.mountDir	fs.device	fs.type	fs.bytes.to...	fs.bytes.u...	fs.bytes.fr...	fs.used.pe...	f
/	/dev/nvme0n1...	xfs	20.0	5.4	14.6	26.9	

Figure 8-39. Sysdig container file system monitoring

Step 5: Select the "Overview" option under Network from the right-side drop-down to view metrics like inbound network bytes, outbound network bytes, and total network bytes, as shown in Figure 8-40.

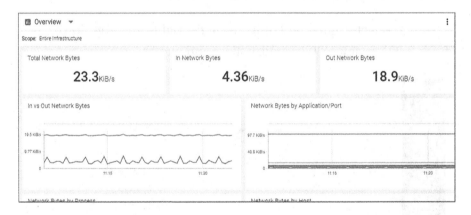

Figure 8-40. Sysdig container network monitoring

Docker Container Metrics

Sysdig provides various useful container metrics in the form of graphs. This information is useful for the sysadmin to monitor the health of the container ecosystem and take an appropriate action; e.g., generating an alert if any container is consuming more memory or CPU utilization. In this section, you will learn how to visualize and analyze the container metrics provided by Sysdig.

Now, let's view container application metrics.

Step 1: To view container-based information for the Sock Shop application (deployed in previous steps), select "Containerized Apps" from the drop-down and then select container names, starting with weaveworksdemos. You will view top pods CPU utilization, memory usage, and filesystem, as shown in Figure 8-41.

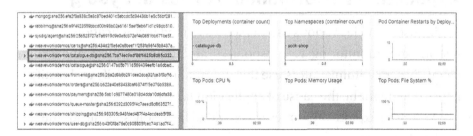

Figure 8-41. *Sysdig containerized application view*

Step 2: To view deployments, select "Deployments" from the drop-down menu and select "Sock-Shop." Select "Kubernetes CPU Allocation Optimization" under the Kubernetes category, as shown in Figure 8-42.

263

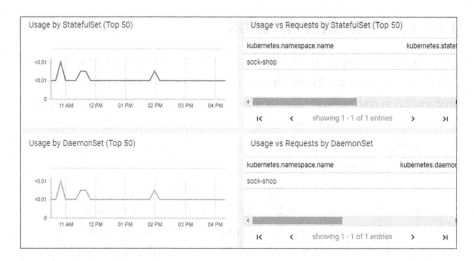

Figure 8-42. *Sysdig Deployment view*

Application Performance Metrics in Sysdig

Sysdig also provides various useful metrics related to application performance monitoring; e.g., response time, latency, request, and error count. System administrators use this information to identify and rectify issues that might be the cause of application failure.

Now, let's explore other metrics provided by Sysdig specific for the application layer.

Step 1: Select "Explore" in the left-hand side panel and choose the "Hosts & Containers" option from the drop-down menu. Select "HTTP" from the second drop-down menu on the right. You will view metrics like top HTTP request, average/maximum request time, slowest URLs, etc., as shown in Figure 8-43.

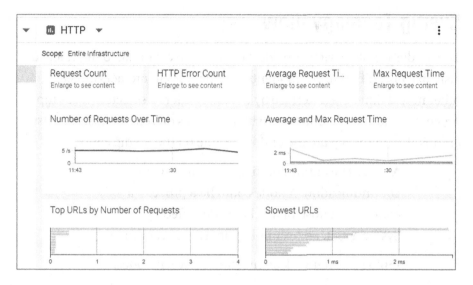

Figure 8-43. *Sysdig HTTP monitor*

Step 2: To analyze the JVM (Java virtual machine) health—e.g., heap size and garbage collector account—Sysdig provides insights. To see the JVM-related metrics, please select "JVM." This will show metrics like allocated heap memory usage by process over time and garbage collector collection time, as shown in Figure 8-44.

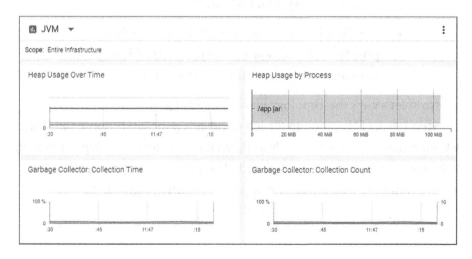

Figure 8-44. *Sysdig JVM monitor*

Sysdig Topology View

The Sysdig Topology view provides an interactive, animated interface to visualize how different components in your system interact with each other in real time. The interface by default renders a selected host's top processes and their interactions with processes on remote hosts or host groups. The following are the entities visible on the Sysdig console:

> **Nodes:** The entities participating in network communication. A node could be a process, a container, a host, or any label identified by the Sysdig agent. For example, `kubernetes.pod.name`.
>
> **Links:** The network connection between nodes.
>
> - Hosts and their child processes (`host.hostName` > `proc.name`) serve as the default grouping for the Topology view. Scaling a Topology view is limited by the number of processes and connections. Sysdig Monitor creates the Topology view by identifying network endpoints (IP addresses) derived from system call data.
>
> - The Topology view in the Explore tab provides pre-defined dashboards to represent CPU usage, network traffic, and response time metrics.

Now, let's view the Topology view from Sysdig.

Step 1: Select "Explore" in the left-hand side panel and choose the "Hosts & Containers" option from the drop-down menu. Select "Topology" and then "CPU Usage." Click on each icon to drill down to CPU usage by application node; a container with topology mapping is shown in Figure 8-45.

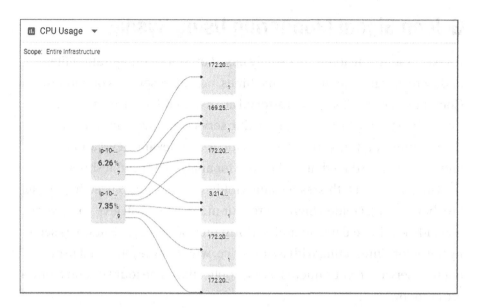

Figure 8-45. *Sysdig Topology view by CPU*

Step 2: Select the "Network Traffic" option from the second drop-down menu instead of CPU usage. You can drill down to view the specific flow; e.g., we selected the Python-based box that shows the network traffic between the Python pod and Mongo DB pod related to our Sock Shop app, as shown in Figure 8-46.

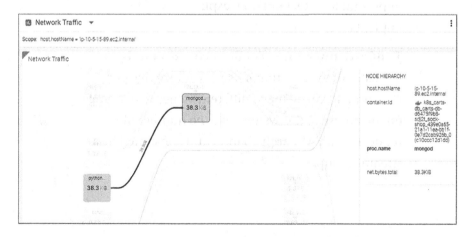

Figure 8-46. *Sysdig Topology view by network traffic*

Golden Signal Monitoring Using Sysdig

Classic monitoring tools are usually based on static configuration files and were designed to monitor machines, not microservices or containers. Containers are created and destroyed at an incredible pace, and it is impossible to catch up without specific service discovery functions.

It is important that we are able to focus on relevant views and alerts and not generate data that is of no use for analysis or troubleshooting.

Google resolved this issue using Golden Signals (term used in Google SRE handbook). Golden Signals are four metrics that will give you a very good idea of the real health and performance of your application as seen by the actors interacting with that service, whether they are final users or another service in your microservice application. The four Golden Signals are as follows:

> **Latency:** Latency is the time your system takes to serve a request against the service. This is an important sign to detect a performance degradation problem.
>
> **Errors:** The rate of errors returned by your service is a very good indicator of deeper issues. It is very important to detect not only explicit errors, but implicit errors too.
>
> **Traffic/Connections:** Traffic or connections is an indicator of the amount of use of your service per time unit. It can be many different values depending on the nature of the system, like the number of requests to an API or the bandwidth consumed by a streaming app.

Saturation: Usually saturation is expressed as a percentage of the maximum capacity, but each system will have different ways to measure saturation. The percentage could mean the number of users or requests obtained directly from the application or based upon estimations.

Now, let's see how we can view Golden Signal metrics using Sysdig.

Step 1: Select "Explore" in the left-hand side panel and choose the "Services" option from the drop-down menu. Select "Kubernetes Service Golden Signals" from the second drop-down menu, on the right. You'll see the Golden Signals metrics, as shown in Figure 8-47.

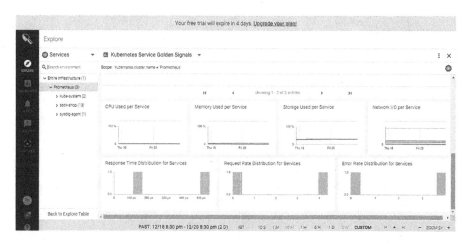

Figure 8-47. *Sysdig Golden Signals metrics*

Summary

In this chapter, we have provided hands-on steps for using Sysdig for container application monitoring. In the next chapter, we will cover how to automate enabling container monitoring using CI/CD-based automated pipelines, along with hands-on exercises.

CHAPTER 9

Automation and Orchestration of Container Monitoring

This chapter will provide hands-on steps for using Infrastructure as Code and the CI/CD pipeline to automate the deployment of container ecosystem infrastructure, applications, and monitoring. We will look at the following:

- Container Monitoring Automation

- Hands-on Exercise for Container Monitoring Automation

Container Monitoring Automation

As infrastructure has evolved and matured over the last decade, the way in which we build and deploy that infrastructure has also changed. With the rise of Infrastructure as Code, we can now reconstruct the whole infrastructure and platform from a code repository. With cloud computing and APIs, we can now truly treat our infrastructure just like an application. With containerization, since the dependencies are packaged with the application, the application can now be ported to any infrastructure, which itself is spun up using Infrastructure as Code.

© Navin Sabharwal, Piyush Pandey 2020
N. Sabharwal and P. Pandey, *Monitoring Microservices and Containerized Applications*,
https://doi.org/10.1007/978-1-4842-6216-0_9

271

A great advantage of Infrastructure as Code (IaC) is that it allows you to build environments rapidly without any human intervention. With IaC, we can now have consistent configuration and builds that are exactly alike.

The following is a high-level view of how IaC tools operate (Figure 9-1):

- You describe the desired infrastructure resources in a file (for example, a virtual network with three public subnets, a compute instance on one of them with a block volume attached to it). You describe what you need; you never describe how to create them—the IaC tool figures out how to create them.

- The tool looks at what you have described in your code and logs in to your cloud account to check if those resources are present.

- If the resources are not present, they are created.

- If the resources are already present with the same attributes, no action is taken.

- If matching resources are found with differences, the IaC tool assumes you want them changed and makes the change happen.

Figure 9-1. *How Infrastructure as Code works*

As DevOps continues to evolve, developers find ways to strengthen the integration of IaC and containers, since they complement each other. Containers incorporate Infrastructure as Code into the development cycle as a core component.

At first glance, a container image appears to be a fully self-contained application: it has all of the code and software dependencies required to run the application. However, once we deploy and operate images in the container ecosystem, we find we need a lot more configuration to scale it out, make it reliable, and make it observable. The monitoring and management of container-based infrastructure and applications brings its own unique elements and complexity.

A containerized application in the cloud might look something like Figure 9-2, where the container image is only part of the full application.

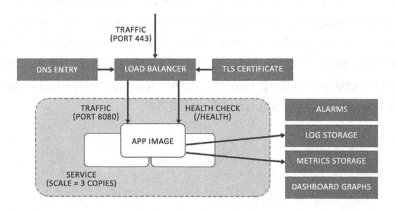

Figure 9-2. *Containerized application components beyond image*

The complete application is really best described with a combination of the container image and an IaC template containing all this configuration. Infrastructure as Code is an important element in release management of an application.

Now, when it comes to automating the container monitoring, there are many use cases possible. Some of the use cases are listed here:

- Enabling container monitoring for base infrastructure and application via CI/CD pipeline and Infrastructure as Code solutions (like Jenkins and Terraform/Ansible). This can include use cases like installing any agent/plugin for Monitoring, creating alarms, configuring threshold etc.

- Self-healing incidents which are created after receiving monitoring alerts using the Runbook orchestration tool. Essentially all the steps that a human performs to troubleshoot and resolve an incident after receiving a monitoring alert are converted into an automated flow, which is automatically triggered to resolve the incident.

- Report generation automation using tools like Grafana or Splunk

When we deploy Infrastructure as Code in a CI/CD pipeline, we can deploy changes in both the microservices infrastructure and the containers in the CI/CD release pipeline. This enables complete visibility of both the application code and the infrastructure code in the pipeline currently deployed in the production environment. A simplified example of our release process is shown in Figure 9-3.

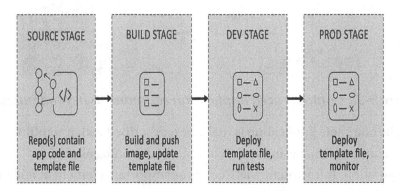

Figure 9-3. *CI/CD pipeline leveraging Infrastructure as Code to automate container monitoring*

The IaC template contains both the container-related configuration and the microservice's infrastructure in the "build" stage of the pipeline. The container image is built and pushed, and the unique ID for the new container image is inserted into the IaC template. Each stage of the pipeline, like "Dev" and "Prod," then deploys the same Infrastructure

274

as Code template. This practice gives us confidence that deployments of the entire application are repeatable. Within this pipeline, we can enable automation to deploy container monitoring as part of a first-time release. In the next section, we will do a hands-on exercise to enable such automation using Terraform and Jenkins.

Hands-on Exercise for Container Monitoring Automation

In this section, we will use Terraform to create a Kubernetes cluster on AWS and configure the Sysdig agent on it, and Jenkins to automate container monitoring. We will use AWS for our target container ecosystem and Sysdig for our container monitoring tool.

Cleaning Up the AWS Environment Namespace

Before we begin, let's clean up the namespace created for the Sysdig agent and Sock Shop application from Chapter 8 for a fresh installation through automation by Jenkins and Terraform.

Step 1: Delete the `sock-shop` and `sysdig-agent` namespaces that we created earlier on the master node by executing the following command, as shown in Figure 9-4:

```
$ kubectl delete namespace sock-shop
$ kubectl delete namespace sysdig-agent
```

```
[saurabht@dryicelabs.com@devops0087 ~]# kubectl delete namespace sock-shop
namespace "sock-shop" deleted
```

```
[saurabht@dryicelabs.com@devops0087 ~]# kubectl delete namespace sysdig-agent
namespace "sysdig-agent" deleted
```

Figure 9-4. Kubernetes namespace clean-up

275

Jenkins Installation (v2.204.1)

We will start with installing Jenkins, which will be used to compose a CI/CD pipeline for our containerized application. We will use our master node (10.1.150.126) server to install Jenkins. We will use a Dockerized version of Jenkins in this exercise.

Step 1: Log into the master node as the root user and execute the following command to clone the Docker file that will be used to install Jenkins. Navigate into the jenkins directory by executing the following command, as shown in Figure 9-5:

```
$ git clone https://github.com/dryice-devops/jenkins.git
$ cd Jenkins
```

```
[root@devops0087 prometheus]# cd jenkins/
```

Figure 9-5. *Jenkins installation directory creation*

Step 2: Create another sub-directory named jenkins-data that will be used as the Jenkins home and that will contain all the required details of the Jenkins server—e.g., workspace, job, configuration details, etc.—by executing the following command, as shown in Figure 9-6:

```
$ mkdir jenkins-data
```

Step 3: Create a Jenkins Docker image with the name jenkins by executing the following inline command, as shown in Figure 9-6, in the jenkins directory that contains the Docker file:

```
$ docker build -t jenkins.
```

```
[root@devops0087 jenkins]# docker build -t jenkins .
Sending build context to Docker daemon  2.048kB
Step 1/6 : FROM jenkins
latest: Pulling from library/jenkins
5cbf04beb70: Extracting [=====================================>]  33.49MB/45.31MB
607093a898c: Download complete
0a8ea045c926: Download complete
4eee24d4dac: Waiting
58988e753d7: Waiting
```

```
root@devops0087/home/prometheus/jenkins                                                      -  σ  ×
  Downloading https://files.pythonhosted.org/packages/e0/d3/9617609b8e1db654ec34753c43a0538d56c1740a5b4d78690ceb93beca15/botocore-1.13.43-py2.py3-non
e-any.whl (5.8MB)
Collecting s3transfer<0.3.0,>=0.2.0
  Downloading https://files.pythonhosted.org/packages/16/8a/1fc3dba0c4923c2a76e1ff0d52b305c44606da63f718d14d3231e21c51b0/s3transfer-0.2.1-py2.py3-non
e-any.whl (70kB)
Collecting pyasn1>=0.1.3
  Downloading https://files.pythonhosted.org/packages/62/1e/a94a8d635fa3ce4cfc7f506003548d0a2447ae76fd5ca53932970fe3053f/pyasn1-0.4.8-py2.py3-none-an
y.whl (77kB)
Collecting urllib3<1.26,>=1.20; python_version == "2.7"
  Downloading https://files.pythonhosted.org/packages/b4/40/a9837291310ee1ccc242ceb6ebfd9eb21539649f193a7c8c86ba15b98539/urllib3-1.25.7-py2.py3-none-
any.whl (125kB)
Collecting jmespath<1.0.0,>=0.7.1
  Downloading https://files.pythonhosted.org/packages/83/94/7179c3832a6d45b266ddb2aac329e101367fbdb11f425f13771d27f225bb/jmespath-0.9.4-py2.py3-none-
any.whl
Collecting python-dateutil<2.8.1,>=2.1; python_version >= "2.7"
  Downloading https://files.pythonhosted.org/packages/41/17/c62faccbfbd163c7f57f3844689e3a78bae1f403648a6afb1d0866d87fbb/python_dateutil-2.8.0-py2.py
3-none-any.whl (226kB)
Collecting futures<4.0.0,>=2.2.0; python_version == "2.6" or python_version == "2.7"
  Downloading https://files.pythonhosted.org/packages/d8/a6/f46ae3f1da0cd4361c344888f59ec2f5785e69c872e175a748ef6071cdb5/futures-3.3.0-py2-none-any.w
hl
Requirement already satisfied: six>=1.5 in /usr/lib/python2.7/dist-packages (from python-dateutil<2.8.1,>=2.1; python_version >= "2.7"->botocore==1.1
3.43->awscli) (1.10.0)
Building wheels for collected packages: PyYAML
  Building wheel for PyYAML (setup.py): started
  Building wheel for PyYAML (setup.py): finished with status 'done'
  Created wheel for PyYAML: filename=PyYAML-5.1.2-cp27-cp27mu-linux_x86_64.whl size=44912 sha256=2ac4a46dbbd4d33ce037c6a8d2540892a90815aaf6e5735cc82a
ee54e623f0bd
  Stored in directory: /root/.cache/pip/wheels/d9/45/dd/65f0b38450c47cf7e5312883deb97d065e030c5cca0a365030
Successfully built PyYAML
Installing collected packages: docutils, pyasn1, rsa, PyYAML, colorama, urllib3, jmespath, python-dateutil, botocore, futures, s3transfer, awscli
Successfully installed PyYAML-5.1.2 awscli-1.16.307 botocore-1.13.43 colorama-0.4.1 docutils-0.15.2 futures-3.3.0 jmespath-0.9.4 pyasn1-0.4.8 python-
dateutil-2.8.0 rsa-3.4.2 s3transfer-0.2.1 urllib3-1.25.7
Removing intermediate container a411a23fe9ec
 ---> 4fefeff7973d
Step 6/6 : USER jenkins
 ---> Running in 87ef2f9d4f95
Removing intermediate container 87ef2f9d4f95
 ---> 004adce89f20
Successfully built 004adce89f20
Successfully tagged jenkins:latest
```

Figure 9-6. *Jenkins Docker image build*

Step 4: Verify whether the Jenkins Docker image was created by executing the following inline command, as shown in Figure 9-7.

If the Docker image was created successfully, then the following command will return "Repository" as Jenkins that we passed in as a tag (-t) in previous step.

```
$docker images
```

```
[root@devops0087 jenkins]# docker images
REPOSITORY                    TAG              IMAGE ID            CREATED             SIZE
jenkins                       latest           004adce89f20        16 seconds ago      778MB
```

Figure 9-7. *Verify Jenkins Docker image*

Step 5: Execute the following command to install Jenkins on Docker, as shown in Figure 9-8:

```
$docker run -u root --rm -d -p 8080:8080 -v /home/prometheus/
jenkins/jenkins-data:/var/jenkins_home -v /var/run/docker.
sock:/var/run/docker.sock Jenkins
```

In the preceding command we used port 8080 on the master node to run Jenkins, so please make sure that this port is open on your Linux VM. You can also pass another port for the VM, but the Jenkins container port would be run on 8080 port only. For more information about the Docker run command, please refer to Docker's official page.[1]

```
[root@devops0087 jenkins]# docker run -u root --rm -d -p 8080:8080 -v /home/prometheus/jenkins/jenkins-data:/var/jenkins_home -v /var/run/docker.sock
:/var/run/docker.sock jenkins
dacfa2869d6a0cadb01f789be9b9a8dfb3328994300a33bf3eae39646e0d1411
[root@devops0087 jenkins]# █
```

Figure 9-8. *Jenkins installation*

Step 6: Execute the following command to verify that the Jenkins Docker container is running fine. Its status should come as up as shown in Figure 9-9.

If the Jenkins Docker container is having any issues, then its status would be `Exited` or `Dead`; in that case, you would have to check the Docker container logs to identify the root cause of the Docker container failure.[1]

```
$ docker ps
```

```
[root@devops0087 jenkins]# docker ps
CONTAINER ID    IMAGE        COMMAND              CREATED         STATUS          PORTS
                NAMES
dacfa2869d6a    jenkins      "/bin/tini -- /usr/1.."  2 minutes ago   Up 2 minutes    0.0.0.0:8080->8080/
```

Figure 9-9. *Jenkins installation verification*

---

[1]https://docs.docker.com/engine/reference/commandline/docker

Step 7: Jenkins requires a secret password during login. Secret passwords are stored in the `initialAdminPassword` file in the `secrets` directory of the `jenkins-data` folder. To get it, please execute the following command, as shown in Figure 9-10:

```
$ cat jenkins-data/secrets/initialAdminPassword
```

```
[root@devops0087 jenkins]# cat jenkins-data/secrets/initialAdminPassword
16b6fbb9f07449508202d1f18606ee41
[root@devops0087 jenkins]#
```

Figure 9-10. *Fetching Jenkins password*

Step 8: Navigate to the following URL to access Jenkins. You will receive a prompt that will require the secret password. Use the secret password fetched in the previous step and click the Continue button, as shown in Figure 9-11.

URL: `http://Master-Node-IP:8080`; e.g., `http://10.1.150.126:8080`

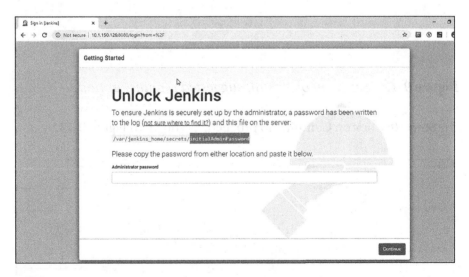

Figure 9-11. *Accessing Jenkins console for first time*

Step 9: Jenkins requires various plugins to create pipelines and to interact with different tools to perform tasks related to CI/CD; e.g., to connect with the GitHub repository and fetch the code, Jenkins required the Git plugin. Jenkins provides two options to install plugins: "Install suggested plugins" and "Select plugins to install." In our case, we selected "Install suggested plugins," as shown in Figure 9-12. If you want to select specific plugins, then choose "Select plugins to install."

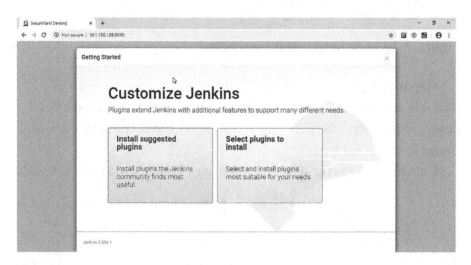

Figure 9-12. Selection of "Install suggested plugins" option

Step 10: Click on Continue to proceed, as shown in Figure 9-13.

✔ Pipeline	✔ GitHub Branch Source Plugin	✔ Pipeline: GitHub Groovy Libraries	✔ Pipeline: Stage View
✔ Git plugin	✔ Subversion	✔ SSH Slaves	✔ Matrix Authorization Strategy Plugin
✔ PAM Authentication	✔ LDAP	✔ Email Extension	✔ Mailer Plugin

Jenkins 2.204.1   Continue   Retry

Figure 9-13. Jenkins first-time login configuration

Step 11: Fill in details for username, password, full name, and email address and click the Save and Continue button, as shown in Figure 9-14.

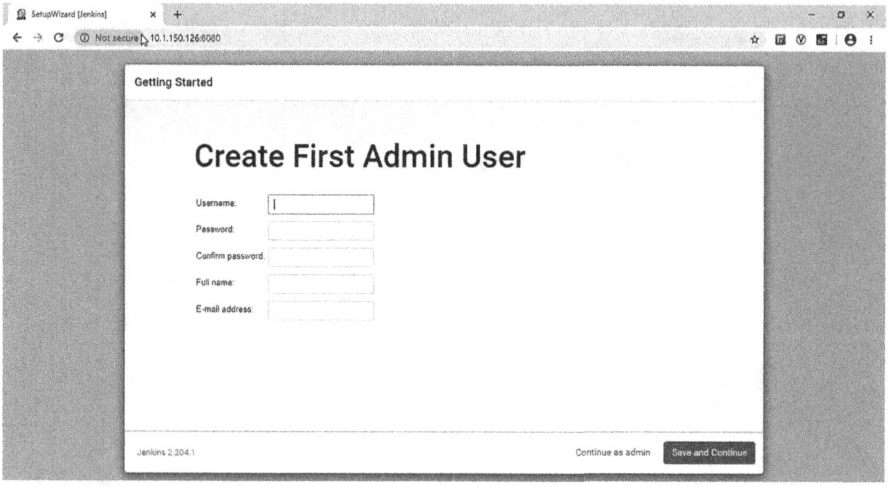

Figure 9-14.   Jenkins first admin user setup

Step 12: Click on Save and Finish to proceed, as shown in Figure 9-15.

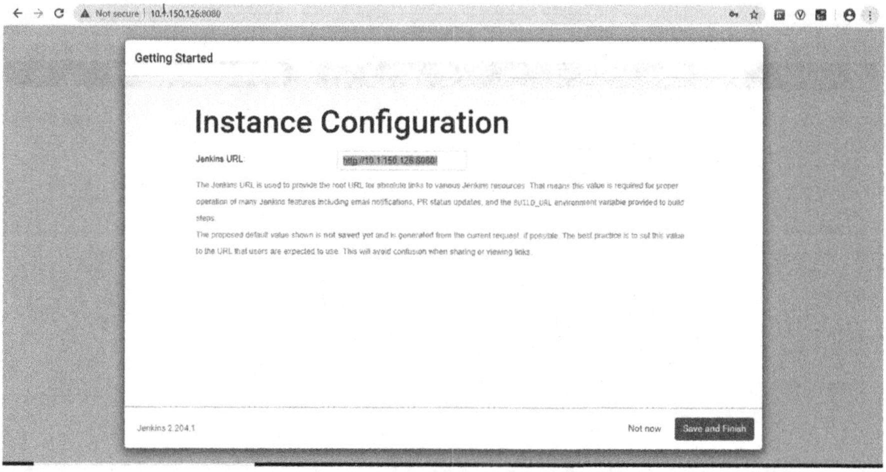

Figure 9-15.   Jenkins first-time login configuration

Step 13: Click the Start using Jenkins button to complete installation, as shown in Figure 9-16.

Figure 9-16. *Jenkins first-time login configuration*

You will see the screen for the Jenkins console, as shown in Figure 9-17.

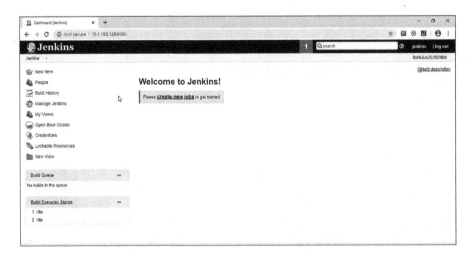

Figure 9-17. *Jenkins console*

Terraform Open Source Installation

We will start with installing Terraform open source, which will be used to compose an Infrastructure as Code module for the containerized infrastructure on AWS. We will use our master node (10.1.150.126) server to install Terraform.

Step 1: Log in to the master node as a root user and create a sub-directory named `terraform` under `/home/Prometheus`. Navigate into the directory by executing the following command, as shown in Figure 9-18:

```
$ cd /home/prometheus
$ mkdir terraform
$ cd terraform
```

```
[root@devops0087 /]#┐cd /home/prometheus/
[root@devops0087 prometheus]# mkdir terraform
```

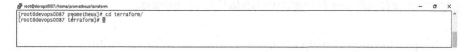

```
[root@devops0087 prometheus]# cd terraform/
[root@devops0087 terraform]#
```

Figure 9-18. *Terraform installation directory creation*

Step 2: Execute the following command to download the Terraform package and unzip it, as shown in Figure 9-19:

```
$ wget https://releases.hashicorp.com/terraform/0.11.11/
terraform_0.11.11_linux_amd64.zip
```

```
[root@devops0087 terraform]# wget https://releases.hashicorp.com/terraform/0.11.11/terraform_0.11.11_linux_amd64.zip
--2019-12-23 19:32:27--  https://releases.hashicorp.com/terraform/0.11.11/terraform_0.11.11_linux_amd64.zip
Resolving releases.hashicorp.com (releases.hashicorp.com)... 199.232.21.183, 2a04:4e42:42::439
Connecting to releases.hashicorp.com (releases.hashicorp.com)|199.232.21.183|:443... connected.
HTTP request sent, awaiting response... 200 OK
Length: 20971661 (20M) [application/zip]
Saving to: 'terraform_0.11.11_linux_amd64.zip'

100%[====================================================================================================>] 20,971,661  17.7MB/s   in 1.1s

2019-12-23 19:32:32 (17.7 MB/s) - 'terraform_0.11.11_linux_amd64.zip' saved [20971661/20971661]
```

Figure 9-19. *Terraform installation package download*

Step 3: Verify the zip file has been successfully downloaded by executing the following command, as shown in Figure 9-20:

```
$ ls -ltr
```

```
[root@devops0087 terraform]# ls -ltr
total 245728
-rw-r--r-- 1 root root  20971661 Dec 15  2018 terraform_0.11.11_linux_amd64.zip
```

Figure 9-20. *Terraform installation package download verification*

Step 4: Unzip the Terraform package by executing the following command, as shown in Figure 9-21:

```
$ unzip terraform_0.11.11_linux_amd64.zip
```

```
[root@devops0087 terraform]# unzip terraform_0.11.11_linux_amd64.zip
Archive:   terraform_0.11.11_linux_amd64.zip
```

Figure 9-21. *Unzip Terraform installation package*

Step 5: Remove the zip file by executing the following inline command, as shown in Figure 9-22:

```
$ rm -rf terraform_0.11.11_linux_amd64.zip
$ ll
```

```
[root@devops0087 terraform]# ll
total 49508
-rwxr-xr-x 1 root root 50695264 Nov 19 03:44 terraform
```

Figure 9-22. *Delete Terraform zip package*

Step 6: Add the Terraform file path to the Linux PATH variable, as shown in Figure 9-23.

```
$ export PATH="$PATH:/home/prometheus/terraform"
$ echo $PATH
```

```
[root@devops0087 terraform]# export PATH="$PATH:/home/prometheus/terraform"
```
```
[root@devops0087 terraform]# echo $PATH
/usr/local/sbin:/usr/local/bin:/usr/sbin:/usr/bin:/usr/java/jre-vmware/bin:/root/bin:/usr/local/go/bin:/root/work/bin:/home/prometheus/terraform
[root@devops0087 terraform]#
```

Figure 9-23. *Update and verify PATH variable*

Step 7: Update the bash.rc file by executing the following command, and append export PATH="$PATH:/home/prometheus/terraform to the end of the file. Save and quit the file.

```
$ vi ~/.bashrc
# .bashrc
# User specific aliases and functions
alias rm='rm -i'
alias cp='cp -i'
alias mv='mv -i'
# Source global definitions
if [ -f /etc/bashrc ]; then
. /etc/bashrc
fi
export PATH="$PATH:/home/prometheus/terraform"
```

Step 8: Verify the updated content by executing the following command, as shown in Figure 9-24:

```
$ cat ~/.bashrc
```

```
[root@devops0087 terraform]# cat ~/.bashrc
# .bashrc

# User specific aliases and functions

alias rm='rm -i'
alias cp='cp -i'
alias mv='mv -i'

# Source global definitions
if [ -f /etc/bashrc ]; then
        . /etc/bashrc
fi
export PATH="$PATH:/home/prometheus/terraform"
```

Figure 9-24. *Verify bashrc file update*

285

Step 9: Validate successful Terraform installation by executing the following command, as shown in Figure 9-25:

```
$ terraform --version
```

```
[root@devops0087 terraform]# terraform --version
Terraform v0.11.11      I
```

Figure 9-25. Verify Terraform installation

AWS IAM authenticator Installation

Now we will install AWS IAM authenticator, which will use AWS IAM credentials to authenticate to a Kubernetes cluster. If you are an administrator running a Kubernetes cluster on AWS, you already have an account to manage AWS IAM credentials so as to provision and update the cluster. By using AWS IAM Authenticator for Kubernetes, you can avoid having to manage a separate credential for Kubernetes access. AWS IAM also provides a number of nice properties, such as an out-of-band audit trail (via CloudTrail) and 2FA/MFA enforcement. We will use our Master Node (10.1.150.126) server to install aws-iam-authenticator.

Step 1: Navigate to the /home/prometheus/terraform directory and execute the following command, as shown in Figure 9-26:

```
$curl -o aws-iam-authenticator https://amazon-eks.s3-us-west-2.
amazonaws.com/1.14.6/2019-08-22/bin/linux/amd64/aws-iam-
authenticator
```

```
curl -o aws-iam-authenticator https://amazon-eks.s3-us-west-2.amazonaws.com/1.14.6/2019-08-22/bin/linux/amd64/aws-iam
uthenticator
  % Total    % Received % Xferd  Average Speed   Time    Time     Time  Current
                                 Dload  Upload   Total   Spent    Left  Speed
00 17.7M  100 17.7M    0     0  1233k      0  0:00:14  0:00:14 --:--:-- 4108k
```

Figure 9-26. Download aws-iam-authenticator

Step 2: Once `aws-iam-authenticator` is downloaded, rename it as `iam-authenticator-aws` by executing the following command:

```
$ mv aws-iam-authenticator iam-authenticator-aws
```

Step 3: Now apply execute permissions on the `iam-authenticator-aws` executable by executing the following inline command:

```
$ chmod 0777 iam-authenticator-aws
```

Jenkins and Terraform Integration

Let's now integrate Jenkins and Terraform. This will set up the base for our CI/CD pipeline, which will have the automation logic for enabling container monitoring while deploying the container infrastructure on AWS. We will configure a Jenkins node on the same server where we have configured Terraform.

Step 1: Navigate to the `/home` directory and create a sub-directory called `Jenkins_node`. Change permission of directory to 700 permission using chmod command so that the root user can only perform read, write, and execute operations on it by executing the following commands. The `Jenkins_node` directory will be used by the Jenkins node to connect and execute the command.

```
$ cd /home
$ mkdir jenkins_node
$ chmod 700 jenkins_node
```

Step 2: Navigate to the following URL to access Jenkins. Use your admin password set up in previous steps. Navigate to Manage Jenkins ➤ Manage Nodes ➤ New Node.

URL: `http://Master-Node-IP:8080`; e.g., `http://10.1.150.126:8080`

287

Step 3: Fill in the form as per the following values:

Root: Select directory as `jenkins_node`.

Name: Mention any name you like.

Remote Root Directory: Path of the `Jenkins_node` folder we created; e.g., `/home/jenkins_node`

Label: Mention label as `Kubernetes_Master`.

Usage: Select "Use this node as much as possible."

Launch Method: Select "Launch agents via SSH."

Host: Mention Kubernetes master node IP address (in our case, 10.1.150.126).

Credential: Click Add button and choose "Jenkins."

Choose Kind as "Username with password" and then fill Username as "root." Password is the root user password of the Kubernetes master node. Also fill in the ID and Description fields. Click the Add button and select the credential, as shown in Figures 9-27 and 9-28.

Host Key Verification Strategy: Choose the "Non-verifying Verification Strategy" option, as we are connecting a Jenkins node by giving a username and password, not by SSH keys, to simplify the Jenkins node setup. If you want to connect the Jenkins node with an SSH key please follow the following link.[2]

Availability: Choose "Keep this agent online as much as possible."

---

[2]`https://support.cloudbees.com/hc/en-us/articles/222978868-How-to-Connect-to-Remote-SSH-Agents-`

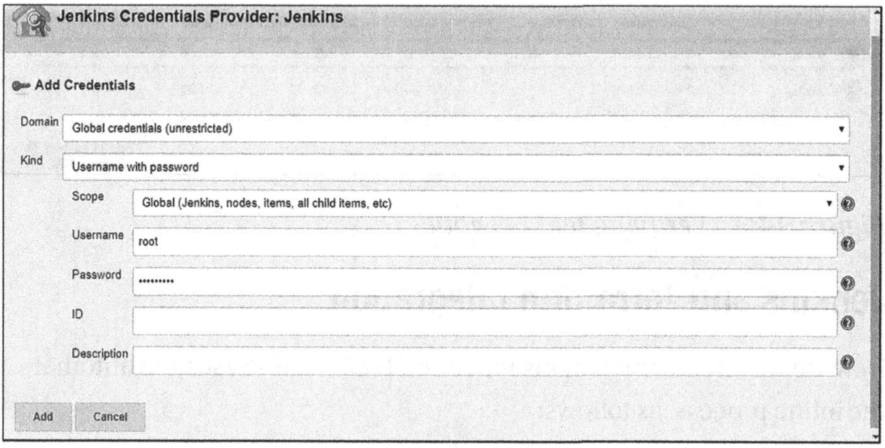

Figure 9-27. Setting up Jenkins node

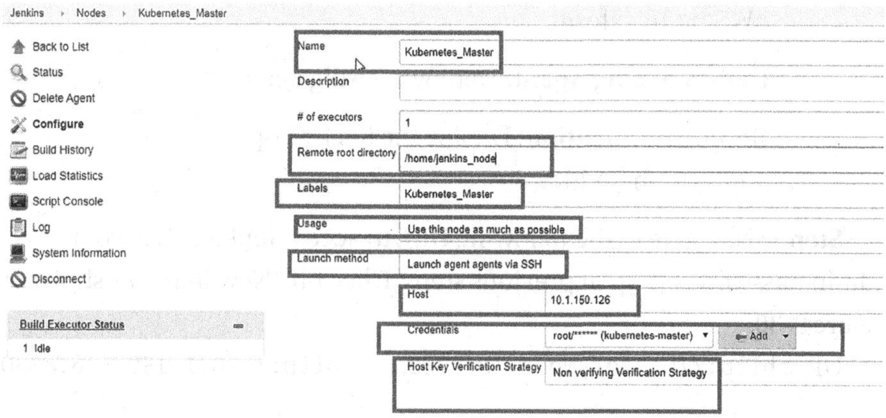

Figure 9-28. Setting up Jenkins node

Step 4: Click on the Save button to proceed.

Step 5: Verify the agent has been configured successfully by reviewing the Jenkins console status, as shown in Figure 9-29.

S	Name ↓	Architecture	Clock Difference	Free Disk Space	Free Swap Space	Free Temp Space	Response Time	
🖥	Kubernetes_Master	Linux (amd64)	In sync	20.87 GB	⊖ 0 B	20.87 GB	20ms	⚙
🖥	master	Linux (amd64)	In sync	20.87 GB	⊖ 0 B	20.87 GB	0ms	⚙
	Data obtained	36 min	36 min	36 min	36 min	36 min	36 min	
							Refresh status	

Figure 9-29. *Verifying Jenkins node*

Jenkins and Terraform Integration

Now we will create the Jenkins Pipeline CI-CD-Kube-Sysdig to automate the inline process, as follows:

Code Clone: Clone the sock-shop code from GitHub.

Create Cluster: Create a Kubernetes cluster EKS on AWS by Terraform.

Deploy Sysdig Agent: Deploy a Sysdig agent on EKS.

Deploy Application: Deploy the Sock Shop application on EKS.

Step 1: Navigate to the following URL to access Jenkins. Use your admin password set up in previous steps. Click on "New Item," as shown in Figure 9-30.

URL: http://Master-Node-IP:8080; e.g., http://10.1.150.126:8080

Figure 9-30. *Creating Jenkins ipeline*

Step 2: Fill the form by making the item name CI-CD-Kube-Sysdig. Choose "Pipeline," as we are using pipeline as code in Jenkins to automate the previously defined process, then click the OK button, as shown in Figure 9-31. Jenkins provides capability of modeling pipelines "as code" where Pipeline definition is written as text or script file (called a Jenkinsfile). This allows pipeline definition to be stored & managed using Version control system.

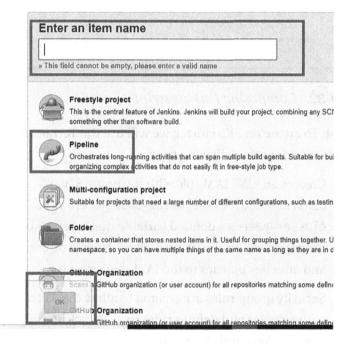

Figure 9-31. *Creating Jenkins pipeline*

Step 3: Click on "Pipeline," and it will display a script box where we will compose our Jenkins script, as shown in Figure 9-32.

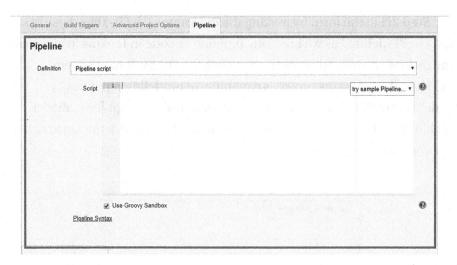

Figure 9-32.   Composing Jenkins script

Step 4: To create an EKS cluster, we will use the Terraform code. The Terraform code does the following tasks:

- Creates an AWS IAM role with the name ${var.
  cluster-name}-eks-cluster-role (where var.
  cluster-name is a defined variable that takes input
  from the user for the name of the cluster to be created)
  and attaches policies to the IAM role created.

- Security group rules are created to allow the API access
  to the cluster and defines rules to access cluster nodes
  from workers and vice versa,

- EKS cluster is deployed by the code with the user input
  name of the cluster. The IAM role created is attached to
  the cluster, the version of Kubernetes is provided with
  a default value, and the end user can opt for a different
  available version of EKS for the deployment.

- EKS worker nodes are configured by passing user data to the launch configuration, while the worker nodes are created by using auto-scaling of AWS to ensure availability of the nodes at all times.

- Security group rules are created for the worker node to allow it to reach out to the EKS cluster and to allow SSH login to the instances.

To deploy the sysdig agent, we will leverage the shell script `sysdig_ agent` to create the namespace's cluster role binding secrets, which will be leveraged by the Sysdig agent to monitor the cluster. Then it deploys the Sysdig agent config map and DaemonSet on the cluster.

Both the script and other Terraform modules are created in the `/home/ EKS_CLUSTER` folder.

Clone the `EKS_CLUSTER` files by executing the following commands from the `/home` directory of the master node (10.1.150.126):

```
$ cd /home
$ git clone https://github.com/dryice-devops/EKS_CLUSTER.git
```

You will see a sub-directory under the `/home` directory named EKS_ CLUSTER. Navigate into that to view the file named `kubernetes_deploy.sh`. This file requires four parameters, as follows:

- `cluster-name`; e.g., Prometheus

- `aws-region`; e.g., us-east-1

- `node-instance-type`; e.g., t3.xlarge

- `KeyName`; e.g., awx

```
$ cd EKS_CLUSTER
```

In the EKS_CLUSTER directory you will also find the sysdig_agent.sh file. In this script, we have to add the key mentioned as (XXXXXXXXXXXXXX) that we used for the Sysdig subscription in the last chapter. Replace the key with your specific value before proceeding to the next steps.

Create an agent-files directory in the /home directory:

```
$ cd /home
$ mkdir agent-files
```

Create the inline files with the same contents as we created earlier (manual process to deploy Sysdig agent):

sysdig-agent-clusterrole.yaml, sysdig-agent-configmap.yaml and sysdig-agent-daemonset-v2.yaml

Step 5: Copy the contents of the Jenkins file into the EKS_CLUSTER folder and paste it into the script box. Then, click the Save button, as shown in Figure 9-33.

Figure 9-33. *Saving Jenkins script*

Step 6: Execute the Jenkins job by clicking on "Build Now" (Figure 9-34).

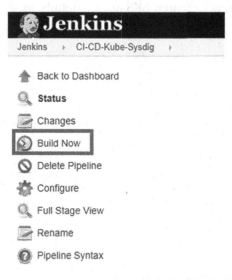

Figure 9-34. *Executing Jenkins script*

Step 7: Once the job has been executed successfully, the following build history will show. If it runs fine, the build number will be blue; if not, it will be red. This history will also show the stages under Stage View. To view logs, click on the build number, as shown in Figure 9-35. Click on Console Output.

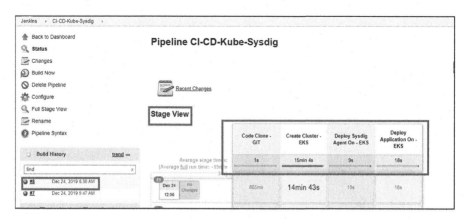

Figure 9-35. *Reviewing Jenkins logs*

In the log console, please scroll three-fourths of the way down the screen to see the newly created EKS node's details, as shown in Figure 9-36.

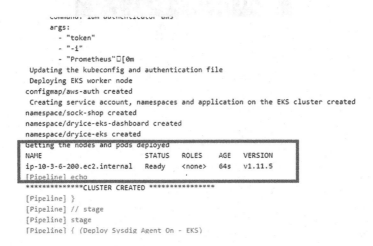

```
                    args:
                        - "token"
                        - "-i"
                        - "Prometheus"☐[0m
     Updating the kubeconfig and authentication file
     Deploying EKS worker node
    configmap/aws-auth created
     Creating service account, namespaces and application on the EKS cluster created
    namespace/sock-shop created
    namespace/dryice-eks-dashboard created
    namespace/dryice-eks created
    Getting the nodes and pods deployed
    NAME                         STATUS   ROLES    AGE   VERSION
    ip-10-3-6-200.ec2.internal   Ready    <none>   64s   v1.11.5
    [Pipeline] echo
    ************CLUSTER CREATED ***************
    [Pipeline] }
    [Pipeline] // stage
    [Pipeline] stage
    [Pipeline] { (Deploy Sysdig Agent On - EKS)
```

Figure 9-36. *Reviewing Jenkins logs*

Step 8: Navigate to your AWS account console and click on "Services," then select "EKS" under the Compute category, as shown in Figure 9-37.

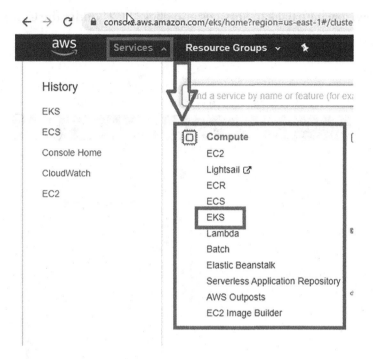

Figure 9-37. *Reviewing the AWS console*

You will see the EKS cluster Prometheus is in an active state, as shown in Figure 9-38, the same that we created through Jenkins and Terraform.

Figure 9-38. *Reviewing AWS console*

297

Now, navigate back to Services and click "EC2" under the Compute category, as shown in Figure 9-39.

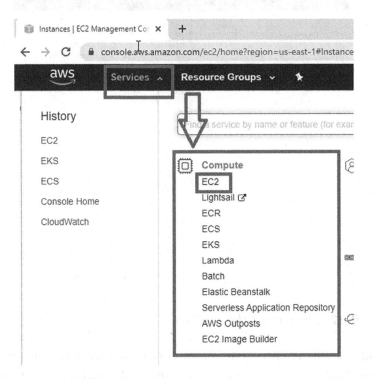

Figure 9-39. *Reviewing AWS console*

Click on "Running Instances" under the Resource category, as shown in Figure 9-40.

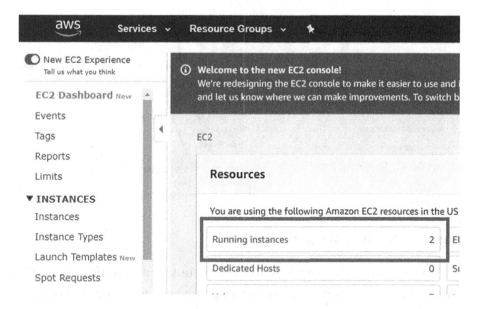

Figure 9-40. *Reviewing AWS console*

You will see the EC2 instance name as Prometheus-eks-node. Select this, as shown in Figure 9-41.

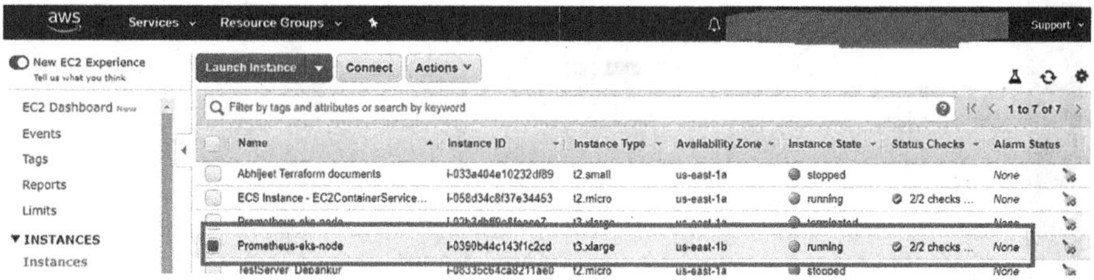

Figure 9-41. *Reviewing AWS console*

In the Description tab, you will get the private DNS. It is same as we have seen in the Jenkins logs, as shown in Figure 9-42.

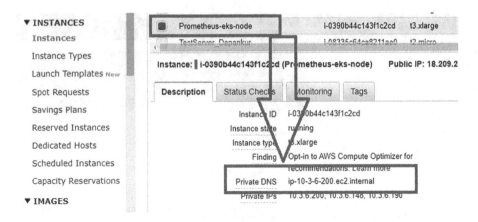

Figure 9-42. Reviewing AWS console

Step 9: Now, let's navigate to the Sysdig console and verify that our EKS cluster has been added under Monitoring. Navigate to Sysdig at `https://sysdig.com/` and log in with your credentials.

Navigate to Explore ➤ Hosts & Containers, and then select "Overview by Container" under the Hosts & Container category. You will see Figure 9-43.

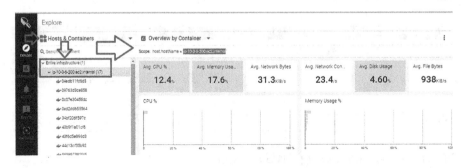

Figure 9-43. Reviewing the Sysdig console

Now, to verify that the Sock Shop application deployed, click Explore ➤ Hosts & Containers ➤ Select Container Limits under the Hosts & Containers category.

Hover over the graph of CPU Shares Used, as shown in Figure 9-44.

Figure 9-44. *Reviewing the Sysdig console*

You will see the Sock Shop container's name, as shown in Figure 9-45.

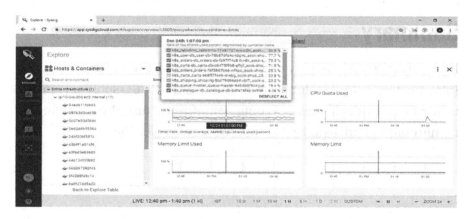

Figure 9-45. *Reviewing Sysdig Console*

Click on Explore ➤ Daemon Sets ➤ Over by Service under Services. You should see something similar to Figure 9-46.

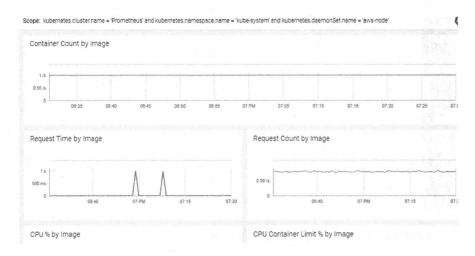

Figure 9-46. *Reviewing the Sysdig console*

Summary

In this chapter, we have provided hands-on steps for using an Infrastructure as Code solution, Terraform; and a CI/CD solution, Jenkins, to automate the deployment of container infrastructure, then enabling monitoring for and deploying a containerized application.

Index

A, B

© Navin Sabharwal, Piyush Pandey 2020   303
N. Sabharwal and P. Pandey, *Monitoring Microservices and Containerized Applications*,
https://doi.org/10.1007/978-1-4842-6216-0

Printed in the United States
By Bookmasters